The Charleston Book

The Charleston Book

A Miscellany in Prose and Poetry

William Gilmore Simms

Introduction and Biographical Notes by David Moltke-Hansen
Bibliographical Notes by Harlan Greene

The University of South Carolina Press

© 2015 University of South Carolina

Cloth original published by The Reprint Company, 1983
Paperback published by the University of South Carolina Press
Columbia, South Carolina 29208

www.sc.edu/uscpress

Manufactured in the United States of America

24 23 22 21 20 19 18 17 16 15
10 9 8 7 6 5 4 3 2 1

ISBN 978-1-61117-477-9 (pbk)

Published in cooperation with the Simms Initiatives, a project of the University of
South Carolina Libraries with the generous support of the Watson-Brown Foundation.
Thanks are also due to The Reprint Company in Spartanburg, South Carolina, for
permission to reprint the text and critical apparatus.

THE
CHARLESTON BOOK

A
Miscellany
in Prose and Verse

Edited by
William Gilmore Simms

With
A New Introduction and Biographical Notes
By
David Moltke-Hansen
And Bibliographical Notes
By
Harlan Greene

THE REPRINT COMPANY, PUBLISHERS
SPARTANBURG, SOUTH CAROLINA
1983

ACKNOWLEDGEMENTS

James B. Meriwether both suggested and made possible this reprint through his encouragement, careful attention to the details of format and funding, and generous sharing of his knowledge of William Gilmore Simms and southern literature.

Equally generous was the gift from the Foundation for American Education. Not only was it generous in itself, it allowed us to seek matching funds for the project. Our thanks go to Charles Scott Hamel, President, and Clyde N. Wilson.

The South Carolina Committee for the Humanities made possible the matching of the gift from the Foundation for American Education with funds from the National Endowment for the Humanities. As always, Leland Cox, Lois Shell, Debbie Foster, and other staff there were extremely helpful.

Petra Gallert and Paul Ragan helped research several of the biographical notes. Harlan Greene, with his unrivalled knowledge of Charleston literature, supplied notes on the writings of many of the authors included in the volume.

As so often is the case, special thanks are due to the courtesy and efficiency of the typists, Pearl Baker and Pat Merriam.

The College of Charleston, the Waring Library Society of the Medical University of South Carolina, and WSCI (Educational) Radio in

Charleston cosponsored the INTELLECTUAL LIFE IN ANTEBELLUM CHARLESTON program out of which this reprint comes. The South Carolina Historical Society administered the program, and partial funding came from the American Council of Learned Societies and the South Carolina Committee for the Humanities, an agent of the National Endowment for the Humanities, a federal agency. Michael O'Brien codirected the program with myself and did so with characteristic deftness. I owe him (and he has) my thanks.

Thomas E. Smith, publisher of The Reprint Company, has made the inevitable complications and misunderstandings in such an enterprise as this manageable, and he has done so with remarkable forebearance and grace. He, too, has my thanks.

D. M.-H.
February 1983

INTRODUCTION

In the late 1830s, the United States saw the publication of a rash of anthologies of writings drawn from individual cities within her borders. There were Boston books, New York books, Philadelphia books, and Baltimore books. All were what we today would call coffee-table publications; each represented what its editors and publishers thought best and most characteristic or promising of the poetry and prose productions of the natives and residents of their city.

In 1841, Charleston book-seller and Reform Jewish leader Samuel Hart, Sr. proposed that Charlestonians join the trend. "[I]t is thought," he wrote, that "we can make a 'Charleston Book,' from the writings of our Citizens, which shall be quite as creditable as the very best of these issues from our neighbors."[1]

At the time, Charleston was the sixth largest city in the country. (Twenty years before, she had been the fifth largest.) It was only natural that she compare herself to Boston and the other American cities which were larger than she. It was natural, too, that she was ambitious to equal these communities culturally.[2]

The Charleston Book indicates the extent to which Charleston fulfilled her ambition. The success of the demonstration derives from the fact that the volume's publisher and editor both knew Charleston writers and their writings well.

Hart, the publisher whose idea the book was, was proprietor of a circulating library and book shop which was "the most fashionable lounging place" of the ladies of Charleston. William Gilmore Simms, the editor whom Hart selected in the fall of 1841, was, at thirty-five, the most famous man of letters in Charleston. According to reviewers, what these two men selected was representative, not only of the interests, but of the accomplishments of Charleston's literati.[3]

While representative, however, the volume was neither all-inclusive nor exhaustive, and at least one reviewer lamented the absence of names "which should have had a place." He had good reason. Selections from only fifty-eight authors were included, and excluded were many of Charleston's best-known writers--for instance, David Ramsay and William Henry Drayton of Revolutionary War fame, scientists J.L.E.W. Shecut and John Holbrook, Bishops England and Capers, politician-lawyer Robert Y. Hayne, U. S. Supreme Court Justice William Johnson, and Simms himself. The omissions reflect both space limitations and the book's final focus. Originally, Hart had conceived of the book as a historical survey based on "as complete as possible" a "search amongst our Chronicles." However, Simms later decided to limit the coverage to people born too late to participate in the Revolution. These were his near contemporaries; he had been born in 1806 and was himself the son of a Revolutionary. It was these contemporaries' writings which he wanted to promote, arguing that northern editors ignored them. Moreover, as he noted, he had too much material for just the one volume. Then too, himself a self-conscious heir of the Revolution and an ardent nationalist as well as sectionalist, he may have wanted to emphasize the accomplishments of the first two generations to mature after American independence. Finally, with polite lady subscribers in mind, he necessarily excluded certain classes of writing. Consequently, theologians, scientists, lawyers, tall-tale writers, and politicians either are not included or are not represented by their more specialized, professional, polemical, or vulgar work.[4]

The final volume, then, presents not all of
Charleston culture, but polite letters in the
city. The book thus is a selective portrait,
rather than a full picture. Like any portrait,
it is an interpretation as well as a represen-
tation of its subject. The interpretation
deserves attention. It does so for three
reasons: it reflects the views of knowledgeable
insiders; it was intended to appeal to the
community's sense of itself; and its challenge
of the stereotype of antebellum Charleston
culture regnant in subsequent historiography
offers a point of departure for future discussions.

The most obvious points suggested by The
Charleston Book are the breadth of Charlestonians' cultural horizons and the up-to-date
nature of their tastes and pursuits. Historians
to the contrary notwithstanding, Charlestonians
were not mired in the eighteenth century, nor
were their horizons noticeably circumscribed
because of slavery. True, Charlestonians' per-
ceptions of their horizons were blinkered, but
those blinkers were commonplace assumptions
about the nature and role of the arts and sciences, the nation, the community, education, and
progress. Many Europeans as well as other
Americans had their visions similarly channeled
in the first half of the nineteenth century.
Like their fellow romantics, Charlestonians conceived of the arts and sciences as at once the
objects and subjects of pleasure, and the
results and signs of refinement. By definition,
refined people were dilettantes educated in the
liberal arts who devoted leisure to cultural
pursuits. This meant that those who would be
fine read the classics, wrote, painted, played
musical instruments, cultivated ornamental gardens, and suffered the various sensibilities
then popular. In doing so, gentlemen were
holding themselves to cultural standards articu-
lated in the Renaissance by Castiglioni, and
ladies were holding themselves to the equivalent
salon standards.[6]

Intermixed with this Renaissance ambition
was a strong dash of nineteenth-century cultural
nationalism. Any of a number of passages in The
Charleston Book could be quoted to illustrate
the point. This which follows is from "Literature and the Fine Arts" by Joel R. Poinsett:

> The importance of cultivating and using
> our utmost effort to improve the liter-
> ature of our country, must be apparent
> to all. It is the vehicle of science,
> and upon its character the dignity and
> reputation of a nation depend.

Allied to this nationalist sentiment was
regionalism. A selection in The Charleston Book
bears the title, "The Necessity of a Southern
Literature." By New England-reared Daniel K.
Whitaker, it argues that the South must contribute to "our country's literature ... as the
South, because ... the North ... has acted as
the North...."[7]

Ambitious, then, to embrace all the arts and
sciences, because it was the civilized thing to
do, and also ambitious to foster American culture and, in so doing, to match the North
article for article, Charleston dilettantes
wrote and wrote and wrote. One of their goals--
and one of the goals which The Charleston Book
was meant to foster--was the making of
Charleston into a center which would support her
citizens' refinement at the same time that it
encouraged American--and Southern--development.

The result was a level of ambition exceeding
the community's ability to produce and a level
of production exceeding the community's capacity
to consume. Not only was The Charleston Book
sent to New York to be printed and bound, it
apparently failed to attract a sufficient number
of subscribers for Simms and Hart to issue the
companion volumes which they had planned. The
failure--if that is what it was--was typical.
Despite considerable growth, Charleston's population of from eight thousand whites in 1790 to
twenty-eight thousand in 1861 could not support
a host of competing publications, each requiring

one-to-two thousand subscribers or more. Wealth, education, and interest were too narrowly concentrated and too variously engaged in the city, while the educated portion of the country population surrounding Charleston was, at an average density of well under four persons per square mile, too scattered, too poorly served by transportation systems, and too buffeted by market changes to fill the resultant gap between production and consumption.

Boston, Philadelphia, New York, and Baltimore were better off in all these regards. They experienced greater and more consistent growth rates and had larger populations, relatively larger middle classes, more general literacy, and more densely populated, accessible, and diversely employed hinterlands. The Charleston Book in its readers' judgements might have competed artistically and culturally with a Boston or New York anthology, then, but Charleston was still not big enough for such a volume to be a commercial success.[8]

Frustration was one result. Retardation of the development of literature as a profession was another. While Charleston had many teachers, journalists, and editors in addition to doctors, lawyers, and artists, as of 1845 William Gilmore Simms was the only Charlestonian to have defined himself professionally as a writer. In a sense, then, it was appropriate that he excluded himself from The Charleston Book, although he was Charleston's most widely circulated and critically acclaimed man-of-letters and had written nearly as much fiction as all the rest of his community put together.

Yet, while Simms's self-definition and production were extraordinary, Simms was nevertheless typical of Charleston in his concern for the community's cultural development. His and his fellow citizens' disappointment in their ambitions for their city only fueled their intense efforts to expand and improve the quality of Charleston's literary life. The Charleston Book serves both to illustrate and explain these efforts. In Simms's view, it in addition illustrates and explains their limited success. His reasoning and conclusions are summarized in his Advertisement to the volume. Artist Charles Fraser, poets Paul Hamilton Hayne and Henry Timrod, and others of Simms's near contemporaries in Charleston made similar arguments at different times. The arguments, as much as the pieces anthologized here, characterize the culture out of which they came.[9]

David Moltke-Hansen
South Carolina Historical Society

1 Mary C. Simms Oliphant et al., eds., The
Letters of William Gilmore Simms, 6 vols.
(Columbia, S.C., 1954-1982), 1:268-269 (herein-
after cited as Simms, Letters).

2 [United States Bureau of the Census],
Historical Statistics of The United States,
Colonial Times to 1970, Population, passim.

3 Louis Fitzgerald Tasistro, "A Theatrical
Visit, 1842," in Thomas D. Clark, ed., South
Carolina: The Grand Tour, 1780-1865 (Columbia,
S.C., 1973), 196; Godey's Magazine, 23 (Oct.
1841), 190; Simms, Letters, I:cix, 283.

4 [Daniel K. Whitaker], Notices, Southern
Quarterly Review, 7 (Jan. 1845), 256-257; Simms,
Letters, 1:268-269; [William Gilmore Simms],
"Griswold's American Poets," Magnolia, 1, n.s.
(Aug. 1842), 117-118.

5 On the stereotypic view in the historiography and its deficiencies, see the Introduction
to Michael O'Brien, All Clever Men, Who Make
Their Way: Critical Discourse in the Old South
(Fayetteville, Ark., 1982).

6 The debt of the South to Renaissance traditions is explored in Raimondo Luraghi, The Rise
and Fall of the Plantation South (New York and
London, 1978), 64-82 et passim.

7 See John C. Guilds, Jr., "Simms's Views in
National and Sectional Literature, 1825-1845,"
North Carolina Historial Review, 34 (July 1957),
393-405.

8 [Whitaker], Notices, 256-257; William Stan-
ley Hoole, A Check-List and Finding-List of
Charleston Periodicals, 1732-1864, (Durham,
N.C., 1936), 4; Frederic Cople Jaher, The Urban
Establishment (Urbana, Ill., 1982), passim.

9 See Gene Waddell, "'Where are Our Trum-
bulls'," in David Moltke-Hansen, ed., Art in the
Lives of South Carolinians: Nineteenth-Century
Chapters (Charleston, S.C., 1979); David Moltke-
Hansen, "The Expansion of Intellectual Life in

Antebellum Charleston," in Michael O'Brien and
David Moltke-Hansen, eds., _Intellectual Life in
Antebellum Charleston_ (forthcoming).

THE

CHARLESTON BOOK:

A

MISCELLANY

IN PROSE AND VERSE.

CHARLESTON:

PUBLISHED BY SAMUEL HART, SEN.,

KING STREET.

1845.

ADVERTISEMENT.

————

THE miscellany which follows is compiled entirely from the writings of native or resident citizens of Charleston. The sources of the compilation are not those of professional authorship. The writers of the South are persons, generally, of other professions and pursuits. What is done among us, in a literary point of view, is the work of the amateur, a labor of stealth or recreation, employed as a relief from other tasks and duties. From this fact the reader will be able to account for that air of didactic gravity, that absence of variety, and of the study of artistical attributes, which would not strike him so obviously had the sources of the collection been found in the more various fields of a national literature. He will discover, however, that in most of the pieces which follow, there is a liveliness of fancy, a fluency of expression, and a general readiness of resource, indicating such a presence of the imaginative faculty, as leaves no doubt of the capacity of the community, from which the work is drawn, to engage with great success in the active pursuits of literature. Should this little miscellany contribute, in any degree, to bring about a result so very desirable, the reward of the publisher will be ample.

It must be mentioned that the collection which follows by no means includes all the writings of repute in Charleston. Many of the distinguished among us, living and dead, have been omitted through the sheer impossibility of finding a space for all in a design so limited. Much of the edited *material*, prepared for this collection, has been left over for future volumes, the publication of which, it is hoped, the success of the present will be found to justify. Should this be the case, the publisher will put forth a second miscellany, to be in readiness as a gift for the holidays of the ensuing year; as this in some measure is to answer a similar purpose for those of the present.

Charleston, October 1, 1844.

CONTENTS.

THE

CHARLESTON BOOK:

A

MISCELLANY IN PROSE AND VERSE.

THE COMPLETENESS AND VARIETY OF NATURE.

BY STEPHEN ELLIOTT, LL.D.

WHAT is there that will not be included in the history of nature ? The earth on which we tread, the air we breathe, the waters around the earth, the material forms that inhabit its surface, the mind of man, with all its magical illusions and all its inherent energy, the planets that move around our system, the firmament of heaven—the smallest of the invisible atoms which float around our globe, and the most majestic of the orbs that roll through the immeasurable fields of space—all are parts of one system, productions of one power, creations of one intellect, the offspring of Him, by whom all that is inert and

2

inorganic in creation was formed, and from whom all that
have life derive their being.

Of this immense system, all that we can examine, this
little globe that we inherit, is full of animation and crowded with forms, organized, glowing with life and generally
sentient.   No space is unoccupied—the exposed surface
of the rock is encrusted with living substances ; plants occupy the bark and decaying limbs of other plants ; animals
live on the surface and in the bodies of other animals ;
inhabitants are fashioned and adapted to equatorial heats
and polar ice—air, earth and ocean teem with life—and if
to other worlds the same proportion of life and of enjoyment has been distributed which has been allotted to ours;
if creative benevolence has equally filled every other
planet of every other system, nay, even the suns themselves, with beings, organized, animated and intelligent ;
how countless must be the generations of the living !—what
voices which we cannot hear, what languages that we
cannot understand, what multitudes that we cannot see,
may, as they roll along the stream of time, be employed
hourly, daily and for ever, in choral songs of praise hymning
their great Creator.

And when, in this almost prodigal waste of life, we
perceive that every being, from the puny insect which
flutters in the evening ray; from the lichen which we can
scarcely distinguish on the mouldering rock ; from the
fungus that springs up and re-animates the mass of dead
and decomposing substances ; that every living form possesses a structure as perfect in its sphere, an organization
sometimes as complex, always as truly and completely
adapted to its purposes and modes of existence as that of
the most perfect animal ; when we discover them all to be

governed by laws as definite, as immutable, as those which regulate the planetary movements, great must be our admiration of the wisdom which has arranged, and the power which has perfected this stupendous fabric.

Nor does creation here cease. There are, beyond the limits of our system, beyond the visible forms of matter, other principles, other powers, higher orders of beings, an immaterial world which we cannot yet know ; other modes of existence which we cannot comprehend ; yet, however inscrutable to us, this spiritual world must be guided by its own unerring laws, and the harmonious order which reigns in all we can see and understand, ascending through the series of immortal and invisible existence, must govern even the powers and dominions, the seraphim and cherubim, that surround the throne of God himself.

Such are the views, such the high and lofty themes which the fabric of nature will present ; which must be embraced in an extended survey of creation. But this task is not allotted to man ; he is not even permitted to behold but through the obscure veil of revelation and of prophecy, the remote boundaries of this great system. His duties and his researches are limited, his business is with that portion immediately connected with the welfare and existence of the human race ; an inhabitant of this globe, his means, his enjoyments, his physical wants are here ; a transient visitor on its surface, it is yet with that surface and its inhabitants that all his temporal cares are entwined—and natural history, as now understood, is confined to earth, and is employed to ascertain and to disclose some idea of the structure of the globe he is destined to inhabit, of the rude and inorganic materials of which that globe is composed, and of the living forms that repose on its bosom, and derive support from its teeming and productive surface.

Every step in this inquiry is interesting to man ; every object combined more or less intimately with his welfare, associated more or less absolutely with his health, his happiness and his prosperity.

Man is altogether and for ever dependent on nature ; the air he breathes, the light and heat by which he is vivified and cherished, the food by which he is nourished, the garments by which he is protected, the roof by which he is sheltered, are all derived from her exhaustless bounty ; but, for the most part, must be acquired and rendered useful and valuable by his knowledge. Researches, therefore, connected with natural history, must, in some form or degree, from the earliest period of his existence, have attracted his attention ; nor is it surprising that as these researches increased in importance, in proportion to the extended and multiplied wants of society, they should have occupied more seriously his time and his reflections.

In the infant stages of society, and in unlettered ages, all that appeared theoretical and abstracted must necessarily have been neglected, and only that knowledge noticed and remembered which was essential and practical. Most of the first efforts of intelligent man were probably misdirected, and many of his original discoveries and opinions have been forgotten ; for triumphant ignorance and barbaric force have frequently swept over the fairest portions of the globe, and defaced or obliterated the brightest records of the human understanding ; yet, vestiges, even if imperfect, remain to prove, that, in the early ages of the existence of our race, there have been illuminated eras; and monuments more ancient than the pages of profane history, attest the improvement, in very remote periods, of some portion of the human species— and indicate that much of our present knowledge has been derived from sources of which the origin is now unknown; has descended to us from ages, and generations, and people, that are now forgotten.

It was no illiterate age, it was no ignorant people who could insculpture on the portals of the temple of Isis, the great mother of nature, its sublime inscription:—"I am whatsoever is, whatsoever has been, whatsoever shall be, and the veil which is over my countenance no mortal hand has ever raised."

*　　*　　*　　*　　*　　*　　*　　*　　*

When we survey this great work of creation, its extent, its harmony, the magnificence of its outline, the perfection of its minute details, we cannot be surprised that its study should have engaged and occupied minds of the highest power, nor that such minds should have failed thoroughly to explain what infinite wisdom has devised, infinite power executed, and what mortal spirits may be permitted only partially to comprehend. Yet let us not despond. In the study of nature we tread in the footsteps of wisdom. We listen to a voice, which is the same yesterday, to-day and for ever. And while the erring and fluctuating opinions of man, his crimes, his follies, his power, pass away and are forgotten, the empire of nature is immutable,— to us eternal the knowledge of nature which is once accurate, is for ever true—the knowledge of nature which is once perfect, may be for ever useful.

When we approach to examine the fabric of nature, so

far as it is subjected to our inspection, we find ourselves immediately placed amidst differing, if not contending, powers. We perceive ourselves inhabitants of a globe, which, science informs us, is but one of an immense system, surrounded by other forms, some similar to our own, some wandering over the earth, roaming in different elements, or confined to one; some, though located in one spot, varying in size and aspect with the passing seasons; or by other substances apparently composing portions of the globe itself, immovable and changing not. The first impression which the mind receives, and that which most attracts the attention, is the wide difference that exists between the earth itself and the diversified forms which occupy its surface; between the silent, still and joyless repose of matter, and the noisy, gay and animated voice of life. The substances which compose that portion of the earth, whether crust, or covering, or projecting masses of its mighty frame, which is alone submitted to our researches, are passive, immovable, insensible; those which inhabit that surface, are, for the most part, active, capable of moving from place to place at pleasure, and possess great sensibility. The former have neither growth nor voluntary action; they have no mode of increase, but by the casual addition of similar particles, united by the strong and universal law of attraction. They can remain unaltered for indefinite periods of time; they have no death, but they perish or rather are destroyed solely by the separation of their component particles. The latter all increase in size through their own agency, by the constant addition of particles which they have the power to collect and assimilate to their substances by the principle of life; they perish whenever this addition and assimilation cannot be continued; and exist only for limited and indefinite periods. The former have no organization, are not produced by similar and pre-existent bodies, but are always and necessarily formed by the accidental contact of similar particles. They have no regular structure, but, under certain circumstances, a modified attraction gives to each particle of matter a definite position, and generates the regular forms of crystallized bodies. The latter are all furnished with organs calculated and adapted to perform the functions, to collect, absorb and assimilate those particles which are necessary for their existence, and they always proceed from similar and pre-existent bodies.

* * * * * * * * *

It is in this vast domain of life, that the order established by divine wisdom is so singularly conspicuous. We perceive beings almost innumerable, forms endless in their variety, creatures infinitely diversified in their habits and in their pursuits, all submitting to the guidance and governance of a few simple, universal laws. All, however varied may be their operations, instinctively labor for the preservation of their own lives and the protection of their future progeny. The butterfly, which sports in the air, and flies from plant to plant on wings as light and brilliant as the flower over which it hovers; wherever she herself may feed, yet deposits her eggs only on those plants which are the appropriate food of her infant caterpillar; the bee and the wasp consume their lives in building cells, and in depositing in those cells honey or insects, or some other food adapted to the support of that offspring they will never know; fish leave the ocean, struggle against the currents, ascend the rapids, leap up the falls of long rivers to deposit their eggs in places which the parent cannot inhabit, but where their young may find security and food:—all bend to some paramount impression, all yield an unqualified obedience to the laws of their instinctive lives. These laws operate with unceasing force ; they are permanent and unchangeable. They have governed the living tribes of nature since their existence began ; they will control them while their races exist. Chance can have no agency in principles so stable and so uniform.

One being alone has been liberated in part from this blind and uncontrollable instinct, has been permitted to compare causes and effects, to know good from evil. To one has been given the awful responsibility of free-will—and instead of the mysterious and unerring impulses of instinct, he has been endowed with that reason which must be his pride or his reproach. Man himself is, perhaps, the most wonderful anomaly in the system of life ; and while he avails himself of his privilege to examine all that surrounds him, all that now exists, and all that has been created, it should be a part of the same study cautiously to investigate his own position, to ascertain his connection with the past, with the present, and with the future.

ROSALIE.

BY WASHINGTON ALLSTON.

Oh! pour upon my soul again,
That sad unearthly strain,
That seems from other worlds to plain;
Thus falling, falling from afar,
As if some melancholy star
Had mingled with her light her sighs,
   And dropped them from the skies.

No—never came from aught below
This melody of wo,
That makes my heart to overflow
As from a thousand gushing springs
Unknown before; that with it brings
This nameless light—if light it be—
   That veils the world I see.

For all I see around me wears
The hue of other spheres;
And something blent of smiles and tears
Comes from the very air I breathe.
O, nothing, sure, the stars beneath,
Can mould a sadness like to this—
   So like angelic bliss.

So, at the dreamy hour of day
When the last lingering ray

Stops on the highest cloud to play—
So thought the gentle Rosalie,
As on her maiden revery
First fell the strain of him who stole
 In music to her soul.

———

THE STUDY OF THE CLASSICS.

BY H. S. LEGARÉ.

IN discussing the very important question whether boys
ought to be made to study the classics, as a regular part
of education, the innovators put the case in the strongest
possible manner against the present system, by arguing as
if the young pupil, under this discipline, was to learn
nothing else but language itself. We admit that this
notion has received some sort of countenance from the
excessive attention paid in the English schools to prosody,
and the fact that their great scholars have been, perhaps
(with many exceptions to be sure), more distinguished by
the refinement of their scholarship, than the extent and
profoundness of their erudition. But the grand advantage
of a classical education consists far less in acquiring a
language or two, which, as languages, are to serve for use
or for ornament in future life, than in the things that are
learned in making that acquisition, and yet more in the
manner of learning those things. It is a wild conceit to
suppose that the branches of knowledge, which are most
rich and extensive, and most deserve to engage the re-

searches of a mature mind, are, therefore, the best for training a young one. Metaphysics, for instance, as we have already intimated, though in the last degree unprofitable as a science, is a suitable and excellent, perhaps a necessary part of the intellectual discipline of youth. On the contrary, international law is extremely important to be known by publicists and statesmen, but it would be absurd to put Vattel (as we have ourselves seen it done in a once celebrated academy, in a certain part of the United States) into the hands of a lad of fifteen or sixteen. We will admit, therefore, what has been roundly asserted at hazard, and without rhyme or reason, that classical scholars discontinue these studies after they are grown wise enough to know their futility, and only read as much Greek and Latin as is necessary to keep up their knowledge of them, or rather to save appearances and gull credulous people ; yet we maintain that the concession does not affect the result of this controversy in the least. We regard the whole period of childhood and of youth—up to the age of sixteen or seventeen, and perhaps longer—as one allotted by nature to growth and improvement in the strictest sense of those words. The flexible are to be trained rather than tasked, to be carefully and continually practised in the preparatory exercises, but not to be loaded with burthens that may crush them, or be broken down by overstrained efforts in the race. It is in youth that Montaigne's maxim—always excellent—is especially applicable, "that the important question is, not who is most learned, but who has learned the best." Now we confess we have no faith at all in young prodigies, in your philosophers in teens. We have generally found these precocious smatterers sink in a few years into barrenness and imbecility, and that as they begin by being men when they ought to be boys, so they end in being boys when they ought to be men. If we would have good fruit we must wait until it is in season. Nature herself has pointed out too clearly to be misunderstood, the proper studies of childhood and youth. The senses are first developed; observation and memory follow; then imagination begins to dream and create; afterwards ratiocination, or the dialectical propensity and faculty, shoots up with great rankness, and last of all, the crowning perfection of intellect, sound judgment and solid reason, which, by much experience in life, at length ripen into wisdom. The vicissitudes of the seasons, and the consequent changes in the face of nature, and the cares and occupations of the husbandman, are not more clearly distinguished or more unalterably ordained. To break in upon this harmonious order, to attempt to anticipate these pre-established periods, "what is it," as Cicero has it, "but, after the manner of the giants, to war against the laws of the universe, and the wisdom that created it?" And why do so? Is not the space in human life, between the eighth and twentieth years, quite large enough for acquiring *every* branch of literal knowledge, as well as they need, or indeed, can be acquired in youth? For instance, we cite the opinion of Condorcet, repeatedly quoted with approbation by Dugald Stewart, and if we mistake not, by Professor Playfair too (both of them the highest authority on such a subject), "that any one may, under competent teachers, acquire all that Newton or La Place knew, in *two* years." The same observation, of course, applies *à fortiori* to any other branch of science. As for the modern languages, the study of French ought to be begun early for the sake of the pronunciation, and continued through the whole course, as it may be, without the smallest inconvenience. Of German, we say nothing, because we cannot speak of our own knowledge; but for Italian and Spanish, however difficult they may be, especially their poetry, to a mere English scholar, they are so easy of acquisition to any one who understands Latin, that it is not worth while even to notice them in our scheme. All that we ask then, is, that a boy should be thoroughly taught the ancient languages from his eighth to his sixteenth year, or thereabouts, in which time he will have his taste formed, his love of letters completely, perhaps enthusiastically awakened; his knowledge of the principles of universal grammar perfected; his memory stored with the history, the geography, and the chronology of all antiquity, and with a vast fund of miscellaneous literature besides; his imagination kindled with the most beautiful and glowing passages of Greek and Roman poetry and eloquence; all the rules of criticism familiar to him; the sayings of sages, and the achievements of heroes indelibly impressed upon his heart. He will have his curiosity fired for further acquisition, and find himself in possession of the golden keys, which open all the recesses where the stores of knowledge have ever been laid up by civilized man. The consciousness of strength will give him confidence, and he will go to the rich treasures themselves and take what he wants, instead of picking up eleëmosynary scraps from those whom, in spite of himself, he will regard as his betters in literature. He will be let into that great communion of scholars throughout all ages and all nations, like that more awful communion of saints in the Holy Church Universal, and feel a sympathy with departed genius, and with the enlightened and the gifted

minds of other countries, as they appear before him, in
the transports of a sort of vision beatific, bowing down at
the same shrines, and glowing with the same holy love
of whatever is most pure and fair and exalted and divine
in human nature. Above all, our American youth will
learn, that liberty, which is sweet to all men, but which is
the *passion* of proud minds that cannot stoop to less, has
been the nurse of all that is sublime in character and
genius. They will see her form and feel her influence in
everything that antiquity has left for our admiration; that
bards consecrated their harps to her; that she spoke from
the lips of the mighty orators; that she fought and conquered, acted and suffered, with the heroes whom she had
formed and inspired; and, after ages of glory and virtue,
fell with *Him*—her all-accomplished hope—*Him*, the last
of Romans, the self-immolated martyr of Philippi. Our
young student will find his devotion to his country—his
free country—become at once more fervid and more enlightened, and think scorn of the wretched creatures who
have scoffed at the sublime simplicity of her institutions,
and "esteem it," as one expresses it, who learned to be a
republican in the schools of antiquity, "much better to
imitate the old and elegant humanity of Greece, than the
barbaric pride of a Norwegian or Hunnish stateliness;"
and, let us add, will come much more to despise that
slavish and nauseating subserviency to rank and title, with
which all European literature is steeped through and
through. If Americans are to study any foreign literature at all, it ought undoubtedly to be the classical, and
especially the Greek.

The very difficulties of these studies, which make it
necessary that so many years should be devoted to them,

the novelty, the strangeness of the form, are a great recommendation. This topic is a most important one, and we would gladly follow it out; but we have already exceeded our limits. We will just observe, that the reason which Quinctilian gives for beginning with the Greek, is of universal application. The mother tongue is acquired as of course in the nursery, at the fire-side, at the parental board, in society, everywhere. It is familiar to us long before we are capable of remarking its peculiarities. This familiarity has its usual effects of diminishing curiosity and interest, and of making us regard, without emotion, and even without attention, what, if it came recommended by novelty, would leave the deepest impression. It is so with everything in nature and in art. "Difficulties increase passions of every kind, and by rousing our attention, and exciting our active powers, they produce an emotion, which nourishes the prevailing affection." Before his eighth year, a boy should be perfectly well grounded in the rudiments of English; and then, if his master be a scholar that deserves the name, he could learn his own language better by having occasion to use it in translations, both prose and metrical, of the ancient languages, than by all the lessons and lectures of a mere English teacher from his birth to his majority. Indeed it would be difficult, in the present state of our literature, to imagine anything more insipid, spiritless, imperfect, and unprofitable than such a course.

THE WOES OF MODERN GREECE: A PRIZE POEM.

BY HENRY T. FARMER.

THERE was a harp, that might thy woes rehearse,
In all the wild omnipotence of verse,
Imperial Greece! when wizard Homer's skill
Charm'd the coy Muses from the woodland hill;
When nature, lavish of her boundless store,
Pour'd all her gifts, while art still shower'd more;—
Thy classic chisel through each mountain rung,
Quick from its touch immortal labors sprung;
Truth vied with fancy in the grateful strife,
And rocks assumed the noblest forms of life.

Alas! thy land is now a land of wo;
Thy muse is crown'd with Druid misletoe.
See the lorn virgin, with dishevelled hair,
To distant climes in wilder'd haste repair;
Chill desolation seeks her favor'd bowers,
Neglect, that mildew, blasts her cherish'd flowers;
The spring may bid their foliage bloom anew,
The night may dress them in her fairy dew;
But what shall chase the winter-cloud of pain,
And bid her early numbers breathe again?
What spring shall bid her mental gloom depart?—
'Tis always winter in a broken heart.

The aged Patriarch seeks the sea-beat strand,
To leave—for ever leave his native land.

No sun shall cheer him with so kind a beam,
No fountain bless him with so pure a stream;
Nay, should the exile through Elysium roam,
He leaves his heaven, when he leaves his home.
But, we may deeper, darker truth unfold,
Of matrons slaughtered, and of virgins sold,
Of shrines polluted by barbarian rage,
Of grey locks rifled from the head of age,
Of pilgrims murdered, and of chiefs defied,
Where Christians knelt, and Sparta's heroes died.
Once more thy chiefs their glittering arms resume,
For heaven, for vengeance, conquest or a tomb.
With fix'd resolve to be for ever free,
Or leave all Greece one vast Thermopylæ.

Columbia, rise! a voice comes o'er the main,
To ask thy blessing, nor to ask in vain;
Stand forth in bold magnificence, and be
For classic Greece, what France was once for thee.
So shall the gods each patriot bosom sway,
And make each Greek the hero of his day.
But, should thy wisdom and thy valor stand
On neutral ground—oh! may thy generous hand
Assist her hapless warrior, and repair
Her altars, scath'd by sacrilege and care.
Hail all her triumphs, all her ills deplore,
Nor let old Homer's manes beg once more.

THE PILGRIMS OF NEW ENGLAND.

BY WILLIAM CRAFTS.

On this day, two hundred years ago, a handful of individuals landed, at an inclement season, on an unknown and barren coast; in the land of pestilence, on the territory of the savage. Fraud or accident had diverted the course of their voyage, and they were placed beyond the protection, weak as it was, of European charters. Neither the church nor the state accorded them the privilege of monopoly or of participation, and they landed with no better plea than their necessities, and no protection but their God.

Providence was not unmindful of them. That they might with scrupulous honesty occupy the soil, its former inhabitants had perished by disease, or wandered into exile; that they might in infancy be secure from Indian warfare, the natives had been withdrawn from the sea shore; and, lest famine should involve them in early ruin, the scanty granaries of the savage became the treasure-trove of the stranger. The soil was rugged and mountainous, indicating the labor and perseverance which its culture required. It had not the baneful reputation of gold and silver mines, the cheap ruin of adventurers and nations. It was primitive and virginal, like the snows that invested it. Scarce a path on its surface but the track of the hunter and his game—scarce a sound in its forests but the rude chorus of the winds.

Well we may ask what worldly inducement impelled

this little band of men, women and children, away from
their friends and their home, in a little barque across the
perilous ocean, to an ice-bound, rocky shore ?   Was it
ambition, that master passion of the human breast, that
knows not difficulties in the pursuit of power ?   To charge
them with ambition were to accuse them of lunacy.   Was
it avarice, that chameleon curse of our nature, which
assimilates to us all climates and all suffering in the pursuit of gain ?   They had no means to traffic, and no arms
to plunder.   Were they convicts doomed to expiate
among the savage, their sins among the civilized ?   They
had been sinned against, not sinning themselves.   It was
that sense of wrong, which he who feels it at all, feels
most acutely, and forgives never.   It was that species
of oppression, which he who endures all else never will
endure, that gave birth to this desperate and heroic
enterprise.   You may invade a man's opinions, one by one,
and dispossess him of them all, until you interfere with
his religious sentiments, and his rights of conscience.
You then strike a spring, whose elasticity increases with
its pressure, rallying every other power in the system and
quickening the motion of them all.   You provoke his
love of truth—his regard for early impressions—his sense
of duty—his hopes of happiness—his pride—his zeal—
his obstinacy—his chagrin and his resentment.   He who
would willingly encounter these, knows nothing of the
lessons of history.   It appears to be the decree of God, that
religious persecution shall avail its authors only shame
and remorse, while it endows its victims with extraordinary
courage, ensures them the Divine protection, and fits
them for heroic suffering and achievement.

  * * * * * * * * *

The ancestors of New England, driven from their home by the persecution of Laud, after a short residence in Holland, where religious and political discussions prevailed with much force and freedom, embarked for America, in the hope of enjoying religious liberty, if not at home, yet under the authority of their monarch. They asked his license to live in an uncomfortable wilderness, crowded with dangers; but so obnoxious were their doctrines, and so slighted their loyalty, that they were refused protection, and only promised indifference. They came, however; and the treachery of the Dutch, who had furnished them a refuge, caused them to be landed far north of their original destination.

Houseless, frozen, miserable outcasts! why not forsake your hopeless enterprise, and leave to the great men of the earth the costly office of planting colonies, enlightening the heathen, and taming the savage?

"It was not," to use their own language, "with them as with common men, whom small things could discourage or small discontents cause to wish to be again at home." They formed on board of their ship a plan of civil and political government, a strict and "sacred bond to take care of the good of each other, and the whole," and disembarked with a fearless intrepidity, inspired by conscience and justified by Heaven.

If the Indian was friendly for a while, the climate made war upon them, and ere they could plant the earth with seed for the living, they opened it to find graves for the dead. They were sorrowful but not disheartened, adhering to their purpose with an intense steadiness of soul, which almost excites the belief that an Angel had revealed to them the glories of their destiny. They endured neglect and oppression, the awards which the world in its charity and its discernment decrees to merit and to genius. Unthinking world! how often thy wrongs are sources of triumph, and thy honors themes of ridicule! A strong affection among themselves — an unbending reliance on Providence—patience in suffering—perseverance in toil—strict honesty, and benevolent regard toward the Indians, were their characteristics. By the aid of these, and the rigid purity of their manners, although peaceable, they conquered a country; although unambitious, they founded an empire ; although obscure, they shall be held in honored remembrance.

* * * * * * * * *

If, on this day, after the lapse of two centuries, one of the Fathers of New England, released from the sleep of death, could re-appear on earth, what would be his emotions of joy and wonder! In lieu of a wilderness, here and there interspersed with solitary cabins, where life was scarcely worth the danger of preserving it, he would behold joyful harvests, a population crowded even to satiety, villages, towns, cities, states, swarming with industrious inhabitants, hills graced with temples of devotion, and valleys vocal with the early lessons of virtue. Casting his eye on the ocean, which he passed in fear and trembling, he would see it covered with enterprising fleets returning with the whale as their captive, and the wealth of the Indies for their cargo. He would behold the little colony which he planted, grown into gigantic stature, and forming an honorable part of a glorious confederacy, the pride of the earth and the favorite of Heaven. He would witness with exultation the general prevalence of correct principles of government and virtuous habits of action; how gladly would he gaze upon the long stream of light and renown from Harvard's classic fount, and the kindred springs of Yale, of Providence, of Dartmouth and of Brunswick! Would you fill his bosom with honest pride, tell him of Franklin, who made the thunder sweet music, and the lightning innocent fire-works — of Adams, the venerable sage reserved by heaven, himself a blessing, to witness its blessings on nature—of Ames, whose tongue became, and has become an Angel's—of Perry,

> " Blest by his God with one illustrious day,
> A blaze of glory, ere he passed away."

And tell him, Pilgrim of Plymouth, these are thy descendants. Show him the stately structures, the splendid benevolence, the masculine intellect, and the sweet hospitality of the metropolis of New England. Show him that immortal vessel, whose name is synonymous with triumph, and each of her masts a sceptre. Show him the glorious fruits of his humble enterprise; and ask him if this, all this, be not an atonement for his sufferings, a recompense for his toils, a blessing on his efforts, and a heart-expanding triumph for the Pilgrim adventurer. And if he be proud of his offspring, well may they boast of their parentage.

SUNSET AT ROME: A PRIZE POEM.

BY A. A. MULLER.

" Roma lieta rideva e pareva ch'ella
Tutti i raggi del Sole avesse intorno."

TASSO.

A DAY hath pass'd in Rome, and round her spires
The farewell sun hath lit a thousand fires ;
Vanquished his strength, the blazing god of day
Sinks from his throne, and hides each quivering ray.
He smiles no more on earth, yet round his shrine,
Gleam the last beauties of his bright decline,
While round each crimson'd cloud, in triumph play,
The transient flashes of expiring day.
That blaze of glory, which at noon unfurl'd
Its gorgeous standard to the gazing world,
Is quench'd not yet ;—and now its mellow'd light
Falls on the far off Tuscan's rocky height,
And sends its last blush o'er the yellow wave,
Where Tyber winds beneath Metella's grave !
See, from yon Alban mount the deep red glow
Throws its broad radiance on the vales below ;
While shadows from the Tarpeian summit fall
O'er the dark ruins of the Cæsars' hall !

Twilight is round me ! and each vestige gone
That mark'd the God in beauty as he shone,
Save, where reflected from his buried car,
One ray yet lingers in the vesper star :

Some sentinel within the silent sphere,
He hails each planet of the viewless air ;
And comes like hope to shed his soften'd light
O'er the dark bosom of affliction's night.
Far fam'd Italia—Saturn's star-crowned coast,
Thus has thy sun gone down—its brightness lost !
That orb, that with thy morn of beauty came,
And rose resplendent o'er thy early name,
No longer lives, nor glows, with light refin'd,
O'er the lost empire of thy perished mind.
That source and centre of Promethean fire,
Whose touch ethereal tuned Apollo's lyre,
No longer warms the soul of cherish'd song,
Nor wakes the thunders of the patriot's tongue.
God of the silver bow !* no more thy sound
Woos the lov'd muse to haunts of classic ground ;
No longer genius leaves his lonely cell,
In thy soft myrtle groves with fame to dwell ;
Nor fair Parnassian maids, around thy shrine,
Bring laurel'd wreaths to grace thy lovely Nine.
As thus beneath the ruin'd porch of Fame,†
The thoughtful muse recalls some honor'd name,
What faded images of glory rise,
From out the tombs where buried greatness lies :
Horatius Flaccus sleeps ! oh, who shall tell
The triumphs of that name ?—the magic spell
Of well-remember'd odes, enchanting lays,
The pride of scholars, and the pedant's praise,
The attic wit, whose spirit fanned the flame

* A title given by Homer to Apollo.
† Temple of Fame.

That lent its fires to guild the Augustan name.
"Integer vitæ"*—who shall wake again
The harp that kindled first that master strain ?
Or who shall boast of satire's pointed song
While Horace sings to charm the list'ning throng.
Virgilius Publius, too,—I write the name,
The treasur'd talisman of Roman fame :
" Arms and the man "†—with epic skill refin'd,
Welcome such music to the classic mind :
Mysterious train of thought—what power combin'd
Thy fairy movements o'er the mortal mind ?
The flight of ages—space—all earth and sea
Prescribe no bounds to thy immensity !

'Tis thus the soul returns to boyhood's prime,
To rescue back one thoughtful hour from time,
To feel once more the magic of that power,
That charm'd the vigils of the midnight hour ;
To hear again the clash of Trojan arms,
See fair Creusa 'mid her wild alarms,
And breathe with Æneas to his aged sire
The filial vow which nature's laws inspire.
'Tis thus at Rome, the pilgrim comes to mourn
O'er faded relics Time hath widely worn ;
'Tis there, from its own pure and bright domain,
The mind of ages comes to earth again,—
While memory, with her fondest theme, renews
Some cherish'd impress of each sleeping muse.
Illustrious Maro—Rome still reigns for thee !

* The beginning of the twenty-second Ode of Horace, Book 1.
† " Arma virumque cano," the known invocation of Virgil to his Muse.

Thy fame decrees her immortality.
Gone are her glories, sunk her mighty throne,
Her kings have perish'd and her victors flown ;
Arts have decay'd, and letter'd wisdom sleeps
Within that tomb,* where lie its treasur'd heaps ;
Yet thy pure spirit lives throughout her clime,
To swell the measure of its deathless rhyme :
And thy proud language still adorns her page,
The charm of youth—the pride of every age.
Long may she boast the triumphs of that skill,
That wak'd o'er Mantuan chords the lyric thrill ;
Long may its echoes fall on every plain,
The purest model of the Tuscan strain ;
Till that proud day when, o'er Apollo's shrine,
Freedom once more shall shed its fires divine ;
And genius from above, its kindling flame,
Resume its torch to light the Etrurian name,
When Rome again shall rule and bless mankind,
Her empire knowledge, and her sceptre mind !

THE MORALS OF ENTOMOLOGY.

BY JOHN BACHMAN, D.D.

Insects are further deserving of our notice from their
various and curious structure, their extraordinary metamorphoses, their remarkable instincts, their wonderful
habits, and the variety and beauty of their colors. But I

* The Vatican Library of Rome.

will not enter into detail under these different heads; it would require many volumes, and the subject would not even then be exhausted. But let it suffice to state, that in almost every department of science or of duty, the study of the insect tribe offers a rich reward to its votaries. The entomologist finds, in examining their organization, enough to fill him with wonder and astonishment. He is struck with their metamorphoses, their instinct, and their industry. He finds that man has been anticipated by this feeble race in many of his inventions and discoveries. He finds that in architecture, insects were before him in rearing houses with stair-cases, arches, domes and colonnades. The white ants have taught him to construct a tunnel twelve times larger in proportion to their size, than that which is now carrying on under the Thames. He finds that paper is no new invention, but was beautifully fabricated by an insect ever since the world began. He finds a spider building his house in the deep water, which he keeps inflated by means of something more ingenious than an air-pump; he descends without getting wet in a natural diving bell, and dwells securely, and is kept dry in the bottom of rivers. He finds insects possessed of instruments and apparatus, more ingenious than those which the ingenuity of man has enabled him to invent; he finds that they are furnished with augurs, gimblets, knives, lancets, scissors, and forceps. From the industry and untiring vigilance they display in guarding their young, he learns a lesson of parental affection. He sees our Carolina mason-wasp, for instance, building its dwelling with an admirable cement, which it is taught to prepare, and which is superior to any mortar. Here it forms its cell, the cradle of its young, and in each cell where it

deposits an egg, it places a certain number of spiders,
that may serve as food for its expected brood. These, it
is taught by instinct, to render air-tight, that the spiders
may not decay till they are needed as food. He sees
certain species of ants (one of which is common with us
and is often found in decayed trees), which are born with
wings; when they have made use of these to convey
them to suitable places where they are to commence their
labors and rear their families, by a powerful effort ridding
themselves of wings, which might be an impediment to
them in the discharge of their new, active and laborious
duties. He sees them when their houses are disturbed,
like the fond mother whose dwelling is in flames, seizing
the larvæ of their young in their mouths and carrying them
to a place of security. If, under these circumstances, they
are bruised and wounded, they still hold on to their beloved charge, let them be cut asunder, or let the flames be
applied to them, and they yet will not relinquish their hold.
And even when that mysterious principle, called life, has
passed away, they are found clinging to their offspring.
He sees all this; he pauses, wonders and adores. He is
at a loss to discern where instinct ends, and where reason
begins. As a lover of the beauties of nature, he is not
insensible to the rich and ever-varying colors with which a
bountiful Creator has adorned many species of the insect
tribe. He sees beetles which outvie in brilliancy the
burnished gold, the emerald, the amethyst and the topaz.
He sees in the wings of several species of locusts and the
libelulæ, a fabrication, infinitely more delicate than the
finest lace. And among the lepidopterous tribes, the but-
terflies, the sphinges and moths, he is dazzled by every
shade and color, vieing with the deepest and purest azure
of the sky.

"Who can paint like Nature?
Can imagination boast amid her gay profusion
Hues like these?"

He has been instructed by the book of God in the cheering doctrine of the resurrection of the body. There he
has been taught that man, the child of the earth, a crawl-
ing worm, when his career is finished here below, casts
off the earthly body and is laid in the ground; that in due
time, that which was sown an earthly body, shall be
raised a spiritual body, endowed with new and augmented
powers, enabling him to wing his way to a purer, a happier and immortal state. And the doctrine which he has
learnt in God's revealed word, he now finds written in
legible characters by the same Almighty hand in the book
of Nature. And here the metamorphoses of insects serve
to strengthen our faith in holy writ. The caterpillar first
crawls on the earth, is sustained by ordinary kinds of food
and engaged in incessant labors. When it has existed a
few weeks or months in this humble form, its work being
finished, it passes into a chrysalis state, resembling the
sleep of death; it is wound up in a kind of shroud and
encased in a coffin, and is buried in the earth, or fastened
to some branch in the air, or sunk in the water. In the
appointed time, earth, air and water give up their several
prisoners; warmed by the sun, they come forth from their
state of torpidity, as a bride out of her chamber, arrayed
in nuptial glory. They are prepared to enjoy a new and
more exalted condition in life, and having arrived to the
perfection of their nature they feed on the nectar of flowers, traverse the fields of air, and love begins its blissful
reign.

I hope I have said enough to convince you, that the

science which has beguiled many a lonely hour of the naturalist, is neither devoid of interest nor utility; and, if I have not succeeded, be assured the fault is in me, not in the study.

But, I have heard an objection urged against the pursuits of the entomologist, which, as it is a very serious charge—no less than that of hard-heartedness and cruelty— I must beg a little more of your indulgence to enable me to refute. We have sometimes been told, that the impaling of insects, as it inflicts on them a torture, may be calculated to destroy the finer feelings of the heart, and blunt those sensibilities which are the highest ornaments of our nature. You may charge the naturalist with being mad; this we can bear, for if it were true, it would only be a visitation of God, for which we would not be answerable; and we would be repaid for the reproach by those numberless and indescribable charms which cheer us on our way at every step we tread on this beauteous earth. But we cannot bear the imputation of cruelty; our nature revolts at the charge. We would pursue no occupation which is calculated to destroy the finer feelings of the soul, or weaken the ties that bind us in sympathy to our race. Hear our arguments before you condemn our pursuits.

Insects, though admirably constructed to the ends for which they were designed, are not as susceptible of pain as creatures who rank above them. From man down to the cryptogamous plant, there is a regular gradation, both in structure and sensibility. From intellectual, reasoning man, whose aversion to pain is occasioned by reflection, and a fear of death, we descend to the brute, who, as far as we know, is only governed by the laws of instinct, or whose reasoning powers are very limited. Descending another step, we come down to the reptiles who are cold-blooded, in consequence of their slow respiration. These require no covering or teguments to retain heat. They are consequently sluggish, and can continue long without food; they may remain in a state of torpidity for many years, as has been ascertained from the living frogs and some kindred genera that have been found imbedded in trees, and even in rocks, where they have remained for centuries. The tortoise is known to walk about long after its head has been cut off, and the polypus multiplies like the cuttings of a plant, by the application of the knife. We descend another step in the creation, and the insect tribe is presented to us. I shall not detain you with a description of their internal structure, and shall simply state, in confirmation of the views which I am supporting, that, so very slight are those organs in insects which constitute the nervous system, the circulation of the blood and respiration, that naturalists have been greatly perplexed in their investigations on this subject. Linnæus wholly denied the existence of a brain in insects; and most of our modern physiologists have arrived at the same conclusions. Lyonet and Cuvier, after the most careful dissections, could find no heart, nor even the slightest traces of any arteries proceeding from, or communicating with it. From the recent experiments of Carus and other naturalists of Germany, organs of circulation have been discovered in some insects, and I think there can be no doubt but they exist in all; but these organs were so minute that it required the aid of glasses of high magnifying powers to render them visible. It may be said, however, that the organs of respiration in insects are in proportion to the size of these diminutive creatures. In answer to

this, I have to observe, that there are many insects much
larger than many species of quadrupeds, and even in
these large subjects, these organs are not visible to the
naked eye. I possess a specimen of a native, and probably undescribed quadruped, obtained by a friend in the
swamps of the Santee, which, though full grown, measures
but an inch and a quarter in length, and in size is no
thicker than the quill of a swan. It is a species of *sorex*
or shrew-mouse. This diminutive animal possessed the
organs of circulation and respiration so distinct, that they
could be examined without the aid of glasses ; and yet
the largest insects, such as the *phasma titan*, which measures eight inches in length, the *prionus gigas*, six and a
half inches, and the *dynastes hercules* (the hercules
beetle), measuring four and a half inches, exhibit no traces
of respiratory organs to the naked eye. Insects have no
lungs, and breathe through spiracles along their sides and
abdomen. Let me not be misunderstood. I do not say
that the insects are not perfect as insects. They may
possess senses with which we are as yet unacquainted.
All I wish to prove is, that, from their formation, they cannot be as susceptible of pain as beings, whose internal
organization approaches nearer to that of man. And the
more we examine their habits, the more sensible we are
made of this truth. The humble bee will continue to
drink honey even when it has been cut in twain. Remove the legs of an insect, and it will continue as lively
and active as if nothing had occurred ; and a butterfly will
fly to the first flower and regale itself, although an insect
pin is pierced through the centre of its body. Now if
insects were as susceptible of pain as man, think you
that they would exhibit such insensibility to pain ? Would

man feel an appetite for his food at the moment when a leg or an arm was amputated, or when a sword was run through his body? The manner in which we deprive insects of motion is also greatly misunderstood. Many of them are found and preserved, after they had died a natural death. An amiable entomologist in New England states, that nearly the whole of his collection was procured on the sea shore. The insects had been driven to sea and drowned in gales of wind, and were washed on shore by the returning tide. When it is necessary that we should deprive them of life for the use of our cabinets, our knowledge of their organization enables us to effect this in a moment, without our witnessing a struggle; an acid, alcohol and steam (all-powerful steam, which seems destined almost to annihilate time and space), are the agents we employ; and if our sensibilities will not permit us even to do this, we then do as you do with the poultry destined for your tables,—we entrust the work to, and divide the responsibility with, a servant. But, my sensitive brother, if I have not yet said enough to convince you that the pursuits of the entomologist are not cruel, then let me turn the tables upon you. For whom are those hecatombs of animals slain, the gigantic ox, the meek lamb, and the gentle pigeon, but for you? Do not exonerate yourself by saying that you had no hand in their extermination; it was, if not by your order, at least for your use. You are, in the eye of the law, a *particeps criminis;* you are the aider, the abettor, the receiver, and the consumer; and if there is cruelty in the act (which I do not admit), you must bear the reproach. You say, however, that it was for the support of life, and you plead your canine tooth. Whilst I agree with you on this, we will all recollect that animal food is not essential to our existence, as we learn from those nations that abstain from its use. But you say you cannot bear to see the beautiful butterfly impaled, and you think it cruel to cause its death. Stop, my friend; what is that grub which you so anxiously search for in your garden and on your trees, and cast to your poultry or crush under your feet, as a thing not fit to live? Why it is that very butterfly in another stage of his life. If you have such a sympathy for him, now is the time to spare him. He is now enjoying his animal life as much as in any other period of his existence; he culls from among all the delicacies of nature, that which he likes best, and he eats twice his weight in twenty-four hours. But when the naturalist seizes upon him, it is at a time when he has passed through all his stages, and in the course of nature is about to die. A few hours, or at farthest, a few days more, and his beautiful wings would be ruffled and broken, and he would become the prey of some ravenous bird or fish. And in return for anticipating the stern mandates of nature, we prize him as gold, we embalm his body, we place him in the temple of science, pronounce his eulogium there, and confer upon him a kind of immortality.

And, fair lady, have you too joined in the cry of cruelty against the poor naturalist? Let us just remind you of your inventions to destroy the cockroach and the fly. That spider, who in the farthest corner of your chamber, as if courting security and peace, had built his house, with its doors and galleries, and his finely constructed net to enable him to obtain the means of subsistence, you cause to be brushed away, and consign him and his works ignobly to the dust. Every worm that assails your pretty plants is hastily devoted to destruction, and a single fumigation of your greenhouse destroys more insects in an hour than the naturalist collects in a year. Away with this affectation of sensibility; this generation will not pass away before the subject will be better understood, and woman, the fairest of God's works, will, instead of condemning, assist us in the study; and, as from the occupation we sometimes form an estimation of the character, let me ask, when and where have you ever found the student of nature a cruel man? He wanders to every land; often without scrip or purse, he carries with him no implements of war, and none of the means of acquiring pecuniary gain. He appears in the simplest dress, with a staff in his hand and his box under his arm, content and happy with his innocent pursuits, and deriving pleasure and instruction at every step he treads, till the very savage of the wilderness, touched with kindred feelings and sympathies, joins in his pursuits, and becomes his companion and protector through his territories. If, in this paper, I shall have been so fortunate as to have removed from the minds of my readers any prejudices that may have existed against the pursuits of the naturalist, and the benefits to be derived from his studies, I shall consider myself amply repaid for my exertions; but double would be the gratification of the few naturalists in our country, to find in the community, an increased disposition to unite in their labors, to go with them and gaze with delighted and inquiring eyes on those things which they have seen, to aid them by their personal exertions, and pecuniary means, in preserving and adding to the rich and accumulating collections in our museums, without which natural history cannot be pursued to any practical purpose. Thus, whilst we will be collecting and preserving, admiring and studying these works of God, in which we behold his glory reflected, we will discover that in advancing the cause of science, and promoting the happiness of our race, we will be better fitted for that higher state of intelligence, and that perfection of happiness, to which immortal minds are privileged to aspire.

———

THE WIFE.

BY ANNA P. DINNIES.

I COULD have stemmed misfortune's tide,
 And borne the rich one's sneer,
Have braved the haughty glance of pride,
 Nor shed a single tear :
I could have smiled on every blow
 From Life's full quiver thrown,
While I might gaze on thee, and know
 I should not be " alone."

I could—I think I could have brooked,
 E'en for a time, that thou
Upon my fading face hadst looked
 With less of love than now ;
For then I should at least have felt
 The sweet hope still my own,
To win thee back, and, while I dwelt
 On earth, not be " alone."

But thus, to see, from day to day,
 Thy brightening eye and cheek,
And watch thy life-sands waste away,
 Unnumbered, slow and meek ;
To meet thy smiles of tenderness,
 And catch the feeble tone
Of kindness, ever breathed to bless,
 And feel, I'll be " alone."

To mark thy strength each hour decay,
 And yet thy hopes grow stronger,
As, filled with heavenward trust, they say,
 " Earth may not claim thee longer ;"
Nay, dearest, 'tis too much—this heart
 Must break, when thou art gone ;
It must not be—we may not part—
 I can not live " alone."

LOVE ASLEEP.

BY WILLIAM CRAFTS.

WAKE him not—he dreams of bliss,
His little lips put forth to kiss ;
His arms entwined in virgin grace,
Seem link'd in beautiful embrace.

He smiles, and on his opening lip,
Might saints refresh, and angels sip ;

He blushes—'tis the rosy light,
That morning wears on leaving night.

He sighs—'tis not the sigh of wo,
He only sighs that he may know
If kindred sighs another move,
For mutual sighs are signs of love.

He speaks—it is his dear one's name—
He whispers—still it is the same—
The imprison'd accents strive in vain,
They murmur through his lips again.

He wakes—the silly little boy,
To break the mirror thus of joy!
He wakes to sorrow and in pain—
Oh, love! renew thy dreams again.

———

THE SECRET OF ORATORICAL SUCCESS.

BY THOMAS S. GRIMKÉ.

IF any competent judge were to be asked in our day
what are the three great elements of oratory, he would be
considered as hardly in his right mind, or as jesting,
should he reply with Demosthenes, delivery is the first,
the second, and the third! How little the eloquence of
Demosthenes could have had in it of the profound and
comprehensive intellect, of the various knowledge and

admirable reasoning, of modern orators, is demonstrated by the fact of his having esteemed delivery *three* times more precious than any of those. How much, also, he must have undervalued the cultivation of *thought*, as the only real fountain of *style*, is obvious from his having *copied* Thucydides nine times with his own hand. Let it not be said that the good sense of the Athenian's method is proved by the result. If he *had not* talents to produce by self-cultivation a style equal to that of the historian, to have copied him a hundred times would have availed nothing. And if he *had* the talents, he needed not to copy a single sentence. The truth is, Demosthenes owed his style to his own talents, industry and ambition. How little credit he deserves for energy of character, and love of study, is manifested by his being able to devise no better method of *keeping himself* at home than shaving one-half of his head; an expedient of weakness in him, but of shrewdness and good sense in the Vendeans, when they treated their prisoners in this manner and then released them. The Athenian's method is as unworthy of a man of virtuous ambition and force of character, as the iron-pointed girdle of Pascal is of good sense and piety. It is undoubtedly true, that a good delivery is important to the modern orator, as a *speaker*, though not as a *writer*. But he needs not all the artificial, theatrical training of the ancients ; much less would he expose himself to ridicule and scorn by adopting their wiles and arts. When the ancient regulated his speaking by a musical instrument, he degraded the orator into the stage-player. When Cicero tells us that Roscius could express a thought as many ways in delivery as he could in words, it does not so much indicate the excellence of the actor as the inferiority of the orator. And when the ancient produced in court the wife and children of his client, or uncovered the bosom of the fair culprit, is it not a confession of his own insufficiency, and of the weakness and sensuality of the judges ? How is the true character of ancient eloquence illustrated by the anecdote of the traitor Manlius ? Whilst he pleaded his cause before the people, *in sight of the* Tarpeian rock, though guilty, and they knew it, they would not condemn him. But when he was removed, and again put on his trial before the people, they condemned him unanimously. St. Basil tells us that painters accomplish as much by their pictures as orators by their eloquence : and Methodius, that a picture of the last judgment converted Bogoris, king of the Bulgarians. We regard both as illustrations of ancient speaking. But we desire as little to see the modern student rely on the pantomime oratory of St. Basil, as the missionary on the pictorial eloquence of Methodius. When the Areopagus resolved to hear causes in the dark, what was it but a direct unblushing acknowledgment of their deficiency in the sense of duty which became them as patriots, and in the moral courage which became them as judges ? Let not the modern orator seek, then, for his models in ancient times, characterized by such facts. And yet I doubt not that Lord Chatham, taking into view his personal appearance, manners, rank, and character, with the age and country in which he lived, surpassed Demosthenes himself, even in delivery.

> " ——————————— Never tone
> So thrilled thro' nerve, and vein, and bone."
> " His eyebrow dark and eye of fire
> Showed spirit proud and prompt to ire ;

Yet lines of thought upon his cheek
Did deep design and counsel speak."
" —————————— With menacing hand,
Put forth as in the action of command,
And eyes, that darted the red lightning down."

If Mr. Burke, who had not more disadvantages to overcome than Demosthenes, had availed himself of the
instruction of Garrick, he would have been *eminent* in the
department of *spoken*, as he is now *pre-eminent* in the
department of *written eloquence*. Let each be an object
with the American student of eloquence ; the former as of
temporary, occasional value, the latter as of the highest and
most durable importance. Let it not be forgotten that it
is his great duty to speak to the people through the
press. His whole country is the theatre for the achievements of his eloquence, not merely a court house, a
popular meeting, or the legislature. The sermons of
Father Lingesdes were received with incredible applause,
when delivered ; but despairing of having them read in
their native dress, he translated them into Latin, and then
printed them in that form. Dante at first intended to have
written his great poem and his treatise on monarchy, in
Latin ; but he afterwards changed his plan, and wrote
them in Italian, that he might instil into the people his
satirical sentiments and political opinions. With the
same general object in view, and the same audience, let
the American orator cultivate composition, as incomparably
more valuable than delivery. Let him resolve to be a writer,
that he may bless and delight thousands, rather than a
speaker, to instruct and entertain only hundreds.

CLAUDE LORRAINE

BY CHARLES FRASER.

RESPLENDENT in the West, the setting sun
Announces day's departure—not a cloud
Fleckers, with envious shade, his glorious path,
Nor veils the dazzling radiance of the scene,
As slow he sinks beneath the landscape's verge.
This was the shrine of thy devotion, Claude!
Here, thy rapt eye its vesper homage paid
To nature's majesty. By this inspir'd,
Thy glowing pencil o'er the canvas pour'd
Its rival splendors,—and with classic grace
Italia's scenes portray'd—the sombre arch,
The consecrated grove,—the slumbering lake,
The azure mountains mingling with the sky,—
Th' Egerian solitude, or Baiæ's shore ;
Whilst o'er each scene, with blended beauty, met
The poet's genius and the painter's art.

———

THE FALL OF JERUSALEM.

BY ISAAC HARBY.

LET us take a rapid glance at the history of our people
since the destruction of the temple, and view the contrast

the Jews of the United States now exhibit in opposition
to the Jews in Europe—the contrast between a once
powerful people scattered by the Almighty's anger, and
bowed in the dust, and humiliated into ignorance, by the petty
tyrants of the earth—and the free-born Jew, the citizen of
these enlightened States, raising once more the brow of
manhood and proud equality! We shudder at the dark,
the ignoble period gone by—I trust for ever. We hail
with pride our present rights and security. We carry our
feelings farther, and fervently pray that religious and
political emancipation may quickly be extended, not only
to our own brethren, dispersed throughout the habitable
globe, but to the oppressed of all mankind.

When the last and fatal blow was given, not only to
Jerusalem but to the Israelitish name, by the son of Ves-
pasian; when the civil controversies of our ancestors
were distracting the wise, and wasting the valor of the
brave; when everything seemed to aid in the accomplishment of that dark prophecy which had foretold of the
dispersion and slavery of Israel,—even in that trying hour,
the spirit of patriotism burned brightest. The factions
of John and Simon were in arms against each other.
While John with wily policy was in the city, aiming at
sovereign authority, Simon unexpectedly returned from
his expedition in Idumea. John and his adherents took
shelter in the Temple of Solomon, and discord presided
in those walls, once the sacred abode of peace and religion,
when the alarm was given that Titus was approaching to
punish those proud rebels against the supremacy of Rome.
It was the time of the Passover, and, from the adjacent
country, there were immense crowds of people assembled
in the city to celebrate that ancient and sacred festival.

The tumult ceased ; the approach of foreign enemies, in a moment put a stop to domestic faction. They drove off the besiegers with great slaughter ; they performed deeds of desperate valor ; they braced every muscle, and hardened every sinew, to defend, and to preserve, this last stand and resting-place of their name and nation. But the dark influence,—the destined hour was on them. They retired victorious from their walls, to wrangle and fight among themselves. Every day saw them victorious ; every day saw them growing weaker by intestine division. The malignant star of Israel was in the ascendant ; and no efforts of valor, no sacrifice of lives, could call down the better angel of the people. Still they fought with the desperation of lost men. They refused to listen to any terms of submission ; their wives, their sisters, their aged parents, their innocent little ones— those ties of nature and humanity which sweeten life and call forth all its cherished virtues—were as chaff before the dread Simoom of fury and of war. We are told by Josephus, that they banished one of their countrymen with ignominy for exhorting them to capitulate on no ignoble terms. Thus determined, they stood prepared to beat off the invading foe, or to perish within the walls of that city, which had been the seat of empire, the focal light of religion, the nurse of arts, the depository of the archives of ancient glory, won and made illustrious by the wisdom and sanctity and valor of their ancestors.

But alas ! all efforts were in vain. The appointed day had come. The visible signs of downfall were presented to their astonished eyes. Famine, fires, earthquakes, portents, unnatural sights, confusion and darkness, all seemed to unite in tremendous warnings, in intelligible

characters, that spoke the fall of Israel. No courage to
be gained from hope, they took resolution from despair.
Although the limited time had come—although the appointed hour had approached—when that nation who
acknowledged no monarch but their God, or one whom
they believed that God, by his special grace, had selected
to govern, were to submit their necks to the unrestrained
yoke of ambitious Rome ; still did your brave ancestors
resolve to hold on. They rallied in, and upon, and round
about the temple of Solomon ; not the one built by the wisest
of men, that had already fallen beneath the sacrilegious
hands of barbarian and heathen conquerors. This was
the second temple, and reckoned among the wonders of
the world. It was the seat of science, and the true
asylum of religion, where the father of a family, with his
wife and children, and the servant raised in his house, and
the stranger within his gates, came to worship the Almighty in truth and simplicity. There was wont to be
heard the sound of "the harp and the psaltery and the
ten-stringed instrument"—the song of praise from hallowed lips, chanting perhaps the inspiring psalm written by
the royal father, the first founder ;—" The heavens are tell-
ing the glory of God, and the firmament showeth his
handiwork. Day unto day uttereth speech, and night
unto night showeth knowledge." Such words, such music,
such heavenward strains were wont to fill those conscious
walls. It was a palace worthy of such ennobling office.
It was a building in which the architect had exhausted
every source, and applied every principle, of the sublime and
beautiful. To preserve this sacred edifice from violation,
the " forlorn hope " of Jerusalem profusely gave their blood.
But when they saw the flames, which had already con-

sumed half the city, beginning to devour this last remnant of their grandeur, this last citadel of their liberties—when they beheld the temple of God crumbling to ashes, or ascending in smoky and lurid volumes to the skies, veiling the fair face of day, and hanging over them even as the funeral pall of Israel, spread by the hands of the destroying angel—then, indeed, the weapons dropped from the hands of the brave,—the feeble and the old raised a melancholy cry to the throne of mercy, and the adjacent mountains re-echoed with the lamentations of women and children. The prophetic intimation was accomplished! The Roman Eagle waved in plumy triumph over prostrate Jerusalem!

> " O Lucifer ! thou radiant star,
>   Son of the morn, whose rosy car
>   Flam'd foremost in the van of day,
>   How art thou fallen ! "

ALFRED: AN HISTORICAL POEM.*

BY WM. SORANZO HASELL.

O'ER Morven's hill, just fading from the view,
The trembling sun-beam, twinkling through the shade,
Gleam'd mournful to the soul.   Th' illumin'd orb
Shone faintly ; then, immerg'd in darkness drear,
The low'ring clouds obscur'd the evening ray,

* Delivered at the public commencement at Yale College, September 11, 1799, by the author, then a youth of eighteen.

And spread a joyless gloom. The raven's cry,
The bittern's mournful sound, sadd'ning yet hoarse,
The gloom augments ; while ever and anon
The dismal wailing of the bird of night,
Comes fitful on the blast. Beneath the cliff,
Stood Alfred, Albion's prince ! Griev'd was his mind ;
A melancholy deep subdued his heart,
And gloom'd his faded brow—long groans his breast
Heav'd forth. Misfortune's bitter cup had reach'd
His lips,—he drain'd the last sad drop. The world,
A desert, wild and desolate ; his hopes
Destroy'd ; while the dear partner of his life
Was left to brave the ruthless spoiler's rage.
His private woes he felt ; but more he felt
His country's wrongs.

  " My friends," the prince exclaim'd,
" My brave companions, banish from your thoughts
Unmanly grief. Upon the Danish arms
Fortune now smiles ; the sov'reign God inclines ;
We must obey, nor dare t' arraign his will.
Here let us part ; first join our hands and hearts
As one, and lift our hopes to brighter days.
In some lone cottage, safe from curious eye,
Clad in the peasant's simple garb, I'll live,
Watchful to rescue from th' oppressor's grasp
My love, my subjects, and my hapless realm.
The bless'd occasion found, soon shall my voice
Arouse, and prove your prowess in the field."
Before the monarch bends each warrior's knee,
And with a sigh, each slowly winds his way.

In gloom desponding, while from distant fires,
The shouts of merriment, and Danish joy,
Went through the woods, and echo'd from the hills,
Alfred, in dreary solitude involv'd,
Pursues his path.　The watch-dog barks; he sees
A light faint breaking thro' the lengthen'd glade;
He knocks; the door unfolds; a lowly hind
Admits the royal guest.

　　　　　　　　　Revolving cares,
Deep in his mind, anxious and restless, long
Without repose, he lay; 'till lost in thought,
A balmy slumber overspread his frame.
Fancy's light wing, in airy visions bright,
Sports playful round; what real day denied,
In pleasing dreams, imagination gave,—
His soul's best treasure clasp'd! his kingdom sav'd!
Before his eyes, while distant ages roll,
Instarr'd with gems, whose constellated pow'r
Shed a new splendor, Albion's glory rose.

　The prince of light, in crimson robes array'd,
From ocean's lucid wave emerges bright;
His beams dance on the misty mountain top,
Gild the soft plumage of the warbling tribe,
Attune their hearts to chant the matin song.
Alfred awoke, the morn's orisons paid,
Trod the light grass, and trac'd his devious way,
From a dark grove, beneath the mountain's brow,
Stretching in full luxuriance to the mead,
With verdure crown'd, a beauteous form appears.
A robe of purest white her limbs adorned;

A zone of azure clasp'd her slender waist;
And zephyrs round her locks disporting play'd.
With ecstasy he view'd; then, panting, cried,
" It must—it cannot be—it *is* Elfrida!"
Warm to his breast he clasp'd her fainting form,
Dissolved in joy extreme. Sweet is th' embrace,
Where souls congenial meet; love, sentiment,
And friendship, pure desire, all blend in one.
Straight to the cottage door he led the fair.

Amid a region wild and desolate,
Where Thone and Parrett roll their turbid waves,
Environ'd round by fens, in woods immur'd,
He fix'd his lone retreat. Hence, from a fort,
Rais'd by a few bold peers, his chosen friends,
Upon the unwary Danes, in sleep dissolv'd,
Or banqueting in mirth, he sallied forth.
They fled in wonder; for they felt the blow,
Yet knew not whence it came.

One morn, while joy
Beam'd from his eye, a messenger arriv'd,
And loud proclaimed, " Hail! happy monarch, hail,
Glad tidings to thy royal ear I bring,
The brave Oddune, prince of Northumberland,
Has nobly fought the foe; bloody the strife,
But glorious victory on his standard perch'd;
Their magic banner, with enchantment wove,
Sad downfall to their hopes, our trophy waves."
New fires now light; new hopes inspire the prince;
He hails the auspicious era, now arriv'd,
To crown his wish. Throughout his realm, quick flies

The royal summons to his lurking bands,
On a set morn, before the day-star dawns,
At Sherwood's wavy grove, all armed t' appear.
Meantime, to view the Danish camps, and learn
Their force, position, strength, the chief resolves.

Pond'ring on this, and clad in deep disguise,
Prepared for bold adventure, at the cot,
Elfrida, mournful, met his raptur'd view.
Rumor had reach'd her ear of his design,
A deed of dreadful name ; th' alarm of death,
All dar'd in battle ; for her tender mind,
The seat of innocence and gentlest grace,
Recoil'd at carnage.   She indeed possess'd
" All that can sweetly charm, or softly please ;"
Still in her bosom, love sole empress reign'd,
Nor knew a rival.   Tremulous she spoke,

" Partner of all my hopes, my other self,
Who shar'st my sorrows and partak'st my joys,
Whom to possess is heaven, to lose is death,
Grant me this boon, deep anguish then shall cease
To rend my bosom.   If, when pleasure calls,
On the same stream we both serenely glide,
Why should I fly when dark'ning tempests low'r ?
Give me to join thee in the field of war !"
" Cease thus to wound my peace " (the prince replies),
God never form'd thy gentle limbs for toil ;
Nor could thy angel spirit e'er sustain
The boisterous tumults of the deathful field ;
But by our mutual love, we here must part,
God grant not long."   Dissolv'd in tears, she stood

In all the silent dignity of grief;
He gaz'd, nor longer dar'd to trust his view.

A minstrel now he goes; tun'd, in his hand
A harp he bore, fit symbol of his mind,
Plaintive, but bold! The din of arms is heard—
Light, airy notes now warble from the lyre;
The Danes receive the sound: In rapture won,
They lead him straight to Guthrum's tent.
The cautious minstrel strikes the trembling strings;
Gay melody quick vibrates from the touch,
Then slowly sinks, and, lost in silence, dies.
Now soothing, tender, wildly plaintive notes
Stream from the harp, and touch the monarch's breast;
The list'ning Danes, to catch the floating sounds,
Thick throng the tent. With praise and presents grac'd,
Alfred retires. His piercing eye had mark'd
Their strength, their numbers and the camp's weak part.
From a dark covert hid, up sprung a youth,
Well form'd and fair, a blush o'erspread his cheek;
Though tremulous his dulcet voice breath'd forth
His proffered aid in battle. Pleas'd, the prince
Welcom'd and led him on to Sherwood's grove.
As down the mountain's side a sudden gust
Swift sweeps, and roars within the vale below,
So hoarse applauses loud rang through the wood,
When the brave nobles, with their loyal bands,
Beheld their monarch. " Gallant warriors, hail!
And you, brave yeomanry," the prince exclaims,
" Arrayed in manly arms, for war prepar'd;
Behold yon blue expanse, yon lurid clouds,
In sullen grandeur roll; the lightnings flash,

There in bright streaks, there in one gen'ral blaze ;
In solemn broken peals, heaven's thunder roars ;
Does this appal you ?   'Tis an omen bless'd ;
The God of worlds frowns on the Danish arms,
And bids you hasten to the embattled plain.
Before him bend the knee, then rise to fight,
And bravely dare for England, and for life."
Now shouts convulse the air, the clarion sounds,
The startled Danes spring from the bed of sleep—
" To arms ! to arms !" tremendous Guthrum cries,
" Bid the trump's clangor sound, the foe appears."
As two contending oceans, driv'n by wind,
Heap their proud waves, and meet, and foam and roar,
So, fierce to combat, rush th' embattled hosts.
Helmets are cleft on high ; on the bright shield,
Harsh clangs the reeking blade ; huge clouds of dust
Involve the plain in gloom.   Swift flew the Danes,
Confounded at the shock.   Holgar, a chief,
Far fam'd through Norway's realm, who chas'd the stag
On the bleak mountain's top, rallies their ranks,
And cries, " Base dastards, turn where vict'ry calls."
Loud as the furious tempests of the north,
The Danes throng round.   He rear'd his falchion bright,
Hew'd through the foe, till Oscar stopped his course.
A blooming youth, his mother's hope and joy,
That, on fair Avon's bank, the sylvan reed
Had tun'd melodious ; woodland nymphs flock'd round,
Danc'd to his lays, but lov'd the youth far more ;
Holgar's keen blade rush'd through his yielding side ;
The vital crimson streamed ; his beauteous limbs
Lay welt'ring in his gore.   Oddune beheld,
And high in air a gleaming jav'lin poised.

Whizzing it flew, and pierced stern Holgar's heart;
Hoarse groans were heard, and clouds of jav'lins shower'd,
The hills re-echo'd—crimson torrents ran—
Earth shook, and uproar wild convulsed the skies.
Fierce Guthrum strode, as whirlwinds sweep the plain,
Mow'd down whole ranks, and spread the streaming gore.
Proudly serene amid the troubled storm,
A watchful radiance blazing from his eye,
Bold Alfred brav'd the chief; in horror lost
Both armies stood, while front to front opposed,
The generous heroes fought.   Upon their swords
Hung empire in suspense.   Each glittering steel,
Now rais'd on high, now swift-descending, clash'd;
Guthrum full on the hero's nodding crest,
Drove the keen blade; shiv'ring it strew'd the ground;
Quick through his breast a jav'lin found its way,
And Guthrum fell.   Loud clamors rent the air,
And the wide concave rang.   Amazed, aghast,
Back rush'd the Danes abrupt.   Lurking behind,
A vile assassin sprung to pierce the prince;
The youth, who side by side with Alfred fought,
Rush'd on the villain, and the monarch sav'd.
" Brave youth, my guardian angel (Alfred cried),
Declare thy rank, thy name, and recompense."
The youth, " My lineage noble; all I ask
Is constant love; in me Elfrida view."
Love, gratitude and pity, wept at once;
Joy warm'd the monarch's heart, the big, round drops
Roll'd down his manly cheeks, with bliss o'ercome.
One gen'ral pardon to the Danes he gave,
And peace, and lands, and safety.

Loose to joy,
The sparkling goblet flew ; the minstrel's song,
Struck to each harp, illumin'd every eye ;
The verdant turf, with mazy dances beat,
Shook with wild ecstasy ; the table's mirth
Re-echo'd from the hills, while proudly roll'd
The smoky columns from the bonfire's blaze.

Then other cares employ'd the monarch's thoughts ;
War, with dread hand, had deeply drench'd the realm
In blood and carnage ; beauteous fabrics razed,
And cities whelm'd in fire. These he repair'd ;
On lofty hills the massy fortress built,
And trained his hosts to war ; for well he knew,
The palm hangs not on valor's arm alone.
Brave were his subjects ; yet, untaught to fight,
Their bands would fall an easy prey to skill.
Lav'd by the wide Atlantic, hostile fleets
Ravag'd his shores. He spoke ; from nodding groves
Huge oaks descend, bend into ships, up-plough
The foamy wave, and guard with watchful care
The queen of isles. Full proudly o'er the main,
Triumphant rides the fleet ; while mighty sails
By prosp'rous zephyrs filled, bear from all climes,
The produce of each soil.

Now learning smiles ;
Now rise Oxonia's walls, by Alfred's hand
Uprais'd. The youths, with bright ambition throng
To taste th' Aönian spring. From heav'n descends
Religion, in her snowy vesture clad,
And all the virtues smiling in her train,

Call'd from long slumbers by his quick'ning voice ;
The tuneful bard awakes, sweet poesy
With music, hand in hand, her sister joined,
Trips o'er the mead, and sings on ev'ry hill ;
The distant mountains catch the gathering sounds,
And echoing vales prolong the raptur'd strain.

Now, sacred law the subject's right secures ;
Not e'en the felon dies, whate'er his crimes,
Till by his peers condemn'd.   The common law,
Offspring of Alfred, into system grows,
And reigns supreme, and guards the spacious realm.
Hail ! prince of princes, hail ! thou first of men !
Born to command, and save, and bless mankind.
Hail ! Albion ! prosperous in thy happy sway ;
Free to all good, as reason would be free.
No furious faction filled thy realm with rage,
And rous'd thy sons to blood.   Foul anarchy
Fled hissing from thy shores.   Fair order rose,
Peace by her side, and smiling, walk'd the land,
Dispensing every joy.   Bless'd in thy prince,
And in thy sons, and in the gifts of heaven,
What raptures filled thy bounds, as time roll'd on ;
Each day with pleasure fraught ; each joyous scene
The morning gilded, and seren'd the eve.

Oh, how unlike, in these degenerate days,
In thoughts, in words, in deeds, philosophists !
Alfred ennobled, they debase the mind ;
He lov'd true liberty, they, rank excess :
Religion's schools, with virtue, science, fraught,
By him supported, flourish'd through the realm :

Schools of impiety, base stews of vice,
Founded by them, corruption wide bespread;
He wove the web of love, they burst the loom.
From carnage wide, from desolation drear,
The land a garden blooms, new nations rise.
Hail! Alfred! father, saviour of the state!
O'er vernal fields, with every beauty gay,
O'er peaceful climes, they bid wild havoc stalk,
Whelm plains in blood, inflame the lofty dome,
While furious sophists light the angry fire.
Just is the portrait; then, Columbia, judge,
Embrace true wisdom, and thy God adore;
The atheist spurn, and real freedom claim.
Thy spacious fields, in gayest vestments rob'd,
Spread wide their golden harvests; India's corn
Rears its green head, and shakes its silken crest;
And fruits of ev'ry form, and ev'ry dye,
Here grace the plains, there bloom upon the hills.
The various tints of color spread around,
From bolder strokes, to shades of nicer touch;
From live carnation, to vermilion's glow;
From azure deep, to hues more delicate;
In lively contrast charm the ling'ring eye.
In simple grandeur winds Ohio's stream,
Old Hudson feels incumbent-freighted barks;
And joyous rolls them to the destin'd port.
Gay scenes of pleasure, innocent as gay,
Amuse the senses, and the soul refine.
Thy Constitution, glorious monument
Of worth and wisdom; where the sister States,
In union, harmony, and love combined,
Sublime around their common centre roll.

Of vice beware, shun vain philosophy ;
And peace, contentment, virtue, and pure bliss,
Conjoin'd shall reign, religion's sun shine forth,
And with unmingled glory light the world.

FRENCH LITERATURE.

BY SAMUEL GILMAN.

WHETHER we can define it or not, we all have a certain
conception of the French character. Many elements of
that character appear in the French literature. I will
venture to point out a few, but do not pretend, in these
desultory remarks, to exhaust the subject.

I suppose, the first idea we have of a Frenchman,—and
I speak it not in a contemptuous sense,—is his *vivacity*.
What other nation so immediately suggests the idea of that
quality ? There is vivacity in his voice, in his replies, in
his eye, and in his motions. He eats, he makes war, he
relieves you in distress, and he guillotines you, with vivacity. The character drawn of the French nation, nearly
a hundred years since, by Goldsmith, still survives
through the storms of their melancholy revolution.

> " Gay, sprightly land of mirth and social ease,
> Pleased with thyself, whom all the world can please ;
> How often have I led thy sportive choir,
> With tuneless pipe, beside the murmuring Loire !
>
> *   *   *   *   *   *   *   *   *   *   *

> Alike all ages. Dames of ancient days
> Have led their children through the mirthful maze,
> And the gay grandsire, skill'd in gestic lore,
> Has frisk'd beneath the burden of three-score."

This, then, is the leading note that rings also through their whole literature. It appears in the tournure of every sentence,—in the construction of every paragraph,—in the modelling of every chapter,—and almost in the fabrication of every book. A French writer appears to entertain an instinctive, shrinking dread of dulness. To vivacity of thought and manner, he is content to sacrifice many important qualities. Not only their essayists, beginning with Montaigne,—their writers of epistles and of memoirs,—their satirists,—their lyrical and comic poets,—abound in this mercurial quality, and surpass other nations in some of these branches of literature, precisely because vivacity is their most attractive recommendation,— but even their historians, philosophers and scientific writers, say what they have to say in a neat, terse, pointed style, explaining difficulties so long as their explanations can be lucid and brilliant, but preferring to assert their profounder conclusions without proof, if there is any risk that the proof will be tedious or obscure. Nay, this same quality is also salient in their gravest and most serious writers. You will discern it in their theologians, their preachers, their epic and tragic poets ; and even a French translation of the Bible is unquestionably more vivacious than an English or German one. As Boileau said of the poet Quinault, that he was so soft and tender in his style, that if he had to say *I hate you*, it would be expressed in a sweet and gentle manner,—so, we may remark, that if a Frenchman makes the most melancholy reflection, there will be in it more or less of liveliness.   He *will* have some antithesis,—something epigrammatic,—something to excite surprise.   Thus Massillon commences his Funeral Sermon on Louis XIV., with the exclamation, *God alone is great.* The effect of this simple sentence, when contrasted with a whole court in mourning, and all the paraphernalia that surrounded the illustrious dead, is said to have been prodigious.   But so dramatic an attempt to produce vivid emotion, would scarcely have occurred to an English preacher.

Another attribute in the character of Frenchmen, which seems to be also embodied in their literature, is a kind of emphatical, exaggerated, histrionic manner, with which they often appear to say and do everything.   Who that is acquainted with their history, will deny that their kings, from Charlemagne down, have exhibited traces of this quality ?   Glory is the idol of France.   She moves as if the eyes of all Europe were directed upon her.   She makes war, and she negotiates peace, as on a theatre.   What was the whole French revolution, but a sort of pompous drama, divided into acts, and subdivided into scenes, and ending with the monologue of one who strutted his hour upon the stage, and affected in all things this super-heroic manner, just because he knew the French character so well ?   Listen to a Frenchman as he tells you the simplest story of the smallest matter of fact.   Will he not be all emphasis and impressiveness ?   It is even said that a Frenchman cannot commit suicide, without long preparations and elaborate accompaniments, altogether unnecessary to the mere act of blowing out his brains or severing his windpipe.   Now, if the *literature* of France be not imbued with this very same quality, I have read it under some spell. I see it not only in the drama, where, by a kind of double reflection, French dramatists make their characters *dramatise* rather than act, but I see it in their poets, historians, writers on science, and preachers. Allow that they often exhibit infinite talent, surprising quickness of penetration, and the very happiest methods of expression, yet do you not see in the midst of, or behind all this, a certain *management*, which you will rarely observe in the writers of any other nation? I fancy that the reason why the *unities* lingered longer in the literature of France than in any other, was because they were so congenial to this feature of their national character. Now, we must not quarrel with, or superciliously sneer at this quality, because it happens not to suit our Anglo-Saxon taste. For, no doubt it has its uses. Ideas are communicated by it with more effect. An emphatic, exaggerated literature, will make an impression on the mind of the world; though we must certainly allow that the highest style of writing, as well as of manner, is that of perfect repose.

The *moral* tone and spirit of French literature, I regard as inferior to that of the English. There is something elaborate, artificial and systematic in the one, very different from the robust, spontaneous and natural morality of the other. Even Fenelon's Telemachus, one of the most directly ethical poems in any language, seems pervaded by a watery, puerile strain, when compared with corresponding productions of the English mind. Much as I admire Telemachus on every account, I can scarcely read it without thinking of some father who promises to fill his son's pockets with sugar-plums if he is good, and threatens to shut him up alone in the dark, if he is naughty. How different from the profound and eternal lessons to be

drawn from, rather than inculcated in, Milton's Paradise
Lost. So, too, read the respective *dramas* of the two
literatures. Shakspeare addresses your moral nature as
Life and Providence address it. He stirs up your conscience,—he starts trains and suggestions which lead
down to the depths of your soul, and agitate all within,—
he moulds you by his plastic examples. But the French
dramatists cram you with their moral lessons to suffocation.
They, indeed, *preach*, in return for the dramatising of the
French preachers. They leave almost nothing to the
reflections of the audience, but beat and hammer out
every duty and every crime, until the theatre seems
indeed to become, what it boasts of being, a school of
morals, rather than a kindling, inspiring mirror of life
and action.

And yet, with all these occasional shady spots, who
would extinguish the glorious constellation of French
literature from the firmament of intellect? The French
mind is certainly a more active one than the English. If
it penetrates not so deep, it spreads farther and quicker
through the upper soils of intellectual culture. If it has not
yet attained its culminating point of excellence, it is probably because it has never yet enjoyed the perfect freedom of
the English mind. In combined gracefulness and precision, it surely surpasses its great rival. There is
something about the French character more classic,—
more Attic,—or, I would rather say, more directly Athenian,
than belongs to any other modern nation. This very
circumstance, besides being an indigenous excellence, has
probably exposed its literature to one other defect, the last
which I shall now notice. France welcomed, with
the utmost ardor, the commixture of Greek and Roman

materials presented for her intellectual sustenance by the revival of letters ; but for a long time she paid them a too absorbing reverence, forgetting her own generous capabilities, and becoming almost ludicrously *pedantic*. At length, the genius of the nation restored itself to a happier equilibrium, under the influence of which sprang out the long line of authors, from Montaigne to Voltaire, who have shed so brilliant a lustre around their country's name. Yet, I am persuaded the French mind has never yet attained its highest destiny. England, we all feel, is scarce likely ever to surpass her existing literature,—but do we feel the same thing with regard to France ? Drinking from the stream of classical literature alone, and almost disdaining to be nourished from other sources, she has ever worn a too artificial and antique impress. Her whole literature savors too strongly of the classic oil. Rousseau, indeed, acknowledged his obligations to England, and especially to England's Richardson, who taught him to draw from his own soul and from nature. But Voltaire, who may be called the very genius of France incarnate, could show no favor, and feel no sympathy for Shakspeare, who was equally the incarnate genius of England. The Revolution shook the mind of France from this too narrow and restricted system. She now seeks everywhere with avidity and docility for intellectual sustenance. England, Germany, Italy, the East, combine to prompt her new and freer impulses ; and although of late she has been defiled and tormented with a demoniac school, which knows no law, critical, moral, or religious, yet even now she is blest by some bright, redeeming exceptions. Whenever her political institutions shall be so adapted and facilitated to her character, as to secure her repose on the one hand, and give to her wing, a wide, free range on the other, how can we doubt that the land of St. Louis, of Henry IV., of Fenelon, of Corneille, of Madame Roland and of Lamartine, enjoying the most felicitous position in Europe, and with so much of pure Athenian spirit in her composition, shall yet accomplish her destiny in assisting to elevate the whole human mind, and thus fulfil the appropriate destiny of beautiful France!

———

SUMTER.

BY JAMES W. SIMMONS.

WHEN Carolina's hope grew pale,
    Before the British lion's tread,
And freedom's sigh, in every gale,
    Was heard above her martyred dead,—

When from her mountain heights, subdued,
    In pride of place forbad to soar,
Her eagle banner, quenched in blood,
    Lay sullen on th' indignant shore,—

Breathing revenge! invoking doom,
    Tyrant! upon thy purple host;
When all stood wrapt in steadfast gloom,
    And silence brooded o'er her coast,—

Stealthy, as when from thicket dun,
   The Indian springs upon his bow,
Uprose, South-Mount, thy warrior-son,
   And headlong darted on the foe!

Not in the pride of war he came,
   With bugle note and banner high,
And nodding plume, and steel of flame,
   Red battle's gorgeous blazonry!

With followers few, but undismayed,
   Each change and chance of fate withstood,
Beneath her sunshine and her shade
   The same heroic brotherhood!

From secret nook, in other land,
   Emerging fleet along the pine,
Prone down he rush'd before his band,
   Like eagle, on the British line!

Catawba's waters smiled again,
   To see her Sumter's soul in arms;
And, issuing from each glade and glen,
   Rekindled by war's fierce alarms,

Thronged hundreds thro' the solitude
   Of the wild forest, to the call
Of him whose spirit, unsubdued,
   Fresh impulse gave to each, to all!

By day the burning sands they ply,
   Night sees them in the fell ravine;

Familiar to each follower's eye,
    The tangled brake, the hall of green.

Roused by their tread from covert deep,
    Springs the gaunt wolf, and flies—while near
Is heard, forbidding thought of sleep,
    The rattling serpent's sound of fear.

Before, or break of early morn,
    Or fox looks out from copse or close,
Before the hunter winds his horn,
    Sumter's already on his foes !

He beat them back ! beneath the flame
    Of valor quailing, or the shock ;
And carved at length a hero's name
    Upon the glorious *Hanging Rock !*

And time that shades or sears the wreath
    Where glory binds the soldier's brow,
Kept bright her Sumter's fame in death,
    His hour of proudest triumph—now.

And ne'er shall tyrant tread the shore
    Where Sumter bled, nor bled in vain ;
A thousand hearts shall break before
    They wear th' oppressor's bonds again.

Oh ! never can thy sons forget
    The mighty lessons taught by thee ;
Since,—treasured up the eternal debt,—
    Their watchword is—thy memory !

THE CHARACTERISTICS OF CIVILISATION.

BY S. HENRY DICKSON, M.D.

WHAT is civilisation but the suggestion of wants and the invention of means to satisfy them? It is an error to affirm, as is often done, that, in this matter, "the demand creates the supply." "The first seats of commerce," says Heeren, "were also the first seats of civilisation. Exchange of merchandise led to exchange of ideas; and by this mutual friction was first kindled the sacred flame of humanity." This is a striking and graphic expression of a great truth. Commerce began by an interchange or barter of the mere necessaries of life. The planter of the river side offered bread in exchange for the salt and dried flesh of the desert hunter. But to this market of food those who had none to offer, brought, to obtain it, spices and frankincense, and gold, and silver, and precious stones, as they could procure them. What can be more evident than that the desire for all these, in turn, was suggested from without, was matter of reciprocal education, a step in civilisation? Here it was clearly the supply that created the demand; the demand reacting has increased the supply. The Hindoo, with the aid of the Englishman, taught the Chinese the delights of opium eating and smoking; the mandarin communicated to "the foreign devils outside, red bristled and barbarous," the aromatic joys of "the cup that cheers but not inebriates." As *love*, in the most exquisite of German stories, *created a soul* in Undine, so a new want gives a new life to whom-

soever feels it, provided it can be gratified; and the
tea-drinking laundress of the present day knows an enjoyment, a refined one too, and admitting of repetition with
fresh delight at " each return of morn and dewy eve,"
which England's virgin queen, at her breakfast of beef and
ale, might have envied, but was perhaps not yet refined
enough to relish or appreciate.

The most artificial of the wants thus generated in the
progress of man from barbarism to civilisation—such as
he has yet attained—is that which we next come to consider as supplied by what are called the fine arts. Concerning the ultimate influence of these upon the well-
being of society, there has been warm and long sustained
dispute ; and not a few stern stoics have denounced them
as injurious to good morals and opposed to useful industry.
It has been argued, that they lead, by their softening
agencies, to instability of character and effeminacy, with
its long train of vices ; and the example has been pressed
of repeated coincidence between their most flourishing
cultivation, and the prevalence of general corruption in
ancient Greece and Rome, and in modern Italy. I allude
here only to music, sculpture and painting; poetry merges
all her peculiar influences in those of literature, already
discussed, and architecture is, at least, equally well
arranged among the useful as the fine arts.

Painting, of which I shall first speak, with all its immediate kindred, etching, engraving, lithography, &c., may
doubtless, like the pen and the press, exert an injurious
effect, and be made efficiently instrumental for harm.
The bad passions and propensities may be addressed
through the eye, with great force and quickness ; and impressions made thus upon the mind, are so tenacious as

often to prove almost indelible. Yet must I differ from those who maintain, that more evil is done by these perverse uses of the pencil, than good by its correct and laudable employment. Apply the test formerly proposed. Obliterate from the canvas, the plate of copper, steel and wood, and the graphic stone, all that the most prolific and prurient imagination has ever traced of indecorous and seductive, and what will you have effected in the cause of virtue ? Vice will have lost from her copious armory little or nothing of importance ; nothing that the dullest of her votaries would need, to spur him onward in his oblique career. On the contrary, how many images of grace and beauty, how many exquisite expressions of virtuous emotion, intensely adapted to soften and purify the heart, and elevate and refine the passions, will have disappeared for ever from our thoughts, as well as from our eyes, if we should lose the immortal works of Raphael, of Guido, of Leonardo da Vinci, of the thrice illustrious Michael Angelo Buonarotti. Immortal, I have said ; Bonaparte was accustomed to sneer at what he was pleased contemptuously to style " the transient immortality of painting," because, in the course of five or six centuries, canvas and colors must both inevitably decay. But the art abounds in every requisite for an undying duration of fame and of influence ; and the names of Zeuxis and Apelles will survive as long as that of the mighty Napoleon himself. And what age or nation will hereafter be ignorant of the fame and of the works of the great masters ? Copies in every variety of delineation, from the brush and the burin, and in the everlasting mosaic, are transmitted to every country, and throughout all time ; and, however inferior in delicacy and living force to the original efforts of inspired genius, will prevail to convey efficiently the form and essence of each worshipped *chef-d'œuvre* to our remotest posterity.

These remarks will apply with still more precision and directness to sculpture ; for, while it enjoys an existence indefinitely prolonged, a duration as nearly approaching eternity as that of the globe itself, it is evident, that the cold and colorless forms of the sculptor must be less potent in affecting the evil propensities of the beholder, than the warm and glowing and life-like images, embodied by the painter.

Music requires to be spoken of with less reserve. It demands no defence ; it needs no eulogy ; it is the most delightful, most unalloyed, and purest of physical pleasures. Scarcely susceptible of being impressed into the service of vice, it offers itself as the ready handmaid of virtue. It refreshes, without exhausting, both the mind and the body ; it costs little or nothing, is easily procured, is always at hand. Next to the sweet smiles of woman, and her soft domestic endearments, it is the most indispensable luxury of existence.

God himself—let me speak it reverently—God himself delights in music. He demands from us, in return for his ceaseless and parental kindness, not a silent thankfulness of heart only, but the loud, uplifted voice of grateful joy ; and the instincts which he has implanted in the higher order of his creation, prompt irrepressibly the utterance of melodious sounds, as expressive of all tender and agreeable emotions.

It would be difficult to estimate how large a proportion of the happiness of the existing race of men, is derived from music. Genius, indeed, can invent no more diffusive or intense addition to the long list of civilized and refined enjoyments, than a new or improved instrument, or the melody and harmony of a fine musical composition. The art, indeed, seems already to have reached perfection. With the pealing organ, the delicate harp, the violin of unlimited tone and inexhaustible capacity, the piano, that domestic treasure, all of them in their present form modern, and comparatively recent inventions, what is there left us to wish for ?

The progress of man in civilisation, his advancement in knowledge, will be found as distinctly impressed upon the character of his recreations, his favorite amusements, as upon his occupations and serious pursuits. First, let us record the disuse of gladiatorial shows, the cherished favorite of the Roman populace, so truly characterized by a Carolinian scholar as " a spectacle fit for fiends." Yet thousands of the daughters of Lucretia and Portia hung with eager interest upon these exhibitions, as many persons even now seek every opportunity of witnessing public executions. Such was the habit of George Selwyn, whom his friends always esteemed " amiable." " For Fouquier Tinville," says a contemporary, " pleasure had no attractions. He was abstemious in his diet, his application was intense, and his business consisted in accusing and condemning. The only relaxation which he ever sought, was to see the victims suffer whom he had sent to the scaffold ; and then his features would appear to melt for the moment, and even to soften into a smile." Next, let the tournament be remembered—the product and passion of Christian chivalry—where the bright eyes of gentle and Christian woman watched the progress of the headlong duel, or gazed on the mingled throng of the

fiery *mêlée*, and adjudged the prize to the panting and
bloody conqueror. These have gone by, though gloomy
and Moorish Spain retains her savage bull-fights ; France
her revolting *combats des animaux ;* and England her vulgar
and disgraceful pugilism. Far more consistent with our
modern refinement of manners and sentiments, the horse-
race, the regatta and the circus, still divide public favor
with the theatre ; where the spectacle, ballet, melodrama
and opera, are mingled with the higher strains of the tragic
and the comic muse. It must be admitted, that in the
conduct of all these various modes of public amusement,
there is still apt to be mingled something blameworthy ;
yet, on many points, the improvement is obvious and
striking. With a stern gravity, sometimes exaggerated
into a gloomy asceticism, many good men, concentrating
their attention upon the incidental evil which has tena-
ciously fixed itself upon these, as all other human institutions, have aimed at their total abolition, nay, have most
sedulously represented all abandonment to gaiety as
indecorous, and inconsistent with proper regard to social
and religious duty. There cannot be a greater or more
mischievous error. It is a fine phrase of Walter Savage
Landor, and true as it is beautiful : " Be assured our
heavenly Father is as well pleased to see his children in
the play-ground as in the school-room." " Socrates,"
says Valerius Maximus, " *cui nulla pars sapientiæ obscura
fuit, non erubuit tunc, cum interpositâ arundine cruribus
suis, cum parvulis filiolis ludens, ab Alcibiade risus est.*"
" If the ways of religion," exclaims the pious South,
" are ways of pleasantness, such as are *not* ways of
pleasantness are not truly and properly ways of religion."
In regard to all this class of subjects, let us consider

that the propensities of man are given to him that they may conduce to his happiness, and therefore it cannot be wise in us to attempt to extinguish, or utterly repress, any of them. Let us inform, regulate, and direct them. No true philosopher or enlightened philanthropist can look with contempt upon the recreations of any community. Men will seek pleasure; they must have enjoyments, both physical and mental. It is an instinctive necessity which forces them thus to unbend and relax, for an occasional interval, the iron grasp of care. Not even the gigantic intellect of Newton would bear the long abstraction and intense thought to which he abandoned himself, but gave way at last under the burden, and sank into temporary imbecility. If we do not guide and instruct the mass, but merely employ our own efforts in checking and prohibiting them, the result will be a defiance of our control, and a much greater preponderance of evil in the course which they will adopt under such injudicious interference. Let us, then, endeavor to enlighten them as to the nature and means of procurement of the truest, safest, and best enjoyments. Let us show them how much of innocent pleasure is within the reach of every one, and let the makers of law and social order contrive to place them as much as possible before the lowest and most destitute of their fellow-citizens. Let there be everywhere parks, and gardens, and public walks, and baths, accessible reading rooms, concerts of music, shows and games, and gymnastic exercises in the bright sunlight and beneath the open sky; and for the evenings, lyceums, and scientific and miscellaneous lectures, debates, oratory and recitations.

THE RESOLVE.

BY MITCHELL KING.

HAPLESS the poor mistaken wight,
Of manners rude and unpolite,
Who, trusting to an honest mind,
Intrudes himself upon mankind ;
Though he possessed Homerian pow'rs,
Could charm the lazy-footed hours ;
By all the magic of the soul,
Alternate raise, depress, control ;
Wielding the passions at his will,
With more than Demosthenian skill ;
Trace learning to the fountain head,
Hold converse with the mighty dead ;
Bid former ages rapid rise,
In vivid lustre on the eyes ;
Collate, unite, correct, increase,
The ample stores of Rome and Greece,
Explaining nature's plastic laws,
And from effects deduce the cause ;
Why planets vast, incessant run,
Their certain circles round the sun ;
The secret laws of comets scan,
Anomalous to the general plan ;
All their eccentric roamings trace,
Athwart illimitable space ;
Why, gathering in their devious way,
They, heaven-directed, re-convey

The electric, all-pervading flame,
Back to the fountain whence it came :
Descry, with optic tube afar,
A sun, or world, in every star ;
And, as each orb its course pursues,
How each, the other's strength renews ;
Or, stooping to the teeming earth,
Say, whence have trees and flowers their birth ;
Explore the subterranean pores ;
Elucidate the mystic stores,
That minerals, plants and fruits bestow,
To soften pain, and banish wo ;
At monarch reason's potent call,
And magic touch, transforming all
Contained within this narrow span,
Subservient to the good of man :—
In lasting characters display,
The Protean manners of the day,
Stamping the present, fickle age,
In living likeness on his page,
Or equal Johnson's godlike art,
Anatomise the subtile heart,
Disrobe of every specious guise,
Error, howe'er concealed it lies ;
Corrode, or leniently assuage
The most destructive passion's rage ;
Invigorate all-powerful truth,
Clothe virtue in immortal youth,
And gain a name that far out-springs
The blood-stained, puny fame of kings ;—
Could he instruct (O, task divine,
The least frequented by the Nine)

To be content with what is given
By the protecting powers of Heaven ;
Who prize not from extrinsic show,
But for the pure ethereal glow
Of modest virtue, truth sincere,
Unbounded love, and conscience clear ;
And, as the lowly, feeling breast,
Internally, with these, is blest,
Alike impartial they regard
A king or beggar, dunce or bard :
Teaching, to reason's dictates true,
What few can find, but all pursue,
The heavenly soul-exalting road
That leads to happiness and God ;—
Although possessed of powers like these,
If void of other arts to please,
Unnoticed, he may trudge along,
Pour to responsive woods his song ;
In gloomy pines companions find,
And talk of virtue to the wind.—
But he, who bends at fashion's shrine,
Digs deep in mammon's dirty mine ;
Who can with an insidious grace,
Cajole and flatter to your face ;
And, loaded by the cumbrous ore,
Deceiving, shifting, still for more ;—
His unremitted, dear employ,
To gain what he can ne'er enjoy ;
How meanly is his smile desired,
His merit praised, his sense admired ;
Though all his shallow pate contains,
Would scarce supply a turkey's brains ;

For men the futile maxim hold,
Worth, genius, wisdom, all are gold :
Poor I, with pockets light as air,
And the politeness of a bear,
Whose cheeks assume a crimson dye,
Whene'er my lips attempt to lie ;
Whose stubborn tongue would never bend,
By flattery to procure a friend ;
Flattery, the fascinating charm,
Which can the coldest bosom warm,
Forming the wise, the good, the brave,
Or to a partizan or slave ;—
For e'en where praise is justly due,
(Ah, justly it belongs to few !)
When it is baseness to restrain
The honors merit ought to gain,
It drawls so slowly from my mouth,
In terms so awkward and uncouth,—
Whate'er the speaker may intend,
The blundering manner must offend.
Now loaded thus, what mortal can
Be company for any man ?
Or loaded thus, what mortal dare
Obtrude his presence on the fair ?
But as 'tis generally confest,
That common-sense, within my breast,
Some partial seeds of worth has sown,
And culture made the fruit his own.
Sometimes the sad misfortune's mine,
To be invited out to dine :
Ashamed politely to deny,
Yes, is the consequent reply ;

And then if any poet saw,
Who could with master pencil draw,
My rustic conduct, blockhead stare,
Confused, nay, downright stupid air,
Each marking with perspicuous ken,
It would immortalize his pen ;
For, certainly, there ne'er has been,
Portray'd so risible a scene ;
And should unlucky stars agree,
That I'd be asked to wait till tea ;
Lounging uneasy through the room,
In all the shame of silent gloom,
I dwindle down to be, at best,
A tedious half-neglected guest ;
The heavy moments slow proceed,
With nothing like a lobster's speed,
Although such beauty bless my sight,—
As even a stoic would delight,
And female wit so brilliant shone,
As might elicit fire from stone !—
At last the painful trial o'er,
Keener than all I felt before,
The lady-visitors conspire,
To think it time they should retire ;
The clock strikes ten, no beaux are come,
I proffer to conduct them home ;
Idea-hunting all the way
For something elegant to say ;
And if, at last, the laboring brain
Produce a thought of modish strain,
'Tis ten to one, the faltering tongue,
Bring forth the weak conception wrong,

Guessing the smile, list'ning to hear,
The titter tingle through his ear;
The bashful, blundering, would-be spark,
Feels happy that the night is dark.
No more shall I harass my life,
Unequal to the giddy strife;
But in this academic shade,
Pursue fair science—heavenly maid!
My future care and time consign
To make her every beauty mine:
Yes, let the proud, ambitious great,
Gemmed in the tinsel toys of state,
Impatient, urge their baleful course
By secret guile, or open force;
Attorneys quibble o'er the laws,
Shaping the worse, the better cause:
Let lovers watch their mistress' nod;
And misers make their gold a god;
If I one hidden truth can trace,
Important to the human race,
'Twill yield more pleasure to my mind
Than they in all their projects find.
Perhaps some fluttering coxcomb may
With puppy simper sneering say,
" The fellow need not go to school,
Or study, to become a fool."—
" Hush," master fopling, not a word!
Your impudence is most absurd,
How dare you offer a pretence,
Even to judge of common-sense?
It is enough for you to know,
The present fashionable show:

The newest mode arrived from France ;
How to evolve the mazy dance ;
The most polite and easy air
To hand the ladies from their chair,
Adjust a tippet, flirt a fan,
Nicely arrange a party plan,
Attend obsequious to the play,
Sad when they frown, glad when they're gay,
Chief-waiter at the tea preside,
Say who will next become a bride,
What Miss unmarried swells her gown,
And all the scandal of the town :
These, and such little trifling arts,
Are fitter for a coxcomb's parts
Than critically to direct,
Beauties perceive, or faults correct.
But Goldsmith, whom we all admit,
A connoisseur on points of wit,
Says, who can steadily pursue
The shade, will catch the substance too,
Nor science ever will beguile
Him, who devoutly courts her smile.
And thou, congenial, pensive Muse !
Do not thy sacred aid refuse ;
Thou, who on Scotia's rugged shore,
Midst cloud-capt hills and torrents' roar,
First taught my humble voice to raise,
The votive lay in virtue's praise ;
Thou, who hast sooth'd my early woes,
And keenest sorrows, to repose ;
When o'er the pathless ocean bound,
Dark, heaving billows roaring round,

Wast ever present in my dream,
And lightedst up the cheering gleam
Of ardent hope, within my breast,
By danger nor dismay represt;
If thou wilt still my soul inspire,
With thy celestial fervent fire,
Let fortune on her vot'ry's head,
Ten thousand, thousand millions shed;
Be mine the lot to live, with thee,
From venal cares and troubles free:
Eccentric from the beaten track,
Pursued by every common hack,
Lead me in some romantic road,
By human footstep never trod;
Bid chasten'd fancy be our guide,
And nature o'er the band preside.
United, we will gaily stray,
Along the lovely, lengthened way;
And, culled from every beauteous field
Of flowers the choicest it can yield,
Teach me with artless strength to twine
Such chaplets for their brows and thine,
As may in fairest verdure bloom,
Till time receive his final doom.
Let no neglected charming spot
In all our wanderings be forgot;
Nor any prospect miss our sight,
That can a noble thought excite,
Let us, before the early dawn,
Trip o'er the dew-bespangled lawn;
Joining the birds on every thorn
To hail the sweetly blushing morn.

When flaming fierce the mighty sun,
His middle course triumphant run,
Shall in the south his orb display,
Pouring intolerable day ;
Within some cool, impervious bower,
Let us defy the sultry hour.
Together, when at evening's close,
Pale night her sable mantle throws
Athwart the bosom of the vale,
Fanned lightly by the breathing gale,
Winding along some rushing rill,
Or climbing slow a rising hill,
Impartial retrospection cast
Over the roll of ages past ;
With candor scan the present view,
Plan wisely what I shall pursue ;
In fortune, and in folly's spite,
Firm fix the dear resolve of right ;
To heaven turn an anxious eye,
And hold high commerce with the sky.
Whatever garb the seasons wear,
Through all the variegated year,
Will add to heighten every joy,
Variety, that cannot cloy ;
Whether gay spring with liberal hand,
In flowers array the smiling land ;
Summer congenial nurse the plain,
Swelling the latent embryo grain ;
Autumn diffuse her blessings round,
Graceful in wheat and olives crowned ;
Or gloomy winter's haggard form
Stride sullen in his bursting storm.

Then when the raging tempests driven
Impetuous through the vault of heaven,
Scatter abroad their boundless sway,
Darkness involves the face of day,
Clouds rolled on clouds horrific lower,
Dense dismal rains in torrents pour,
Tremendous thunders downward hurled,
Shake the deep centre of the world,
And livid fires inflame the sky,
Flashing destruction on the eye ;
Then on some huge stupendous rock
High reared above the awful shock,
May we, superior and serene,
Enjoy the dread terrific scene !
Thus free from all that man alarms,
Will nature ope her matchless charms ;
Fancy in glowing language dress
Whate'er her sister can express ;
And thou, with voice sublimely strong,
Exalt the energetic song,
Make coward vice dejected stand
Trembling beneath thy scourging hand ;
Raising the lovely moral lay,
Crown merit with unfading bay ;
Bid fear, or joy, or grief prevail,
As winds the soul-commanding tale.
With native vigor strong rehearse,
In Milton's powerful epic verse,
Or pure immortalizing rhymes,
The noble theme of olden times.
If these, thou never wilt bestow,
But dull and trite my numbers flow ;

If vainly I essay to raise,
On fashion's base, the fane of praise ;
Should fear or faction e'er control,
Or sordid interest sway my soul ?
Should I, insensible of shame,
In honor deck a villain's name ?
Meanly desirous to deceive,
Insidiously attempt to weave
A wreath for him, but which adorns
His forehead with convulsive thorns,
Or darkly aim the poisoned dart
Of envy, at an honest heart ?
Then let my lyre no more be strung,
And lasting silence seal my tongue.
Firm, independent may I tend
Onward, to meet a placid end,
Surrounded by a chosen few
Of old companions tried and true,
When reverend age has thinly spread
His hoary honors o'er my head ;
Retaining still the fire of youth,
Tempered by sage experienced truth,
Then be the task delightful mine,
To form the human soul divine,
Aspiring virtue careful rear,
Curb folly in her first career,
Direct to shun the devious course
That leads to guilt and dark remorse ;
Nor prune the wild luxuriant bough
With captious hand and sullen brow,
But teach the daring plant to climb
Majestic in the vale of time,

Until the branching tree expand
Its fragrant odors o'er the land,
And when a long respected age,
Shall quit life's busy bustling stage,
Bless'd by my God, at peace with all
My brothers on this fleeting ball;
Unfeignéd may the mournful tear
Of weeping friendship dew my bier,
Leaving behind a spotless fame,
And, Oh fond hope, a deathless name.

I SIGH FOR THE LAND OF THE CYPRESS AND PINE.

BY SAMUEL HENRY DICKSON, M.D.

I SIGH for the land of the Cypress and Pine,
  Where the jessamine blooms and the gay woodbine;
  Where the moss droops low from the green oak tree,—
Oh! that sun-bright land is the land for me!

The snowy flower of the orange there,
Sheds its sweet fragrance through the air;
And the Indian rose delights to twine
Its branches with the laughing vine.

There the deer leaps light through the open glade,
Or hides him far in the forest shade,
When the woods resound in the dewy morn
With the clang of the merry hunter's horn.

There the humming-bird of rainbow plume
Hangs o'er the scarlet creepers' bloom ;
While 'midst the leaves, his varying dyes
Sparkle like half-seen fairy eyes.

There the echoes ring through the livelong day
With the mock-bird's changeful roundelay ;
And at night when the scene is calm and still,
With the moan of the plaintive whip-poor-will.

Oh! I sigh for the land of the Cypress and Pine,
Of the laurel, the rose, and the gay woodbine ;
Where the long gay moss decks the rugged oak tree—
That sun-bright land is the land for me.

————

THE TRUE GLORY OF AMERICA.

BY JAMES L. PETIGRU.

BUT military fame constitutes the least part of the honor due to the soldiers of America. War, after all, is the reign of violence, and violence is the scourge of the human race. And it is the peculiar glory of that army which bore the brunt of this sharp contest, that when the war was over, they laid aside with the sword the love of war, and with peace resumed the peaceful arts in the retirement of private life. Honored in all times be that patriot soldiery who served a bleeding country in all its privations, and bore the delay even of the modest recompense due to their toils, with the fortitude of the soldier and the modesty of the citizen. What are the boasted triumphs of those who have dyed the earth in blood, compared with the fame of that army, which, after a successful war, laid down their arms before their own claims were satisfied? That a stable government, with the resources arising from a perfect command of the civil force, should raise and disband troops at their pleasure, is the common privilege of a well-governed State. But this was a revolutionary army, enlisted, not in the name of obedience, but of resistance to the established authority. An army which had made all the sacrifices of a hard service without the emoluments of the camp—which had felt the steel of the enemy, without feeling the cares of a Government even for the supply of their wants. They had, by their arms, set up the civil power that now disposed of their claims to justice. Every selfish feeling prompted them to take justice into their own hands, and the most plausible arguments were at hand to excuse the step. They were organized, and the weakness of the government required an infusion of energy. The State stood in need of reformation, and their wrongs cried aloud for justice. How easy in such circumstances to cover ambitious designs under the cloak of the public good! To their everlasting honor, they resisted the temptation, and imposed on themselves a forbearance without example. With arms in their hands, they submitted to the civil authority, as men who had no weapons but persuasion. So rare an instance of duty has deservedly raised the character of military men, and made them, in this country, objects, not of jealousy, but of popular regard. But such moderation could only be expected from men under the most enlightened influence, and is accounted for by the pre-eminent character of their leader. They trusted in Washington, and set the seal to the gratitude of posterity, by yielding an implicit obedience to his counsel and example. A nation may well be proud of military fame ; but the character of Washington has added to the estimation of mankind, and forms part of the inheritance of the human race. We may boast of the valor of our troops, but submission to the law, and respect for the liberties of their country, are the crowning glory of the patriot army that fought the battle of Independence. They laid no sacrilegious hand upon the ark of liberty, and showed themselves formidable only to the enemies of their country.

The example of the army was well calculated to increase the joy with which the return of peace was hailed, and to inspire a hope that the reign of justice had commenced. But peace had its dangers ; the authority of the laws was inadequate to the preservation of the public defence ; and the government was neither able to obtain nor to enforce justice. The task was still incomplete, and many doubts and fears were still to be overcome before the fair temple of liberty could be reared upon the soil of Columbia. Hitherto, liberty was resistance, and her cause was the law of the strongest. But now liberty was to be made an institution, and freedom reconciled with power. And although to the generality of mankind, dazzled with show, and inattentive to the silent causes, which, in the moral as in the natural world, bring about the order and harmony of things, the organization of a community may seem to be easy, yet to the reasoning mind no enterprise is so arduous. Too long, indeed, have men been accustomed to pay unbounded homage to those abilities that are most conspicuous in the service of selfish ambition. But when civilisation shall have more widely diffused its benignant sway, they will learn to reserve their highest praise for those whose labors are most eminently conducive to the happiness of mankind. Who will compare the bloody laurels of the conqueror with the mild lustre that surrounds the brow of the magistrate, who gives laws to mankind; or hesitate to postpone the boisterous orator, or keen politician, to the simple and modest student of nature, who has so recently enriched the human family with the present of the magnetic telegraph? What does it signify that some have fought and bled, and signalized the bloody arena of their toils by great exhibitions of moral or physical strength, if the result has been barren of any real good or solid benefit to society? But they who have developed the resources of their country, who have increased the amount of rational and innocent enjoyment, or diminished the evils of human life, are justly hailed as the bene-factors and fathers of mankind. And who so justly entitled to this distinction as those who have bestowed on their country, by wise institutions, the permanent blessings of justice? In this class the great men of America are entitled to a distinguished place, and we may celebrate this anniversary not merely with the honors due to a brilliant feat of arms, but as the opening of a new and better state of things. For when the toils of war were over, the American people dedicated the liberty which they had won, to the noble purpose of establishing among them, for generations, the blessings of freedom, justice, and equality of rights. By this result the true value of liberty is known, and by the success of the Federal Constitution, the real amount of good obtained by American Independence must in the end be estimated. For liberty is but a name, where the weak are not protected against the strong, nor justice armed with the power of defending the innocent, and punishing the guilty. And it is here that experience warns us of the rocks on which men in the pursuit of liberty have so often split, and calls on us to admire and maintain the work of the authors of the Constitution. To reconcile the greatest degree of freedom with the perfect security of private and natural rights, has baffled the skill of the wisest of mankind. For who shall control where all are equal, or how shall the people restrain the will of the people ?

To accomplish a work to which the wise might look with despair; to give to the world an example of a republic that might recall the glories of that proud name in ancient times, without admitting the elements of discord which so often shook the frame of those celebrated States ; to emulate the vigor of those ancient commonwealths, without impairing the safety and sanctity of private rights, so essential to modern civilisation—these were the general aspirations of the men of the revolution, and the consummation of that great struggle, to the memory of which we dedicate this day.

MIRIAM.*

BY PENINA MOÏSE.

AMID the flexile reeds of Nile a lovely infant slept,
While over the unconscious babe his mother watched and
wept.
Nor distant far another stood whose tears flowed fast
and free,
'Twas Miriam the beautiful, the bright star of the sea.

With breaking heart that parent bids farewell to her
doomed child,
Commending to Almighty God his spirit undefiled.
The sister lingers yet to mourn o'er tyranny's decree,
And bitter was thy agony, fair maiden of the sea.

The palace of the Pharaohs now sends forth a noble train,
Thermutis comes, by Heaven led, to break her father's
chain.
And who is she that homage yields upon her bended
knee ?
It is the graceful Miriam, the brightener of the sea.

Trembling she rose and timid stood upon the water's edge,
When lo ! the princess marks the boy slumbering amid the
sedge.

* This name signifies star of the sea, lady of the sea, the exalted,
the brightener, the enlightener.

A fairy ark and foundling too ? 'Tis Fortune's gift to me,
Joy to the heart of Miriam, the fair star of the sea.

A nurse for this deserted babe, cried Pharaoh's gentle
    daughter,
Whose name, my nymphs, shall Moses be, thus rescued
    from the water.
A woman of the stranger's race I'll quickly bring to thee,
Said the delighted Miriam, the day-star of the sea.

She turned aside, nor tarried long, for soon her infant brother,
On the familiar bosom lay of his own Hebrew mother.
And bounding onward by her side, full of triumphant glee,
Went Miriam the beautiful, the bright star of the sea.

Time fleets—the child, to manhood reared, has left his
    proud abode,
And royalty's bold protegé has broken Egypt's rod.
The oracle of Israel has set his nation free !
Then sung melodious Miriam, enlightener of the sea.

But why hast thou at Hazeroth thy timbrel cast aside,
And dared to lift thy voice against the legislator's bride ?
For this shalt thou be smitten, till thy brother's prayer for
    thee
Restores again thy loveliness, rash lady of the sea.

A wail is in the wilderness, a deep and solemn wail,
The prophetess who soared beyond mortality's dark pale,
Has to the *spirit's promised land* departed pure and free.
Farewell, inspired Miriam, thou lost star of the sea !

THE SPIRIT OF THE AGE.

BY HENRY L. PINCKNEY.

THIS is the age of science. Antiquity had but little
s cience, in the strict signification of the term ; but in every
department, moral, intellectual and physical—in everything relating to mind or matter—everything that can
illustrate the geography of the heavens or the earth—
e verything that can reveal or contribute to the security
and elegance of life—the present century is illuminated
with a flood of light. And, as it is the peculiar
property of science to know no limit, so even its present
elevation may justly be regarded as a point from which
it will continue, with undazzled eye and unwearied wing,
to ascend the greater and still greater heights. Each
r olling year will still come laden with improvements, and
e very step in the march of mind will either develope
some new and valuable principle, or increase the power
of those with which we are acquainted, by applying them
to purposes to which as yet they have never been
directed. And thus every known science will continue
to advance, and new ones will be constantly added to
their train, going on steadily to the *ultima thule* of human
knowledge, and imparting, as they go, all that is essential,
in every department of society, to the dignity and happiness of the human race. And it is the age of *elegant
literature and the arts*. It is true, however, respecting
this assumption, that antiquity may rise up and dispute
the palm. She may take us to the villa of Cicero, or

the tomb of Virgil. She may show us the ruins of the
Coliseum or Parthenon. She may exhibit the agony of
Laocoon, struggling with the serpents, and the noble self-
sacrifice of Alcestis, as she dooms herself to death for
the preservation of her husband. And she may ask,
where are *your* Polydorus and Euripides ? What have
you, superior to the Venus of Apelles ? Who has yet
touched the lyre with the plaintive sweetness of Tibullus ?
Where is the invention in modern architecture, that
rivals the luxuriant elegance of the Corinthian, or the
graceful beauty of the Ionic order ? And, above all,
what have you, in eloquence, comparable to the energy
of that soul of fire, " Who shook the arsenal, and
fulmined over Greece, to Macedon and Artaxerxes'
throne ?" But it is not my purpose to respond to these
inquiries. It would be sacrilege to disturb her repose,
by plucking a leaf from the laurel that adorns her tomb.
There is no classic heart who would not that it should
bloom for ever with unfading freshness. In everything
susceptible of improvement we have left her far behind ;
and it ought not to mortify us, that, in those things which
she could, and therefore did carry to perfection, we have
been unable to surpass her. Science admits of endless
progression, and is therefore constantly progressing. But
imagination may fly at once to the highest heaven of
invention, and as this was effected by ancient poetry, no
modern wing can ascend beyond it. This is the
difference between science and literature, as contradis-
tinguished from each other. The one is emphatically the
production of intellect, requiring patient research and
profound investigation. The other is the offspring of
those faculties of the mind, which are usually employed

in the creations of fancy or delineations of nature, in portraying character or exhibiting the passions of the human heart. Hence the vast superiority of Euler and La Place over Ptolemy and Euclid, or, in other words, of modern over ancient science, while Homer still remains the prince of poets, and sculptors and painters still take their lessons from the great models of antiquity. But even admitting the claims of the ancients, and to the fullest extent to which their warmest admirers consider them entitled to admission, it is still demonstrable that the present age not only far surpasses all that have preceded it in the number and variety of its authors and its artists, but will bear an advantageous comparison with any in the extent of their learning, the originality of their genius, and the sterling merit of their works. In proof of this assertion, abundant testimony might easily be adduced from England, France, and the classic soil of Italy. But as my limits will not permit me to dwell upon this topic, I proceed to remark, in the next place, that a prominent feature of the present age is *the general diffusion of popular intelligence*. Amongst the ancients, the benefits of education were confined to a few. The Spartans were barbarians, and even an Athenian populace was an ignorant mob. Since the invention of the art of printing, however, information has become easy and accessible, and in every Christian country, therefore, the people have received an extraordinary degree of moral and mental cultivation. Of late years, particularly, the attention of patriots and philanthropists has been powerfully directed to the great object of popular education. Knowledge is now carried to the humble dwelling of the poor, as well as to the splendid mansion of the rich. Like the sun, it diffuses its light indiscriminately upon all, and all, in consequence, have become enlightened. But a still more conspicuous feature of the present age, is *the unprecedented extent to which the dominion of man over physical nature has been carried.* This is truly the era of steamboats and railways, of canals and tunnels. The prophecy of *Darwin* has been more than realized. *Watt* and *Fulton* have subdued the elements. Unconquered steam not only rides, like a sea-god, on the bosom of the ocean, but moves with resistless power and rapidity over every obstacle on land. And who can prescribe a limit to its conquests ? Who can designate the barrier that it shall not pass, or name the river or the wilderness, however desolate and solitary now, that it shall not cause to roll down gold, or blossom as the rose ? And it is *the epoch of exploration and discovery.* Governments are laudably vieing with each other in the cause of science. New accessions are constantly making to the stores of knowledge. The spirit of adventure examines land and sea ; the Niger and Columbia, the Pacific Ocean and the American wilderness ; and while it daily discloses new wonders of nature, and new mines of knowledge, it also lays open new avenues of commerce, and new and extensive sources of national prosperity. But while nations are thus engaged in exploring and subduing physical nature and its elements, they have not forgotten to investigate and establish the principles of government and the rights of man. This is peculiarly *the age of civil and religious liberty.* The ancients had nothing that deserved the name. Grecian liberty was always wild and tumultuous, and the Romans knew no medium between licentiousness and servitude. These great principles

originated in the era of the Reformation, when Luther
and Zuingle, and their bold co-adjutors, broke the chain
of ecclesiastical oppression, and proclaimed freedom of
conscience to a captive world. From that period they
have gone on regularly, "conquering and to conquer."
They shone triumphantly in England, in the memorable
revolution of 1688, and they gave the impulse to our
revolutionary war, and laid the foundation of the American
Constitution. And the triumph of liberty here, awakened
the enthusiasm of the gallant French. But, unfortunately,
they knew but little of regulated freedom ; and their revolution, therefore, instead of ending like ours, in the success of
the principles in which it had its origin, terminated in the
establishment of a military despotism. Since then, however, the Catholics of Ireland have achieved their emancipation, and English Dissenters have been admitted to the
full enjoyment of their birth-right. Man no longer dares
to legislate for Heaven, or to regulate conscience by penal
laws. In many other points, too, important advances
have been made in enlarging the freedom of the British
Constitution. A very numerous portion of the people,
formerly denied all participation in the affairs of government, are now entitled to the exercise of the elective
franchise ; and the period is rapidly approaching when
the odious principle, that one denomination of religionists
shall be compelled to sustain another, will be finally
abolished. In France, all connection between Church
and State has been dissolved, and in consonance with the
spirit of the glorious revolution of '31, a republican
system has been engrafted on its monarchy. There is,
indeed, everywhere a constant contest between freedom
and oppression. Even in old Spain, the spirit of liberty

heaves and throes, though Pelion has been piled upon Ossa to crush it to the earth ; and at this very moment, it nerves the arms and animates the hearts of a gallant band in the neighboring territory, who, with the true nobleness of the Anglo-Saxon blood, have firmly resolved to achieve their independence, or to perish in the effort. And may we not hope that they will succeed ? While we weep over the scene of the Alamo, may we not rejoice at the brilliant victory of San Jacinto, and the consequent capture of a tyrant whose deeds of blood have disgraced humanity ? And may we not trust that the period is near at hand, when the people of Texas shall indeed be our brethren, and when the chorus of freedom shall reverberate from the Hudson to the Sabine, and from the banks of the Colorado to the heights of Bunker ! But, again, *this is the age of liberal principles and free inquiry.* The human mind is no longer chained down by despotism, nor locked up in darkness. Antiquity is no longer the shield of error, nor dogmatic authority the evidence of argument. Nothing now can stand, that is not sustained by truth and reason. Every system is subjected to the severest scrutiny, and the consequence is that while every valuable principle is strengthened, and every good system refined and purified, by the ordeal of discussion, all pernicious and untenable doctrines are tottering and falling, and new and better ones erected on their ruins. And " though last, not least," it is *the age of active piety and enlarged benevolence.* After whole centuries of apathy, the Christian Church has at length awakened to the full performance of its duty. It has undertaken the great enterprise of the conversion of the world, and organized a system of moral machinery admirably adapted to the purpose ; and its suc-

cess has been commensurate with the god-like principle
upon which it acts. It has established thousands of nur-
series, in which myriads of children receive the benefits
of religious education. It has revolutionized society by
the great engine of the temperance reform. It has placed
heralds of salvation on Moslem minarets and on pagan
walls. It has kindled the light of Revelation in Alpine
solitudes and on Himalayan heights. It has planted the
standard of the cross on the banks of the Ganges, and in
the isles of Polynesia. In one word, it has brought on
the dawn of the millenial day; and it will go on prosper-
ously, like an army with banners, invading kingdoms and
subduing nations, till the pure spirit of Christianity shall
spread like a sea of glory, over a reformed and civilized
world.

THE BELL-BIRD OF BRAZIL.

BY WILLIAM HAYNE SIMMONS.

It is generally supposed that the woods abound with birds, whose
flight and note continually enliven the forest; but nothing can be
more still and solitary than everything around — the silence is
appalling, and the desolation awful; neither are disturbed by the
sight or voice of any living thing, save one, which only adds to the
impression. Among the highest trees, and in the deepest glen, a
sound is sometimes heard, so singular, that the noise seems quite
unnatural. It is like the clinking of metals, as if two lumps of
brass were struck together; and resembles sometimes the distant
and solemn tolling of a church bell, struck at long intervals. This

extraordinary sound proceeds from a bird called the Araponga, or Guirapongo. It is about the size of a small pigeon, white, with a red circle round its eyes. It sits on the tops of the highest trees, and in the deepest forests; and though constantly heard in the most desert places, is very rarely seen. It is impossible to conceive of anything of a more solitary character than the profound silence of the woods, broken only by the metallic and almost preternatural sound of this invisible bird, coming from the air, and seeming to follow you wherever you go. I have watched with great perseverance when the sound seemed quite near me, and never but once caught a glance of the cause. It passed suddenly over the top of a very high tree, like a large flake of snow, and immediately disappeared. —*Notices of Brazil, by the Rev. R. Walsh.*

Whilst we lay in the noon-day heat, shadowed under the thick wood, the very peculiar and romantic cry of the Campanero, or bell-bird, would be heard at intervals. It is white, about the size of a pigeon, with a leathery excrescence on its forehead; and the sound which it produces in the lone woods, is like that of a convent bell, tolling at a distance.—*Transatlantic Sketches, p.* 29. *By Captain J. E. Alexander.*

THE CAMPANERO.

HERE Nature, clad in vestments rich and grey,
Sits like a bride in gorgeous palace lone—
And sees naught move, and hears no sound all day,
Save from its cloudy source the torrent tumbling,
And to the mountain's foot its glories humbling;
Or wild-woods to the desert gale that moan—
Or far the Campanero's note deep tolling
From the pine's glossy spire, where the breeze,
Disporting o'er the green and shoreless seas,
Impels the leafy billows ever rolling.
It comes again, sad as the passing bell,
That solitary note—unseen whence swell

The tones so drear—so secret is the shade,
Where that coy dweller of the glooms has made
His perch on high ; behind his verdant screen,
He nestles, or like transient snow-flakes flash,
Or flying foam that winds from torrents dash.
Plunges to stiller haunts, where hangs sublime
The wandering water-vine,* its pitcher green
Fill'd from the cloud ; where but the bear may climb,
Or thirsting savage, when the summer ray
Has dried each fount, and parched the desert way.
There safe he dips refresh'd his pearly bill,
In lymph more pure than from or spring or rill.
No longer by the wandering Indian shared,
The dewy draught he there may quaff unscar'd ;
For vacant now glooms every glen and grove, .
Where erst he saw the quiver'd red-man rove—
Saw, like the otter's brood upon the stream,
His wild-eyed offspring sport, or 'neath the tree,
Share with the birds kind Nature's bounty free.
Chang'd is the woodland scene, like morning dream,
The race have vanish'd to return no more—
Gone from the forest side, the river shore.†

* (*Tillisandria intriculata, and liquelata.*) The leaves are
protuberant below and form vessels like pitchers, which catch and
retain the rain water, furnishing cool and limpid draughts to the
heated traveller, in elevations where no water is to be found. The
quantity of fluid contained in these reservoirs, is sometimes very
considerable, and in attempting to reach the flower-stem I have
been often drenched by upsetting the plant.—Walsh, p. 170.

† During the administration of the Marquis De Pombal, these
people (the Indians) were protected, and it was decreed that no
Indian should be reduced to a state of slavery. * * * By a
mistaken humanity, however, permission was given to the Bra-

Is it for this, thou lone and hermit bird,
That thus thy knell-like note so sad is heard
Sounding from every desert shade and dell
Where once they dwelt, where last they wept farewell;
They fled, till wearied with the bloody chase,
Or stopt by the rich spoil, their brethren pale
Sated, the dire pursuit surceas'd a space.*
While memory's eye o'er the sad picture fills,
They fade, nor leave behind or wreck or trace;
The valiant tribes forgotten on their hills,
And seen no more in wilderness or vale.

ETRUSCAN REMAINS.

BY JOEL R. POINSETT.

THE attention of the literary men of Europe having
been much excited by the recent discovery of Etruscan
remains on the estate of Lucien Bonaparte, Prince of

zilians to convert their neighbors to Christianity. * * * The
Indians were everywhere hunted down for the sake of their
salvation. Wars were excited among the tribes, for the laudable
purpose of bringing in each other captives, to be converted to
Christianity. The consequence was, that all who could escape,
retired to the remotest forests, and there is not one now to be found
in a state of nature, in all this wooded country.—Ibid., p. 47.

* The Portuguese settle only where they meet with mines, and
leave the richer lands, with which the country abounds, unculti-
vated.—Ibid.

Canino, situated near the Maresmas of Rome, I have thought some account of them might be acceptable.

While ploughing up a field round Mount Columella, the oxen attached to the plough broke through the ground, and fell into a deep vault or grotto. The laborers discovered in this place two vases, broken into fragments, for which, however, they found a ready sale. The agent of the estate immediately set to work, and opened several similar vaults and made further discoveries of vases, which were sold to a collector. The circumstance became knownto the government, and was immediately communicated to the proprietor, who repaired in person to the spot and commenced regular works, opening the earth in every direction round the mount, where there were any indications of subterranean grottos. The enterprise of Lucien Bonaparte has been crowned with complete success, and more than two thousand beautiful Etruscan vases have been brought to light. Lucien Bonaparte has published a work in which he describes these vases, and gives explanations of the paintings with which they are ornamented. It would be impracticable in an article so limited as this must necessarily be, to follow him throughout these explanations, which occupy a quarto volume, and which are intended to show that the arts were known in Italy before they were in Greece. It is a synopsis of his argument, and proofs derived from other sources, which we intend to lay before our readers in order to support the position assumed by the Prince of Canino.

The subjects of the paintings are taken from scenes of the Iliad and Odyssey, or of the heathen mythology, or from customs peculiar at the period to the Etruscans. One of the most striking, records the death of Hector.

Achilles is represented mounting his car, to which he has attached the dead body of Hector; and the shade of Patroclus is seen hovering above them, enjoying this act of vengeance; a white greyhound and a winged figure, probably that of victory, precede the horses of Achilles. The death of Achilles is represented on another vase, with some difference from the account of that event given by Homer. He is seen stretched on the field of battle, despoiled of his armor, and defended by Ajax and his son Neoptolemus, not an infant but a man grown. On another, Ajax sustains the body of Achilles in his arms, and excites the Greeks to defend it. Neoptolemus is on the right of Ajax, engaged in combat with Æneas; on the left, Menelaus combats Paris, having at his feet a warrior whom he has overcome. Peleus and Thetis, with Achilles, and the Centaur Chiron, are frequently represented, and on these vases Chiron has the fore feet human. There is on one vase a beautiful picture of the flight of Æneas with his family. He has a helmet on his head, his sword by his side, and two spears in his left hand, while with his right he supports the feet of Anchises, whom he bears on his shoulders. The old man clings to the neck of his son with one hand, and carries a sceptre in the other. The little Ascanius is behind the group, running to keep up with his parents, and Crëusa precedes Æneas, with her head turned towards him, as if to hasten his flight. There is an inscription on this vase, the letters of which are perfectly clear, but the language quite unintelligible. On a large vase is represented Ulysses, suspended beneath the ram and issuing forth from the cave of Polyphemus; and on another he is standing before Penelope. Several of these paintings represent the superstitious rites of

the Etruscans ; in some, soothsayers are seen examining the entrails of victims ; in others, they are figured
in processions ; on several, the four-horse car is
represented with the driver leaning eagerly over the
horses and urging them forward to the goal ; on many,
Hercules is painted in his combats with Centaurs and
wild beasts, and in repose ; Bacchus with his Cornupotorio and the accompanying fawns, satyrs and Bacchants.
Minerva with her casque and lance, and covered with the
Ægis, is a favorite subject ; and the rest are made up of
combats and nuptials, warriors and horsemen, nymphs and
matrons.

The forms of these vases are beautifully graceful, and
the figures are exquisitely finished. They are painted
yellow and white, and violet color, upon generally a black
ground. It is supposed that they were drawn upon the
terra cotta after it had been partially baked, with a pointed
instrument. The whole design is drawn in lines ; and the
opinion is that it was necessary to trace every line with
one continued stroke of the pencil. The relief and light
and shade are all produced by the disposition of these
lines. The colors are vivid, and the varnish so admirably
tempered, that an antique Etruscan vase may be steeped
for twenty-four hours in aquafortis, without the varnish or
the colors being, in the least degree, affected by the acid.
I saw a collection of these vases from Canino, which were
exhibited in London a few years since, and thought them
generally more perfect than those I had formerly seen in
Naples, and quite equal to the most beautiful of the collection described by Sir William Hamilton.

Lucien Bonaparte is persuaded, that the hill of Columella, an artificial mount round the base of which the

researches were made, stands on the site of the ancient city of Vitulonia, and near the famous baths of Caldana. He is confirmed in this belief by the discovery of a small, but beautiful statue of Higeia, and by the inscription on one of the vases having the name Vithlon, under the group of a man and a woman, presenting their homage to an old man, with a crown on his head, whom he supposes to be the genius of Vitulonia. It may as well, however, be a Bacchus, for it has a cornupotorio in one hand.

The most difficult subject connected with these vases, is the letters and the language of the inscriptions. Tiraboschi assures us, that the genius and the nature of the Etruscan language have never been understood by the moderns, and there is more of ingenuity than of truth in the interpretations given to the ancient Etruscan inscriptions. It appears, certainly, to have undergone many material changes in the lapse of ages, and the characters to have been frequently altered. A very general opinion appears to have prevailed, that in the first written language of the Etruscans, they used the Phœnician characters; while some of the existing monuments prove, that they used, at an early period, the letters of the Pelasgians. These are the same as those of the inscriptions in the temple of the Ismenean Apollo at Thebes in Bœotia, as copied by Herodotus. After the early method of the Phœnicians, the Pelasgians, and the Greeks, the Etruscans wrote at first from right to left; but this similarity is not sufficient evidence, nor even a corroboration of the identity of the Phœnician and Etruscan characters. That these early settlers in Italy emigrated from Asia, there can be no doubt; and the Asiatic nations still write from right to left. In one of the oldest fragments of Etruscan

history, I have found this passage ; speaking of Aruns, one
of their earliest kings, it says, " *sub cujus imperium
hebraica lingua corrumpi cœpit,*" under whose reign the
Hebrew language began to be corrupted.   This passage
renders it probable that the root of the language was
Hebrew ; that it afterwards became corrupted by the intimate connection of the Etruscans with the Pelasgians,
introducing the letters of the latter and corrupting the
original tongue, as their subsequent intercourse with the
Greeks contributed still further to change it ; for the inscriptions of that period are Etrusco-Greek, as those of a
later epoch are Etrusco-Latin.   This is only true, however, of the characters in which the inscriptions are written ; the language is still the same, and, except the proper
names, equally unintelligible.   I have before me one
written entirely in the Roman character, which no knowledge of any dead or living language with which we are
acquainted, will enable us to understand.   The words
are,—

SVPKI V,SIS ISVI ISVI IOTELNE ISVIV ISVT ISVPE

The mixtures of characters, and the changes they have
undergone, may be seen in the famous Eugubian tables.
These inscriptions, engraved upon several tables of brass,
were discovered in the year 1444, in a subterranean
chamber, near the theatre of Eugubium, and have ever
since been carefully preserved in the archives of Gubbio,
a town built upon the ruins of the ancient Eugubium.   The
two first are in the Pelasgian character, others in pure
Etruscan, and others in Roman letters, but in the Etruscan
idiom.   There is one poem, or lamentation, as it is called,

on these tables, of which a translation has been attempted ; and if we are to rely wholly upon the conjectures boldly put forth, of the learned, who published these tales, that poem was composed 247 years before those of Hesiod and Homer. Still, however, it is certain, that these and other inscriptions have rather been interpreted than translated ; and as Tiraboschi assures us that the root, nature, and genius of the language are not yet understood, we must wait until another Champollion arises, to give the true interpretation to these numerous inscriptions.

We are equally at a loss for the origin of this extraordinary people. The first rise of ancient nations is generally fabulous, uncertain, or totally unknown, and this is especially true of the Etruscans. According to Herodotus and Strabo, they were first called Thyrrenians, from the name of Thyrrenus, under whose conduct they landed in Italy ; but, according to other authors, they landed and took possession of Italy under the conduct of Janus, son of Japhet, son of Noah. Others, again, say, that they were led out of Armenia by Esar, who was deified, and to whom the great temple at Volterra was dedicated. All that we know with any certainty is, that the Pelasgians, who arrived in Italy one hundred years after the deluge of Deucalion, united themselves with the Thyrrenians ; that their first colony was called Kitim, which gave its name to all that part of Italy afterwards called Magna Grecia ; that their country was after some years called Eturgia, corrupted to Etruria, and the principal city called Volterra, from Volturnis, a favorite chieftain ; that they became great navigators, and gave the name of Thyrrenian to the sea which borders the coasts of Italy, and were withal famous pirates ; that the Lydians sought new settlements

in Etruria, and, after the example of the Pelasgians, united
themselves intimately with Etruscans, who subsequently
conquered and colonized all the country on both sides of
the Appenines. These mountains were so called from
Apis, who reigned over Etruria, and conquered that part
of Italy. The numerous Etruscan medals are proof of the
dominion of this people over all the places where they
were struck, and that includes all Italy. Etruria was at
the highest point of its grandeur about a century before
the taking of Troy, and its decline and fall were so sudden,
that they were attributed to the wrath of the gods.

The Etruscans are known to us in three distinct epochs.
The first comprehends the period of their dominion over
all Italy, which they governed as colonies; the second,
when they enjoyed free institutions and a federative government, and elected annually their executive under the
title of Lucumon: and the third, after they fell before the
mighty power of Rome.

In the first epoch they appear to have cultivated the
arts and sciences with success, and if they did not extend
their researches so far, or carry their inventions to such
perfection as the Greeks, they had the advantage of preceding that illustrious people in architecture, sculpture and
painting. We will not follow the example of some Italian
authors, who attributed so many discoveries in the arts to
the Etruscans, that a zealous Hellenist said in derision, he
expected soon to be told, that they had invented the art of
breathing; but we think there is sufficient evidence to
show, that architecture, engraving on stone, sculpture and
painting, were cultivated by the Etruscans of the highest
antiquity, and that they were original among them. They
could not have borrowed them from Greece at a period

when, according to Thucydides, there was very little communication with that people by sea or land, and when they were yet uncivilized—nor did they obtain them from Egypt, because, according to Herodotus, they could have had at that time no communication with that nation,—so that the learned conjectures of Buonarotti, who imagines he sees by the manner in which the ancient Etruscans have treated the arts, traces of their Egyptian origin, prove, in reality, nothing more than that inventors in both countries, having met with the same difficulties, employed the same means, and, in the first stages, produced nearly similar works. This appears to be the case in every country where the arts have originated.

The specimens of sculpture found in Mexico, resemble the early attempts of the Etruscans and Egyptians.

The Mexicans possessed the art of carving upon the hardest stone, and the specimens we have of that art and of their sculpture, and even of their architecture, resemble so much those of Egypt, that many persons have believed Mexico to have been originally peopled from that country. Although we think the evidence is against the Etruscans having descended from the Egyptians, or having borrowed their arts from them, it is certain that, at a subsequent period, they had an extensive commerce with that people. For this fact we have the testimony of Strabo. He again lays too much stress upon the similarity of their monuments, and, especially, that both nations erected pyramids for the sepulchres of their dead. The Mexicans did the same, and the pyramids near Teoleohuacan, on the plains of Mexico, are inferior only to the largest of the pyramids of Egypt. There is other evidence of the intercourse of the Etruscans with the Egyptians, as there is of their communication with the Hebrews. Some of the kings of Egypt, when driven out of their country, are known to have taken refuge in Etruria; and we find that, during the Lucumonship of Saturnus Francasius, six legates were sent from Volterra to Solomon, King of the Jews, and they were accompanied by two priests of the College of Augurs, in order, says the annalist, that they might hear the words of wisdom which fell from the lips of that celebrated monarch. On the following year, in the Lucumonship of Lucœus Salinius, these ambassadors returned, bringing presents of great value, which the wisest of kings sent to the people of Etruria. But whether descended from the Hebrews, the Phœnicians, or the Egyptians, all we contend for, is, that the similarity of the early efforts of the arts among those people is no proof of their descent from either.

According to Vitruvius, the first edifices raised by man served for the models of the architect. The rustic roof of the hut, which necessity had taught man to erect, was changed into the pediment, the rafters into architraves, and the rough hewn trees which supported the building, into beautifully proportioned columns; and it is to be presumed, that all inventors, whether Etruscans, Egyptians, or Mexicans, would follow this natural order. Very few monuments of Etruscan architecture remain to us. The colossal wall of Cortona and Volterra, and the temples at Pœstum, are all that we know of. The origin of the latter is still a subject of dispute among learned antiquaries; but a very superficial examination of those magnificent ruins, would convince any one conversant with the subject, that they are not of pure Grecian architecture—they resemble the Doric, but they have neither the proportions, nor the distances, given by Vitruvius to that order, or found in the remains of any Greek temple which now exists. Both Sir William Hamilton and Mr. Forsyth, while they acknowledge these differences, still deem them Grecian. There exist, however, in the walls of the town, Etruscan inscriptions with letters of great size, and tinged with red, which mark the walls to be Etruscan, and the ruins of the temples they inclose may be so likewise. Forsyth speaks of the ruins of Pæstum in language, to the truth of which my own feelings bear testimony ; he says, " taking into view their immemorial antiquity, their astonishing preservation, their grandeur, or rather grandosity, their bold columnar elevation, at once massive and open, and their severe simplicity of design, I do not hesitate to call these the most impressive monuments that I ever beheld upon earth." The ancient annals furnish ample proof of this branch of the arts having been carried from Etruria to Greece by the Pelasgians. Diodorus Siculus tells us, that they were the first to invent the portico, to keep off the noise of servants and clients, " *ad avertendum turbæ servorum et clientum strepitus !*" The use of the portico introduced the first order of architecture, the Tuscan, which gives a high idea of their original genius in the arts. It is a singular fact, that the antiquities of Thebes, in Upper Egypt, the remains of the Etruscan walls and edifices, and the ruins of Palenque in Mexico, exhibit the same style of architecture.

It has been already stated, that the liberal arts owe their origin to the religious feelings of mankind. The savage hut was converted into a temple to be worthy of the Gods they worshipped ; and the earliest attempts of sculpture were made to convert the stones, trees and pillars, which, we are told, received divine honors in the east, into statues representing the attributes of their Deities. The earliest attempts in this art have been alike in every country where it originated. In Etruria, in Egypt, and in Mexico, it commenced by fixing up blocks of stone or wood, a little longer than they were broad, with a round stone at the top, to figure the head ; next, these blocks were tapered away so as to assume somewhat the form of the human figure, and the features of the face were grossly delineated on a circular stone ; then the feet were made to appear below these Hermes, and the arms were indicated, but still stuck fast to the sides, and the statue bolt upright.

At length a determined proportion was given to these Hermes. It having been observed that the length of a man's foot was nearly one-sixth part of his height, that rule was adopted for the height of the Hermes, and different heads placed on the top indicated the different deities they were intended to represent, which were sometimes further denoted by an inscription. After a time, the sculptor, seeking to imitate nature more exactly, succeeded in bringing the features out in bold relief, and, at length, in fashioning the stone into the form of the head, and giving an imperfect copy of the " human face." They, at the same time, found out the means of presenting the appearance of the human form in some of the most simple of the infinite variety of positions in which the body may be placed. In the museum of the Literary and Philosophical Society of South Carolina, some specimens of the early attempts of Mexican sculpture may be seen ; but in that of the American Philosophical Society in Philadelphia, there exists a series of examples from the very earliest efforts of the art, to the perfection to which

it had attained in that country at the time of the conquest—
these exhibit an exact similarity with those of Egypt and
Etruria. The first efforts of the Greeks, before the arts
were introduced by the Pelasgians, were still more rude ;
and it is curious to trace the progress of sculpture in that
country, from the first statue of Minerva, which was
worshipped in the Acropolis at Athens, and which Tertul-
lian represents to have been a rough block of wood,
" *sine effigie rudis palus et informe lignum*," to the statue
of the same goddess, placed in the Parthenon by Phidias :
but this inquiry would lead us too far from the present
subject. There are two Etruscan statues of great beauty,
and exhibiting great perfection in the art, in the Florentine
museum ; they are, the statues of the Soothsayer and of
the Chimera, which bear the clearest proof of their being
Etruscan, from the inscriptions upon them. For beauty,
symmetry and grace, these statues bear a comparison
with the finest models of antiquity. Pliny speaks of a
colossal statue of Apollo, an Etruscan monument, which
stood in the Augustan temple, and which, he tells us, was
of admirable beauty.

Most authors agree, that the Etruscans were the earliest
painters in Europe. Pliny tells us that painting had
already acquired all its force and beauty before the age of
Demaratus, who first introduced the art into Greece ; and
it is a remarkable circumstance that Homer, in neither of
his poems, makes any mention of painting. The nearest
approach to it is the description of the shield of Achilles.

Now, there is sufficient evidence to show, that the art
was cultivated in Etruria before the siege of Troy. We
have no remains of Etruscan paintings except what are
seen upon the vases. And when we consider the

extreme difficulty of painting upon a cylindrical surface, and upon a substance which required each contour to be drawn with a continuous line, the artists who executed these paintings must have possessed greater knowledge of their art, and talents of a higher order than would appear from these works, although they unite, in a high degree, the beauties of grace, simplicity and expression. The forms of these vases, which are of an infinite variety, vary with the uses for which they were intended. Some were destined for votive offerings, some to contain the sacred oil given to the victors of the games ; others to adorn the depository of the Lares ; others for domestic uses ; and others again were cinerary, and contained the ashes of the dead, and the precious things which were buried with them. This custom was common, too, to the Etruscans and Mexicans. All the vases of the former have been discovered in vaults, destined for depositions of the dead, where we found, likewise, engraved stones, small vases, and ornaments that resemble the toys of children. The finest vases of bronze, of porphyry and chalcedony, now existing in the museums of Naples, were found in some of these sepulchres, which were subterranean vaults, walled up on every side. In some of them were sarcophaguses of marble, or of *terra cotta.* Now, it is very remarkable, that the same customs should have prevailed among the Mexicans. I have myself been present when some of these subterranean chambers were opened. They are generally situated in the centre of a small mound or pyramid, called there a teocalli. On opening them, we invariably found a number of vases of *terra cotta ;* and, in one or two instances, a sarcophagus of the same material, shaped like a large vase, and filled with human bones. These vaults were filled with toys made of earthenware, lamps and vases of different forms, and some painted with considerable taste. There is one of *terra cotta* in Philadelphia, which is encircled with a painting resembling very much an Etruscan border. In one of the tombs opened under my inspection, was found a perfect mirror, made by polishing a single pyrite and a number of hawk's bells, which the Spaniards exchanged with the Mexicans for gold, besides a variety of ornaments in shells and cut stones,—all these denoted the rank of the chief as well as the epoch of his death. In some of these tombs have been found vases of alabaster of graceful forms and highly ornamented— (there are two of these in Philadelphia)—and masks of the human countenance carved in alabaster, in porphyry, and even in obsidian, denoting great perfection in the art, whether we regard the workmanship or the expression. But to return to the Etruscans. There is little of their history by which we can judge of their progress in science ; but so intimately connected are the liberal arts with science, that one cannot flourish without the other ; and where architecture, sculpture and painting were carried to the high state of perfection which they are known to have attained among the Etruscans, it is reasonable to believe that the sciences were likewise cultivated with success.

It is manifest, that neither painter, nor sculptor, nor architect, could attain any celebrity in their several arts, without being acquainted with the rules of proportion, the nature of colors, and the laws of perspective, and other things of a similar nature, which require a knowledge of science. If, then, we have shown that the Etruscans were remarkable for their proficiency in the liberal arts, we must grant that they cultivated the sciences at the same time with equal success. Livy says, that the Roman youth were formerly taught the language and erudition of the Etruscans, as they now are those of the Greeks. Dionysius Halicarnassus recounts that the Greek Demaratus caused his children to be instructed in the Etruscan literature. Their account of the creation of the world resembles so much that recorded in the book of Genesis, that Tiraboschi founds an argument upon it to show that they must have descended from the Hebrews, or from some nation bordering upon them. We know that, although Etruria was called by ancient writers the " *mother of superstition,*" and that the principal occupation of their philosophers was the examination of the entrails of animals, and observing the signs in the heavens, and especially the lightning, still, it is certain they had some exact notions of physic, and were aware that the lightning proceeded from the earth as well as from the heavens. They made great advances in navigation, and first invented the use of the rostrum and of anchors. The warlike trumpet was invented by them, and the Romans derived from them many of their customs.

They first instituted public games. They had, from time immemorial, a high priest of the augurs, and a college of soothsayers; temples dedicated to Vesta, and vestal virgins to officiate at her altar. Their chief magistrates were accompanied by lictors, and were elected annually by the people, under the title of Lucumons; an institution which may be traced back to a period long anterior to the siege of Troy. It is written, that, on the landing of Æneas on the shores of Italy, there arose a dispute among the Lucumons of the several Etruscan cities, some of them espousing the cause of the Trojan hero, and others taking part with Turnus. But the glory of the Etruscans had passed away long before the fall of Troy. Posterior to that epoch, their meagre annals record little else than the annual elections of their Lucumons, their feeble wars and discordant factions, which prepared the way for their downfall and final destruction by the power of Rome. It is curious, in looking over these annals, to observe the resemblance between the contests of the Etruscan people and the nobles, with those which took place between the two estates during the stormy period of the Italian Republics. The incidents and the characters are very nearly similar. The Etruscans, in the early ages, are represented to have been industrious, prosperous and happy. The ancient poets placed the golden age at the period of the reign of the wisest and greatest princes of that people, probably during that of Janus, who reigned sixty years, and during whose government the Etruscans received wise and wholesome laws, and all Italy enjoyed profound peace ; and during that of Saturn, who reigned over Latium, after he was expelled from his kingdom by his eldest son. When the Etruscans drove out their kings and changed their institutions, they adopted a republican and federative form of government, under which they enjoyed great prosperity. The cities sent delegates to the general council, according to their population, and this assembly decided on peace and war, made and altered laws, decided controversies between the states or cities, and compelled submission to their decrees. They constituted a court of appeals from the decisions of the Lucumons and other tribunals in the cities and colonies.

The Lucumon had both criminal and civil jurisdiction, but he was compelled to decide according to the laws, and, in all criminal cases, to call in six impartial men, with whom he consulted on the guilt and the punishment of the accused. In judging all civil cases, he associated with himself four prudent men. Was not this somewhat like the trial by jury? All the elections were popular, and it is difficult to conceive a freer, happier or more prosperous people. Their downfall was sudden, and their ruin irretrievable. They attributed it to the wrath of the Gods; but, for many years preceding, we find in their annals the history of dissensions and factions, and this lamentation is frequently repeated,

" Imperandi cupiditas pernicies est Reipublicæ."

" The lust of power is the ruin of the Republic."

THE PILLAR OF GLORY.

BY EDWIN C. HOLLAND.

HAIL to the heroes whose triumphs have brighten'd
  The darkness which shrouded America's name;
Long shall their valor in battle that lighten'd,
  Live in the brilliant escutcheons of fame:
    Dark where the torrents flow,
    And the rude tempests blow,

The storm-clad spirit of Albion raves ;
 Long shall she mourn the day,
 When in the vengeful fray,
Liberty walked like a god on the waves.

The ocean, ye chiefs,—(the region of glory,
 Where fortune has destined Columbia to reign),
Gleams with the halo and lustre of story,
 That curl round the wave as the scene of her fame :
  There on its raging tide,
  Shall her proud navy ride,
The bulwark of freedom, protected by Heaven ;
  There shall her haughty foe,
  Bow to her prowess low,
There shall renown to her heroes be given.

The pillar of glory, the sea that enlightens,
 Shall last till eternity rocks on its base,
The splendor of fame, its waters that brightens,
 Shall lighten the footsteps of time in his race :
  Wide o'er the stormy deep,
  Where the rude surges sweep,
Its lustre shall circle the brows of the brave ;
  Honor shall give it light,
  Triumph shall keep it bright,
Long as in battle we meet on the wave.

Already the storm of contention has hurl'd
 From the grasp of Old England the trident of war,
The beams of our stars have illumined the world,
 Unfurled, our standard beats proud in the air :

Wild glares the eagle's eye,
Swift as he cuts the sky,
Marking the wake where our heroes advance ;
Compass'd with rays of light,
Hovers he o'er the fight ;
Albion is heartless—and stoops to his glance.

———

HYMN OF THE EXILE.

BY WILLIAM H. TIMROD.

FATHER of light, of life, of love,
Before thy lofty throne we bow,
Thy presence brightens all above,
Thy presence gladdens all below ;
In darkest clouds of human wo,
Thou beam'st, and all is calm and fair ;
And brightest scenes that earth can know,
Are darkness, if thou be not there.

Long ere we crossed the trackless sea,
We praised thee at our natal fanes,
Nor shall we cease to call on thee
In free Columbia's happy plains ;
At home, the regal tyrant reigns,
Who claimed our wealth, our blood, our toil ;
Rescued by thee, our grateful strains,
Now heavenward rise from freedom's soil.

And late, when storms of civil feud,
  Rent our adopted country—when
The boldest hearts affrighted stood,
  We quailed not—thou wert with us then ;—
  What is the power of mightiest men,
Great Lord of power, compared with thee !
  Thou broke their iron hearts—again
Peace smiled, and owned thy proud decree.

And now once more, before thy throne,
  The native, the adopted kneel,
Thy strong sustaining arm we own,
  Thy kind, forgiving love we feel ;
  Be ever nigh, oh Lord ! to heal
The madness of our wayward hearts,
  And evil from our breasts will steal,
As night before the morn departs.

THE DUNGEON AND THE GALLOWS.

BY JOHN BLAKE WHITE.

WE were called to the prison, on professional business, the evening previous to the execution. At the instance of the jailer, we went down with him to the ground cells of the prison, where he unlocked a door, which opened into an extensive apartment. The furniture of this gloomy chamber, illumined only by a lantern, which our guide

carried in his hand, consisted of several deal coffins, a
gibbet, whose disjointed parts lay lumbering against the
wall, some fragments of rope, a spade, a pick-axe, and a
few like implements of death and the grave. The jailer
proceeded to examine the machine, and to ascertain that
all its parts were complete, and fit and ready for the morrow. The gibbet had served many a turn, since the execution of the hapless youth, Dennis, to the present time ;
and we were told of many particulars concerning the
several victims who had suffered beneath it. Two proper
sized coffins being selected and delivered over to an
attendant, we followed the jailor to another cell, at a remote corner of the building. After repeated calls, a voice
at length answered from within, as from a sepulchre. The
door being unbarred and opened, we beheld, stretched upon
the floor, a being that appeared to be anything rather than
human. Haggard, pale, emaciated, it began, slowly, to
rise from the floor, growling like some glutted hyena at
being roused from his lair. It stood, at length, erect before us, resembling more an anatomical preparation than
a true and living man. "Thus am I served," muttered he,
" whenever you want my work. But give me something
to drink. I must have drink, and I will be contented."
This was the executioner ! Yes, we stood in the awful
presence of a minister of justice, and we shrunk with reve-
rential horror at his glance !

This solitary, this mysterious being, lived alone in creation. Neither wife, nor child, nor kinsfolk, had he ; and
he acknowledged no human tie to this world. He was a
pensioner upon the sheriff for mere food and scanty rai-
m ent, and had been so for a long time upon the bounty of
many a predecessor. Here, then, stood before us, in un-

sophisticated reality, the murderer of state, the pensioned
cut-throat, the day-laborer of death, one who did his work
for pay with fidelity and skill, and all by virtue of law and
under the sacred sanction of justice. This miserable man,
being extremely intemperate, it became necessary to con-
fine closely when his services were about to be required.
Again and again, he entreated to be supplied with liquor,
which was positively refused, though with the assurance
that, after the execution, if well performed, he should have
as much to drink as he desired. A transient, but ghastly
smile flickered for an instant on his cheek, when the door
of his cell was again closed and bolted. On the ensuing
day, at the particular request of the sheriff, we attended at
the jail. A minister of the gospel had been for some time
in private with the convicts, humanely endeavoring to
prepare them for their awful change. From their cell,
sighs, sobs, and moans were heard, and sometimes loud
and lengthened lamentations ; then all was silent, and now
frantic shrieks broke upon the ear. The door of the cell
remained closed, and we remembered that this was the
culprit's privacy: the eve, to him, of a new and untried
life—his preparation for eternity !

In the lobby, silently awaited the sheriff and his attendants. At the farthest end of the gallery stood the executioner, arranging, with professional skill, the slip-knot and
the noose, and stretching to their utmost length the fatal
cords. The moment at length arrived, and the order was
given to prepare the convicts. The door was thrown
open, and what a scene was then exhibited ! The miserable man and his wretched wife were both before us. Two
finer forms the sculptor's fancy has seldom sketched ; tall,
graceful, we might almost add, majestic ; but, alas ! fallen,

helpless, degraded to the very dust! As the door opened, the eyes of the hapless woman fell upon the ghost-like apparition of the executioner, when she sent forth a shriek that chilled every heart with horror. After a long parley and much difficulty, and even resistance on her part, the jack-ketch adjusted the cords and pinioned his victims. His task was performed with indifference the most cold, and with skill the most perfect. To depict, with justice, the horrors of this scene, would require the pen of a Maturin, a Byron, or a Scott. It was made up of a thousand minute incidents, too much so to note, yet which essentially tended to fill up the whole picture with terrible and affecting interest.

The prisoners had provided themselves, at their private expense, with loose white garments, which they put on over their clothes. They threw themselves once more into each other's arms, and bade each other an eternal adieu. From this moment, the executioner appeared to take possession of this devoted pair, and thenceforth to claim them as his own. He left them not for an instant, but stood forth a conspicuous figure in this melancholy group. It may be considered presumptuous to dive into the human heart, and scan its secret and mysterious operations; but, in contemplating this extraordinary individual (whom to behold once, was never to forget), it was impossible to consider him but as one of the most debased and abandoned of the human race. The all-scrutinizing eye of Heaven may alone define the space between the hangman and the culprit; our finite judgment cannot determine it.

The unhappy victims descended the stairs, arm-in-arm, to a coach in waiting at the prison door, and the proces-

sion slowly moved forward, flanked by a company of
cavalry. It was a melancholy, though novel sight, to
behold a female led out to execution, and it attracted an
immense concourse of spectators, wonderful to add, of
both sexes, and of all ages and conditions! Arriving
within sight of the gibbet, which was erected a little way
out of the city, even now we remember the horrible
picture of despair exhibited in the countenance of Fisher,
when he first beheld the frightful reality. His cheek
assumed a livid paleness; his eyes involuntarily closed;
a tremor shook his frame; he almost sunk into the
arms of the master-spirit that now presided over his
destiny. He made, at this moment, a prodigious effort to
recover himself. He drew his wife, with a convulsive
grasp, to his bosom, and in a few seconds looked up,
nerved for the issue. The coach now reached the spot.
The culprits and the jack-ketch descended. Fisher
mounted the scaffold, and cast his eyes mournfully around
upon the immense multitude. Not so his wife. She
positively refused to go up. Neither remonstrances, nor
persuasions, nor threats, could avail. The constables
were at length constrained to resort to bodily force, and
she was almost dragged to the stand. This unhappy
woman could not believe it possible that she was then
destined to die. She called upon the multitude to rescue
her, and stretched forth her trembling arms, imploring
pity. At one moment she would rant and blaspheme,
and stamp and rave, with incoherent wildness; and now,
with execrations the most shocking, she would imprecate
perdition on the executive who would consign a woman
to an end so ignominious. Silence, like that of death,
hung over the vast assembly, broken only by the shrieks

(truly demoniacal) of this very maniac upon the verge
of eternity! Nothing could be more appalling. She
was totally unprepared to die. It was pitiable; it was
truly heart-rending, to behold this unhappy husband,
himself just about to perish, and needing every moment
for his own soul's sake, bending, with interest the most
intense, towards his frantic wife, and, in the tenderest
accents, conjuring her to make her peace with heaven.
All was unheeded. Her whole mind seemed engrossed
by the one absorbing thought—the hope of pardon. The
accidental examination of a written document, at this
moment, by the sheriff, shed a false gleam upon her.
Grasping at this incident (a frail plank in the tempest of
despair that raged within her bosom), she was ready to
leap from the scaffold, which the cords and the executioner only prevented. The sheriff, discovering the error
under which she labored, hastily re-folded the paper, and
in a sober and impressive voice, assured her that her
expectations were wholly groundless, that her moments
were few and numbered, and that she must assuredly
die. No human tongue can adequately describe the
intense interest of this moment. Happily, the words of
the sheriff were electric. She seemed to pierce with her
eyes into his very soul. For a moment she was mute.
Her execrations were hushed, and now, with frantic
gesticulations, she called upon heaven to have mercy
upon her, and to save her soul alive. Brief exclamations,
hurried ejaculations, half uttered but glowing words, flowed
from her lips with rapidity quicker than thought. All
was terror, hurry, dismay. Tremendous conflict! The
time was brief: she felt that she had delayed too long to
make her account with heaven; and now, the dreadful

messenger of death tugged at her despairing heart. Her prayers, though late, we fervently trust, ascended to the throne of grace, and pleaded, trumpet-tongued, in her behalf for mercy!

While these agonizing scenes were passing, the executioner we beheld, mounted aloft, on a ladder, hovering, like a vampire, over these devoted beings, engaged in making fast the cords, and adjusting the caps over their faces. One more thrilling pause ensued. This ill-fated pair stood trembling upon the narrow isthmus between time and eternity! A private signal passed from the sheriff—the platform gave way—they fell—all was hushed and still—their loose white garments only floated on the breeze!

For our own part, we disclaim all that morbid sensibility which might induce some persons to take part with every culprit the moment he is condemned, and to convert him into a martyr when he has expiated his crime. If it be the settled and deliberate will of the legislator, that capital punishments shall be inflicted for capital offences, we, of necessity, are bound to acquiesce. What we do earnestly desire is, not that crimes should go unrestrained, much less unpunished, but in the place of death, that milder and, as we submit, more efficient punishments should be substituted. It is the sacred duty of society to provide a substitute. Who can pretend that it was indispensably necessary to the welfare of the State, that these unhappy fellow-beings (though no doubt very wicked and depraved) should have been cut short in the prime of their existence? Might not their lives, with perfect safety, have been spared? Might they not have been reformed, and even rendered useful, perhaps virtuous, fellow-citizens; or, if not reformed, why, we ask, might they not have been required to pass their remaining days in solitary confinement, or, even in perpetual servitude? We would have it ever seriously remembered, that the vilest culprit is still a fellow being, and that we, as men, dwelling under the benign influence of the Christian dispensation, should not deal with him, however guilty in our eyes, as one unworthy of pardon in the eyes of an all-wise, just, and merciful God;—that, while life exists, there is ever hope of repentance, but that death seals the destiny of all, whether for time or for eternity! The penitentiary system is in perfect accordance with the principles of Christianity, and until it shall be adopted in its fullest extent through our thrice blessed and happy land, we, as a people, can never enjoy the consoling reflection, that we have conformed to the desire and example of Him who died to establish "peace on earth and good will towards men."

THE POWER OF BEAUTY.

BY MAYNARD D. RICHARDSON.

WHAT shall compass Beauty's dow'r—
Who shall sing of Beauty's pow'r—
Who is weak that Beauty arms—
Who is dull that Beauty charms?—
Though the Minstrel slumber long,
Beauty wakes him into song;

All his human bands she breaks,
All his heavenly ardor wakes,
Bids him ride on eagle wings,
Soaring to celestial things.

In her bow'r long days he lies,
Raptures sealing up his eyes,
'Till she prompt him with a glance,
And he lifts the lyre and lance ;
Throws aside his apathy,
Learns to live and dares to die,
Nor the storm, nor piercing wind,
Stays the ardor of his mind.

From his limbs the locks are hurl'd,
And he rushes o'er the world ;
All his spirits now awaken,
From his eye the scales are taken,
And his living song is given,
To that brightest form of heaven :
To the world's eye she is shown,
As her charms have fill'd his own,
'Till, as mad as he who sings,
All the million put on wings,
Soaring for the embodied glory,
Of that wild-eyed Poet's story.

They would compass Beauty's dow'r,
They would witness Beauty's pow'r,
They would revel in her arms,
Blest with all her sacred charms—

But she keeps the charms and spell,
For the bard who sings them well;
Though, for him, the prince of verse,
They are yet the care and curse.
She has bound him in her chain,
And he never sings again,
Ruling not his fellow men,
He has lost his empire then—
Hush'd the lyre that once delighted,
And the wreath of bay is blighted.

WOMAN.

BY CHARLES R. CARROLL.

WHEN we compare the present with the past condition of woman, we congratulate ourselves on the change in her disposition and the accomplishments of her mind. She lives among us, a being of sentiment and love, folding her affections around the other sex, animating his nature, and infusing into his heart the wholesomest lessons of peace. Unlike the women of other times, who were masculine and sensual, she possesses the responsibilities of a moral agent, and virtues and attractions absolutely necessary to elegant society. In a word, she differs from her ancient kind, in the measure of her estimation among men. She is now a part of the moral economy of states—a person of intelligence, not of sense; of sociability, not of exclusion; of sentiment, not of appetite. It would be interesting,

could we spare time, to trace her history up to this period,
as it appeared in different ages. The result would exhibit
her progressively improving with the moral and intellectual
culture of society. We would behold her, at one time,
amid barbarians, servile and disgusting; with no accomplishments for social converse; and having no communion with the other sex, save in the gratification of passions
common to animal life. At another time, we would see
her advanced one step further in civilisation; that is, extending her privileges and adding new charms to the graces of her person; and, then, we would see her next in
the chivalrous age—the age of emprise and gaudy romance;
of love-sway and brilliant feats of arms; of talismanic
keepsakes and the daring gage; when the brave knight,
amid the deafening applause of the thronged circle, kneel-
ing before his lady Queen, and, presenting her, on the
point of his spear, the emblem of his affection, wet with the
blood of a vanquished rival, she forsooth smiled upon him.
In that age, her influence doubtless produced admirable
effects upon society. Not to say much of the punctilious
laws of knight-errantry, then substituted for merciless
assault and private assassination, her situation at that time,
as the fascinating meed of the brave, elevated her in the
admiration of men, and prepared the way for her social
improvement; and, of course, for the dissemination of
those principles of religion, which inculcate peace. With
this era commenced her legitimate sway; for, surely, her
charms seem fairest under an unclouded sky. True, she
can bare her bosom to the wars, and stand before misfortune with a fortitude as unbending as the bravest heart;
yet, after all, unalloyed pleasure is to be mostly enjoyed
with her in days of peace. The dazzle of arms and the

strifes of public life, wean the affections of man from home ; it is only when the heart goes on in the even tenor of its course, unagitated by stirring events, that it throbs for the amiable endearments of the female presence. And the apparent hankering of the world now for peace ; the substitution of negotiation for war ; and the umpirage of the law, instead of arms, have so predisposed the other sex to enjoy the delicate pleasures of her society, that she is more than ever essential to his comfort and his felicity.

We have remarked, that she is now esteemed a being of intellect, and one of the elements of a moral intercourse. This constitutes the height of her commendation. Considered in any other light, she appears of very little more value than an object pleasing to the *senses*. Some of the French writers may say to the contrary, but we are confident there is a love without even a blush of what is called passion. We know that a beautiful woman will awaken desire ; that the languor of her eye, the flush of her cheek, and the developments of her figure, will, and ought, as so ordained by our Creator, to excite pleasurable sensations ; but, at the same time, we contend, that there is an emotion arising from the reciprocal and intimate endearments of the sexes, more lasting and grateful than any passion. It is a love, growing out of their peculiar relations ; vivified by a chastened imagination ; and, over all, graced with a sentiment, that brightens up the realities of life into an adorning romance.

An author has somewhere remarked that love ends with the first kiss. If he alludes to those who love without sentiment, we may grant what he asserts ; but if he means that, after marriage, there can be no love, as we have heard a learned professor once affirm, we must declare that his paradox

befits a sensualist, and one who claimed no higher communion after death, than the mingling of his remains with
the dust of brutes. It is to authors like him, that we must
attribute the disinclination of some to matrimony—the
holiest of connexions—of all others, the most dignified
and productive of unsullied felicity. We here speak of
the union of two persons of moral principles, and of well
attempered dispositions. Their love comes from a mutual
pride, a mutual interest, and mutual endearments—a pride
that blends their reputations into one name and one destiny,
teaching them that the merited reproach of either would
be agony to both ;—an interest that induces them to
depend on concerted prudence, to obtain either the luxuries
or the necessaries of life, as their conditions may be
elevated or humble ;—and mutual endearments to create
sentiment, and move in their hearts the indescribable
emotions of a romantic affection. These influences are
necessary to connubial happiness ; and naturally result
from that principle of our laws, which considers the parties
to the marriage bond one person in all the concerns of
life. By this means, their hopes and their fears, their
fames and their fortunes, their pains and their pleasures,
are identified. Whatever redounds to the credit of one,
reflects credit on both ; and there is seldom, if ever, a
rivalry between them, except it be to set off one another
to the best advantage. Envy, too, that source of almost
every sort of human anguish, can rarely come between
them, to fester their hearts and turn their sweets into
bitterness and hate. The difference in their physical and
moral constitutions precludes this ; for their attractions
are peculiarly interesting, because of the separate spheres
in which they revolve. She is timid, confiding, and sub-

missive ; he is bold, arrogant, and self-willed. She limits
her wishes to the precincts of home, to the innocent
prattle of her "little ones," and their young features
reflecting in her fond anticipations a name of excellence ;
—he courts the bustle of the world and its loud praises.
She lives under an Italian sky, lit up by the pale moon,
and modest stars blushing in the distance ;—he endures
the heat of the sun, and gazes at it with the eye of an
eagle. His aspirations are for thrones and large dominion ;
she is queen of the household ; her diadem is the social
affections ; her sceptre, love ; her robe, chastity, pure
as the driven snow, enveloping her form, so that the imagination can find naught to blush at, even in the impro-
priety of an attitude. Her measures are those of peace ;
her ministers, the virtues ; and her smiling subjects, the
children of him to whom she owes fealty, as the paramount
lord of her heart and her treasure.

These are the matters of her exclusive dominion, these
the charming influences flowing from her intellectual and
social refinements. Did man bring himself to look on her
in this posture, with a feeling of sentiment, she would
always be to him as nature designed her—his solace and
his passion ! We repeat the word sentiment ; for, as the
appetite can be cloyed, so sure as one mixes no romance
in his affections, will he tire of the partner of his house.
We do not mean that morbid sentiment, which expects
more of a lady than nature has allotted her. Far from it ;
it is a healthy mood, which, being insensible to her trifling
frailties, gains its pleasure from contemplating her excellence ; which does not busy itself to find out spots in the
sun, but admires it, and is exhilarated when it rises. It is
a disposition like this, which distinguishes the benevolent

from him, who sees all things through a cynical medium—
a disposition, moreover, easily acquired, since we know
that the frequent contemplation of an object not sensual or
disgusting, will attach to it an interest far above its real
value, so as to exclude whatever of unpleasantness may be
incident to it, more especially if it affords satisfaction to
his pride or his propensities. Besides, men generally
forget that sensibilities the most attenuated quicken the
female heart—that she is all impulse, and sensitive as
that plant which shrinks from the slightest touch. Her
love is not what some have imagined. It is not a burning
passion, exhausting itself by its own intensity ; it is not a
sublime impression, lessening every time the object which
produced it, is gazed at. It is a prolonged emotion of
beauty, filling her soul with the most delightful images and
the gentlest pleasures. Delicate in nature, he that would
retain her affections must approach her in demeanor respectful, and with language refined. The quiet of her
pastimes conduces to raise in the mind creations of romance, of sentiment and warm anticipations. She looks
up to man for protection, and should he assume a self-
superiority and frown upon her, so as to make her feel it,
that instant will her heart wither in hate, or break with
grief. Would he, then, have her fulfil the destiny for
which God hath created her, let him place her nigh his
bosom, as a precious and beautiful flower, requiring the
nicest attentions to preserve its fragrance and its bloom.

Constituted, then, as woman now is, with virtues to
adorn society, the next question is, what should be the extent of her acquirements ? They should be, in our
opinion, such as will make her an object of social attraction. Her pursuits, whether literary or otherwise, should

not, for a moment, interfere with her domestic duties. Those embellishments which are the offspring of a delicate taste, she should cultivate—such as music, polite literature, poetry, history, painting, and, in fine, every study which will enable her to impart information to her children, and render home interesting to the partner of her love. Let our fair friends dwell on this last remark, for we assure them it unfolds the secret of female influence. Her pride should be, to convert home into a paradise, to fix her affections there, and to have an eye to this in everything she says and does. For this is her proper place, wherein she shines most, and is everywhere else a stranger. If she have no content here—if home be not a temple, at whose altar she can offer the incense of her love—what other spot will she find so sacred ? She cannot go into the world like the other sex, and catch pleasure in the shifting scene ; she cannot outlive unrequited affections in the whirl of public life and the schemes of a vaulting ambition. If there be no solace at home, the universe beside is a troubled sea, whereon she can find no resting-place. This truth, then, should urge her to consecrate her dwelling with every refinement, so that, if her love have a sympathy there, it will, with these embellishments, be enlivened ; and if not, such a misfortune she can alleviate by her own resources of intellectual enjoyment.

THE LAST PLACE OF SLEEP.

BY MARY E. LEE.

Lay me not in green-wood lone,
Where the sad wind maketh moan,
Where the sun hath never shone,
　　Save as if in sadness ;
Nor, I pray thee, let me be
Buried 'neath the chill, cold sea,
Where the waves, tumultuous, free,
　　Chafe themselves to madness.

But in yon enclosure small,
Near the church-yard's mossy wall,
Where the dew and sunlight fall,
　　I would have my dwelling ;
Sure there are some friends, I wot,
Who would make that narrow spot,
Lovely as a garden plot,
　　With rich perfumes swelling.

Let no costly stone be brought,
Where a stranger's hand hath wrought
Vain inscription, speaking naught
　　To the true affections ;
But, above the quiet bed,
Where I rest my weary head,
Plant those buds, whose perfumes shed
　　Tenderest recollections.

Then, as every year, the tide
Of strong death bears to my side,
Those, who were by love allied,
    As the flowers of summer;
Sweet to think, that from the mould
Of my body long since cold,
Plants of beauty shall enfold
    Every dear new-comer.

DEATH OF HUGH S. LEGARÉ.

BY RICHARD YEADON.

OUR whole community was thrown into gloom and
sorrow, by the heavy tidings—the unexpected and stunning intelligence of the sudden decease of this eminent
citizen of our republic—this gifted and cherished son of
our State and City. The melancholy and lamentable
event which has given this illustrious victim to the grave,
occurred early in the morning of the 20th June, 1843,
at Boston, whither he had gone, high in health, in spirits
and in fame, to unite with President Tyler and the
other members of the Cabinet, in the Bunker Hill Monument celebration, on the 17th. His indisposition,
however, prevented his attendance on the festivities of
the occasion, and, on the third day after, he died of an
inflammation of the bowels. The death of such a man is
indeed a national loss, and is universally felt as a national

affliction ; in the language of the fitting allusion to him
at the late celebration, he was " a statesman of the whole
republic—a citizen of the whole republic of letters ;—"
combining, as he did, in their highest excellence, the
gifts of the scholar, the orator, the jurist and the statesman, he was a rare possession to our country, and one of
the lights of the age ;—entrusted as he was with the
high office of Attorney General of the Union, and temporarily with the yet higher one of Secretary of State,—an
office which he was eminently qualified to fill, and which
he has disappointed his destiny in not living to fill for a
more extended period—his death, at the present juncture,
mingles a sense of the embarrassment of national affairs,
with a deep and pervading grief for his untimely end.
But great as is the national appreciation of this calamity—
it is here, here in his native home, where his young
genius budded and bloomed and unfolded its glorious
promise of ripened excellence—here, where kindred
and friends rejoiced in the honors of his youth and
maturity, and were watching with anxious interest the
probable climax of his soaring career—it is here that the
sad event is felt and mourned as a domestic grief, a fire-
side sorrow, which refuses to be comforted, and causes
the full heart to swell out in tears and lamentations.   Our
city has lost a son, our people a brother, our State one of
the proudest and noblest ornaments she has ever given to
the councils of the nation—cut off, too, in the meridian of
life—in his 47th year—when destiny stood ready to
crown him with higher usefulness and higher honors.

Rare as were the gifts and acquirements of the illustrious deceased, he was altogether our own. He was educated at a Charleston Grammar School, having been the

pupil of the Rev. Dr. GALLAGHER and the Rev. MOSES
WADDELL ; and he received his diploma from the South
Carolina College in the year 1814, bearing off from his
competitors the first honor of the institution. Having
devoted himself to the study of law, he familiarized himself with its principles as a science, and soon became an
ornament of the profession, winning its laurels by a display
of ability and eloquence, rarely surpassed in any forum.
At an early age, he was returned to the Legislature of the
State, and there maintained the highest reputation as an
orator and legislator. In the year 1830, he was elected
to the Legislature at the head of the Charleston delega-
tion, and before the close of the session was chosen Attorney General of the State. In 1831, he was called into the
diplomatic service of the nation, having received from
President JACKSON the appointment of Minister to Belgium.
Returning from this service in 1836, with a mind improved by foreign travel, association and study, he was immediately chosen a Representative to Congress by the people
of this District ; and served out his official term with a
large increase of his already brilliant and commanding
fame. In 1841, he was appointed by President TYLER
Attorney General of the United States, and on the resignation of Mr. WEBSTER from the State Department,
he was also entrusted with the seals of that Department as
acting Secretary of State ; and he filled both these important offices at the time of his death.

   In addition to his eminence as a jurist, an orator, and a
statesman, Mr. LEGARE reached the highest distinction in
literature. He was perhaps the ripest scholar of our country, if not of the age ; deeply versed in classic lore, and
skilled in the literature and languages of modern Europe.

His contributions to the Southern Review, of which he was for a time editor, and his later ones to the New York Review, entitle him to rank among the highest in the republic of letters. He was a man, too, of pure feelings and high sensibilities, amiable in disposition and kind in heart; above the petty intrigues or warfare of party politics; a true patriot, recognizing no rule of statesmanship but his country's good. In life we admired him for his high endowments, and loved him for his virtues and amiable gifts; in death, we add our individual tribute of sorrow for his loss, and honor to his memory.

MY GARDEN.

BY CAROLINE GILMAN.

My garden, fresh and beautiful!—the spell of frost is o'er,
And earth sends out its varied leaves, a rich and lavish
    store ;
Thy heart, too, breaks its wintry chain, with stem and leaf
    and flower,
And glows in hope and happiness amid the spring-tide
    hour.

'Tis sunset in my garden—the flowers and buds have
    caught
Bright revelations from the skies in wondrous changes
    wrought ;

And as the twilight hastens on, a spiritual calm
Seems resting on the quiet leaves; which evening dews
    embalm.

'Tis moonlight in my garden ; like some fair babe at rest,
The day-flower folds its silky wings upon its pulseless
    breast;
Nor is it vain philosophy to think that plants may keep
A holiday of airy dreams, beneath their graceful sleep.

'Tis morning in my garden ; each leaf of crisped green,
Hangs tremulous in diamond gems with emerald rays
    between ;
It is the birth of nature : baptized in early dew,
The plants look meekly up and smile, as if their god they
    knew.

My garden, fair and brilliant !—the butterfly outspread
 Alights with gentle fluttering on the wallflower's golden
    head,
Then darting to the lily bed, floats o'er its sheeted white,
And settles on the violet cup with fanciful delight.

My quiet little garden !—I hear the rolling wheel
Of the city's busy multitude along the highway peal ;
I tread thy paths more fondly, and inhale the circling air,
That glads and cools me on its way from that wide mart
    of care.

My friendly little garden !—few worldly goods have I
To tender with o'erflowing heart in blessed charity :

But, like a cup of water by a pure disciple given,
A herb or flower may tell its tale of kindliness in heaven.

My small herbescent garden!—what though I may not raise
High tribute to thy fruitfulness in these familiar lays—
Yet, when thy few shrunk radishes I pluck with eager
    haste,
They seem a daintier food to me than gods ambrosial taste.

And as for those *three* artichokes, the fruits of toilsome
    care,
And my angel-visit cucumbers that come so scarce and
    rare,
And the straggling ears of corn that shoot so meagre, thin
    and small—
To me they still outweigh the hoards that crowd the mar-
    ket-stall.

I own I have mistakenly oft trained a vulgar weed,
And rooted up with savage hand some choice and costly
    seed,
And boiled a precious bulbous-root, of lineage high and
    rare,
And planted onions in a jar with most superfluous care.

But truth springs out of error, and right succeeds to wrong,
Mistakes that wound, and weeds that vex, give morals to
    my song,
That bid me clear my mental soil, and calmly look within,
To check the growth of earth's wild weeds, of passion and
    of sin.

To nobler themes, and hopes, and joys, my garden culture
    tends.
To that high world, where only bloom without the weed,
    ascends,
I lift my soul in reverie, enraptured and alone,
Still coining links of thought that wreathe my spirit to
    God's throne.

Yet sadness sometimes fills my mind, as each unfolding
    sweet
Springs up in ready beauty beneath my household's feet,
For some young hand that gathers now the plants that
    gaily wave,
May shortly lie in withered bloom within the dreary grave.

My faith-inspiring garden!—thy seeds so dark and cold,
Late slept in utter loneliness amid earth's senseless mould;
No sunbeams fell upon them, nor west-wind's gentle
    breath—
But there they lay in nothingness, an image meet of death.

Now, lo! they rise in gorgeous ranks, and glad the eager
    eye,
And on the wooing summer-breeze their odor passes by;
The flower-grave cannot chain them, the spirit-life up-
    springs,
And scatters beauty in its path, from thousand unseen
    wings.

My garden! may the morning dew rest lightly on thy
    bowers,

And summer clouds distil around their most refreshing
    showers ;
And when the daily sun withdraws his golden tent above,
May moon and stars look watchful down, and bless thee
    with their love !

THE DEATH OF ALBERT RHETT.

BY J. M. CLAPP.

> Oh ! why has worth so short a date,
>   While villains ripen grey with time ?
> Must thou, the noble, generous, great,
>   Fall in bold manhood's hardy prime ?
>
> BURNS.

> Ostendent terris hunc tantum fata, neque ultra
> Esse sinent.
> Heu, miserande puer ! si qua fata aspera rumpas,
> Tu Marcellus eris.   Manibus date lilia plenis.
> Purpureos spargam flores, animamque nepotis
> His saltem accumulem donis, et fungar inani
> Munere.
>
> VIRG. ÆN.

DEPARTED this life on Sunday night, the 29th of October,
Albert Rhett, aged thirty-three years. For him, it is
enough that, as a Christian man, forgiving all, loving all,
facing death without a shudder, and bowing humbly before Him who giveth and recalleth life, he sunk into peaceful sleep from which he waked not. Noiselessly and un-

reluctant, the gates of life opened, and the spirit went forth to its home. Sufficient for him, that having truly and manfully worked, while it pleased God to lay the tasks of life upon his neck, he now rests from labor. Earth never took back to her bosom a truer child, and the hand of the mother will press lightly upon his beloved head.

But to the living, who have still their appointed work, there remain duties to fulfil toward the dead and toward each other. Albert Rhett—the world knows not and cannot know, what magical power is in that name to those who loved him—how exhaustless the fountains of tenderness that open and gush forth at its spell—how all its deep import of truth, gentleness, generosity, and self-devotion, maketh now and will long make even his ashes an altar of refuge, where all the household virtues, all the sweet charities of life, hover and renew their gracious ministry!

But the world knows this—that, young as he was, he had proved himself, beyond all doubt and question, one of its master-spirits. The world has felt and acknowledged the power of his indomitable will, his clear intellect, his lofty manhood, his heroic earnestness. And the qualities that made him so early in life one of the lights of the State, already enriching the present and casting its resplendent shadow over the future, also make him a proper subject of public contemplation, as his loss is pregnant cause of public sorrow.

Of his profession Mr. Rhett had the noblest conception; judging well that the profound struggles toward system, the vast complexities, the elaborate subtleties of the law, were its least claims to admiration and reverence—were in fact but the necessities of its grand moral scope, the weakness of human reason seeking with inadequate strength to in-

carnate the spirit of justice. With him the law was only
a name for the great bond of society, whose elements are
truth, justice, and patriotism. He never disconnected it from
morals, and the more deeply he pondered upon its meaning and embraced its majestic course, the more clearly did
he feel that its very soul and mission in the world was for
the enforcement of right, the guardianship of innocence,
the good of man. We have never conversed with him on
the subject of his profession, without feeling the earnestness with which he cherished in his heart this view of its
dignity and value. In the mere learning of the law, too,
he was deeply read, and in such way as made learning not
a burden, an incumbrance, an unsorted storehouse of
foreign goods—still less a shallow pretence and gaudy
show-case, courting ephemeral admiration—but at once a
pure light, and a most efficient weapon to his reason.
Taking, then, the highest view of his profession, using it
for the most beneficent purposes, and bringing to its ministry all the powers of an intellect, clear, bold, ardent, and
comprehensive, it is no exaggeration to pronounce him a
great lawyer.

Not less was he an enlightened legislator, looking ever
in that character to the whole State, unfettered by preju-
dice, unshaken by popular outcry, judging with stern
impartiality old customs and new projects, shrinking from
no responsibility that principle involved, fearing no consequences that principle demanded, wearing in his inmost
heart the honor and good of the State. It is difficult to
do him justice in his character of a public man. His
youth, his boldness, his contempt of the arts of popularity,
the utter absence of all self-seeking, his overmastering
earnestness in debate, that sometimes gave an appearance

of asperity to his manner and language, have all contributed each in its way to thwart an unprejudiced judgment of his worth. He is gone; and by the chasm his
death has made, the State will measure his noble qualities, and then we scruple not to say the feeling will be
universal, that a great man has fallen. The title of great,
the world will never consent to fix to a young man living.
It belongs to the past, and whatever their powers or
achievements, we refuse to judge the young but by the
future—the vague, nameless future, over which rule hope,
doubt, dread, desire—shadows colored by all the infinite
lights of imagination. Yet, with his grave fresh before
us, gazing upon the adamantine door closed for ever upon
him, we cannot feel that with him the future is all unreal.
Such was the stern consistency of his principles, such
his inflexible perseverance, such the living and elastic
energy of all his varied faculties, such the unaffected
humility with which he looked upon a past that had
dazzled all others, that we feel as if we had a right to
count as his, all that he was capable of achieving; as if
the dim outlines of hope should deepen into the fixed
graving of history, and the future should be held as the
soul, quickening, ennobling and immortalizing the past.

If we are not a calm or an impartial judge; if the
memory of twelve years of friendship, rooted in the
imperishable associations of youth, strengthening and
spreading with each step in life, shaken by never a
passing doubt of his good faith, his candor, his love of
the right, his generosity, his self-devotion—darkened by
not even a look we could wish to forget, or a word we
could wish unsaid; if his death has brought a night of
sorrow, through which we see feebly, yet God judge us,

as out of the depth of sincerity we say, this man was great,—great in the noble powers of his intellect, in the lofty morality of his principles, in the disinterestedness of his life, in the sincerity and depth of his affections.

THE FLIGHT OF TIME.

BY MARY E. STEWART.

" Time is ever silently turning his pages."

Yes ! as his icy fingers fly,
   How many a sweet and hallowed name,
Dear to the bosom and the eye,
   Is blotted from the book of fame.

Oh Time !—thy pinions never stay,
   Swift o'er the path of life they dance ;
And joys, which swell the heart to day,
   Melt as to-morrow's hours advance.

When pleasure spreads her silver sail,
   And hope sits laughing at the prow :
One touch of thine throws up the veil,
   And smiling pleasure, where art thou ?

Deep sunk beneath the teeming wave,
   Thy brilliant spirits all are dead :

No hand their sinking forms could save,
   With time they lived, with time they fled.

Then lift the heart, exalt the voice,
   Pass these low scenes of trial o'er ;
Look to that land where saints rejoice,
   When *Time* itself shall be no more.

———

THE VALUE OF THE ARTS AND SCIENCES TO THE PRACTICAL MECHANIC.

BY WILLIAM D. PORTER.

THE importance of the mechanical arts, and the real dignity which attaches to their pursuit, must be obvious upon the slightest consideration. They spring up necessarily with the first rudiments of society ; and, in a more advanced stage of improvement, are inseparably connected with the comforts and luxuries of life, and with the resources and glory of the state. The axe that fells the tree, and the roof that affords a kindly shelter against the blasts of the elements, as well as the stately ship, instinct with life and beauty, that in peace goes forth upon the waters of waters, to return after many days, laden with the products and the wealth of distant climes, and in war rears her wooden walls, the chief and glorious defence of the nation —are alike the creation of mechanical skill. The elements and substances of the natural world, various and multiform though they be, are inadequate in their native state to the demands of social life ; the aid of the mechanic is necessary to change their forms, to modify their action, and multiply their uses. By the process of this art, shapeless inert matter is endued with comeliness and motion, and the mighty forces of inanimate nature, instead of lying dormant, or becoming the objects of terror and dismay, are made to work together for the useful purposes of life. The wind bloweth where it listeth ; the cataract pours down its never failing volume of living waters ; and steam hides within its bosom a principle of transcendant strength, the possible effects of which can neither be measured nor imagined. But the mechanic has constructed machines, by means of which all these wonderful phenomena are pressed into the service of man, are made obedient to his bidding, and subservient to his wants. Indeed, in every part of the artificial world which has been built up around us, from the smallest utensil that serves our daily convenience, to the loftiest piles of architectural beauty and grandeur, is the workmanship of his hand conspicuously seen. What calling, then, can be more useful or more honorable than that which ministers so largely to the accommodations and embellishments of life, and which assists so materially in extending the dominion of mind over matter ?

The wants of man, natural and artificial, may be considered one of his chief blessings. They form a great law of his progress ; for he finds in them his most powerful stimulus to improvement. In a primitive state, these wants being few and simple, his social progress is slow ; but in proportion as new desires are developed and gratified, so does he advance in the scale of civilisation. In this point of view, the application of machinery to the arts has exercised a greatly beneficial influence on his condition. By economizing labor, and adding to the rapidity and perfection of manufactures, it has led to the cheap and almost indefinite multiplication of articles that contribute to the convenience and refinements of llfe. The inventions for cleansing, spinning, and weaving cotton, our own great staple—to take a single illustration—have reduced the price of the most essential article of clothing more than one half, a reduction which has greatly multiplied and extended its uses with the whole family of man. By this and similar means, thousands, nay millions, are let into a participation in blessings which were before denied them. Thus are luxuries converted into comforts, and comforts into necessaries ; the desires and gratifications of the few extended to the many ; the arts tasked to open new and enlarge former sources of enjoyment and by a necessary consequence, the sum of human happiness is accumulated, and t he great work of industrial improvement carried steadily forward. If it be true that civilisation consists in the creation of wants and the invention of means to satisfy them, then are the arts the great instruments of civilisation, and their cultivators the true benefactors of their kind. F ulton, himself an honor to his race, said that Arkwright, Whitney, and Watt, did more for the good of mankind than any of their contemporaries ; and these men were mechanics—sprung, too, from an humble condition in life. All cannot hope to achieve as much for their own glory, and t he benefit of their species, as did the inventors of the s pinning jenny, the cotton gin and the steam engine ; but all may study their example with profit, and learn to imitate the habits of application and perseverance which led them to such brilliant results.

History shows that the arts have always gone hand in hand with civilisation. The cultivated states of antiquity held them in high estimation, and encouraged them by the rewards of honor and emolument. In Egypt, Greece and Rome, the first seats of refinement, they illustrated themselves by achievements which still excite the wonder and admiration of the world. It is to be regretted that so much of the traditions respecting them has been forgotten and lost. Much would it delight and instruct us to know, who were the founders and improvers of early art ; and with what means and instruments they plied their work ! But even their names are buried in the shades of a far antiquity. The mighty monuments of their labor and skill have outlived the fierce assaults of time and the barbarian ; but the processes by which they worked in stone without iron, and the combination of powers by which they piled up their immense structures till they pierced the clouds, are matters with which the ingenuity of speculation has been exhausted in vain. Proud as may be the achievements of art in our day, there are losses in the past it cannot supply ; mysteries it cannot explain ; wonders it cannot reveal.

By the application of science to the arts, in modern times, the powers and triumphs of both have been greatly enlarged. Discoveries in philosophy have opened the way to inventions in the arts. Franklin did not rest content with the discovery of the identity of lightning with the electric fluid, but proceeded to give it a practical application by devising means whereby the thunderbolt has been robbed of half its terrors, and is conducted harmless through our dwellings. A series of brilliant experiments in chemistry led Sir H. Davy to construct that most beautiful and useful invention of late days—the Safety Lamp,

—which enables the miner to carry on his work with security a thousand feet below the surface of the earth, and in the midst of an atmosphere of inflammable gas. In the construction and management of curious and complicated machinery, which now plays so conspicuous a part in the economy of labor, theoretical knowledge is as necessary as practical skill. It cannot be denied that important inventions have been made by unlettered men; but, on inquiry, we shall find that these instances are less frequent than is generally supposed, and that they are chiefly confined to the earlier stages of civilisation, when the common arts of life were deemed unworthy the attention of the philosopher, and when scientific inquirers disdained the aid of the practical mechanic. But, in our day, the workshop has been brought into close alliance with the laboratory; and the occupant of each has been a great gainer by the connection. The man of science has ceased to be a mere speculator; whilst the artisan, enlightened in the principles on which his art depends, has risen to the level of the philosophical inquirer. A lucky thought, or an accidental combination, may suggest, to mere ingenuity, some useful improvement; but if to that ingenuity be added an exact and thorough comprehension of principles, with how much more ease and certainty will the experimenter proceed to remove the obstacles that lie in his way, and to give to the thing of his imagination a perfect bodily shape. Who can tell how many valuable conceptions have glimmered through the minds of uneducated men, and died away, perhaps, in abortive experiments, from want of the scientific information necessary to carry them into practical effect? Great discoveries and inventions are, in the nature of things, slow and gradual in their progress; very rarely have they advanced at once to maturity. It is not often that the whole idea is grasped at first; and even if so, the means of illustrating and executing it are imperfectly attained. Defect is removed after defect, improvement is added to improvement; and it is in the suggestion and adaptation of these, till the full conception stands completely bodied forth, that science finds a wide field for its display. An illustration may be found in the history of the steam engine—in its progress from the first rude machine of the Marquis of Worcester, in 1663, to that most powerful and perfect of mechanical agents, which, after successive improvements by Savary, Newcomen, and others, it became a century afterwards in the creative hands of Watt. It was not genius alone, but scientific research, an accurate investigation into the action of fluids, and the laws and properties of heat, that conducted Watt to the happy conception of "separate condensation," in which, by his own acknowledgment, lay all the merit of his invention. And to what a saving of human labor, not to speak of its other results, has that conception led? Before the improvements of Watt, steam found its chief employment in draining mines and raising water; now it works with countless hands, and with a precision and uniformity more than human, in all the departments of operative industry—almost superseding the toil of man, and daily inviting him to new and more extensive applications of its powers. It has been calculated that "the amount of work now done by steam machinery in England alone is equivalent to that of between three and four hundred millions of men, by direct labor." What a relief to human toil! What an addition, not only to the power of the nation, but to the resources of general civilisation!

There can be no reasonable doubt that the arts are destined to further and nobler triumphs. Though much has been accomplished, they have not reached the point of attainable perfection. Science has yet to unfold principles, by which their processes shall be made shorter—their fabrics cheaper and more exquisite. The mechanician has yet to invent new modes of combining skill with strength, and of applying them to the elegant and useful purposes of life. Ingenuity has not been exhausted; nor have the materials upon which it works. Philosophy gives us reason to believe that there are many elements of power around us which still await discovery and application. It is a curious fact in natural history, that so little an animal as the bee is acquainted with principles and powers of which we are profoundly ignorant. Can it be that instinct has led where reason cannot follow? And that insects are familiar with useful processes, to which man, with all his God-like apprehension, can never attain? How wonderfully is the whole economy of nature adapted to teach us, that the progress of improvement is indefinite, and that in the highest cultivation of our moral and intellectual faculties is the only worthy fulfilment of the ends of our being!

One of the objects of this society, as set forth in its constitution, is to encourage skill in the arts, and to excite emulation among apprentices, by premiums and by public commendation. It is in pursuance of this object that we are now assembled. Though the specimens on this occasion be few, it is to be hoped the experiment will not be abandoned; but that our young mechanics will be incited hereafter to lay before the community in large numbers, the fruits of their industry and skill. By early

and successful efforts brought before the public eye,
they will lay the foundation of that professional excellence and popular favor, which lead to competency and
independence. The schools and institutions in England
have found it highly beneficial to make a public award of
premiums.

In our great sister cities of the north, a mechanics'
exhibition is one of the most imposing spectacles that can
be witnessed. Who that has visited one of these exhibitions, where the achievements of art seem almost to rival
the wonders of nature, has not been struck with admiration at the richness and variety of the productions to
which the inventive mind and cunning hand of man, in
a single city or state, have given birth? Upwards of
20,000 articles, tools, fabrics and pieces of mechanism, in
almost every branch of art and manufacture—all illustrating some new combination, curious handicraft or useful
improvement—are spread before the delighted eyes of
thousands of spectators, who throng in from the whole
surrounding country. It is thus that the arts are trained
to excellence, and their cultivators taught to respect their
calling and themselves. Why should not our mechanics
imitate so noble an example? One of the greatest of
philosophers has said that the people of the South are in
general more ingenious than those of the colder regions of
the north. If we have the aptitude, let it no longer be
our reproach that we want the courage or the application
to excel them. May the time not be distant, when our
city shall have its annual exhibition; and when this
hall shall be fitly decorated with the manifold and beautiful creations of southern art.

To the young and intelligent mechanic I would say—

you have before you every motive to exertion—every prospect of an honorable career. Respectability, fortune, influence—all prizes of the social state, lie within the reach of your well directed efforts. You should propose to yourself, at the outset of life, a high mark of attainment. Be not guilty of the fatal error of supposing that all has been accomplished, when you have mastered the mere details of your art. The faculties within you are intended for higher and nobler uses. Who can tell to what reach of invention, to what heights of achievement, those faculties may be carried by skilful and assiduous cultivation? If you would become a native workman, in the noblest sense of the word, you must first serve an apprenticeship to books as well as tools, to science as well as art. It was thus that Watt, the humble mathematical instrument maker, became one of the greatest benefactors of his country and the world. It was thus that Franklin, the poor printer boy, rose to be the first philosopher, and one of the first statesmen of his day. But why multiply examples with which you are already familiar? Be proud of your vocation, for it has been illustrated by names that will live, through all time, in the grateful memories of men. Be worthy of it, for " in the great temple of nature, whose foundation is the earth, whose pillars are the eternal hills, whose roof is the starlit sky, whose architect is God,—there is no ministry more sacred than that of the intelligent mechanic."

THE FROZEN DEW-DROP.

BY LEWIS C. LEVIN.

How lavishly the moon to-night,
   Her silver o'er the landscape throws ;
The stars pour down their crystal light,
   The dew sleeps sweetly on the rose ;
Yes ! night has shed her pearly tears,
   The drooping flowers of earth redressing,
And beautiful each bud appears,
   A sparkling drop of light caressing.

'Tis morn ! each flower that sprang so fair,
   Is withering on the bending stem,
The moistening dew is frozen there,
   And shines a cold but glittering gem ;
And find ye, where yon ruins lie,
   Of drooping, weary, wasted flowers,
An emblem of our destiny
   In youth's gay sunlit fleeting hours ?

Go, ask that one, whose early year
   Reflected blending love and bliss ;
She'll point you to her image here,
   And weeping say—" 'Tis this—'tis this !"
Within her eye, upon her brow,
   Once virtue's image bright was beaming,
Oh ! wrecks of hopes but linger now,
   And wintry wreaths are wildly streaming.

If e'er a glance of light should break
  Through clouds that brood in endless storm,
'Twill brighten o'er a frozen lake,
  But ne'er the chilling waters warm.
Then nurse thy grief, despair and pain,
  Till death shall calm the heart that's broken,
There, long an angel's tear has lain,
  But frozen is affection's token.

———

SONG.

BY MARY J. B. DANA.

I SEE thee in my dreams,
  Thou who hast gone before me ;
And faithful mem'ry seems,
  My loved one to restore me !
Thou'rt clad in robes of light,
  Thy face with joy is beaming,
Thus, dearest ! every night,
  I see thee when I'm dreaming.

The songs we loved so well,
  I heard my dear one singing,
And sweet, o'er hill and dell,
  Melodious notes are ringing !
The tears bedim my sight,
  Which in my eyes do glisten,

While, trembling with delight,
   I hold my breath to listen.

I stretch my arms to thee—
   But suddenly awaking,
My love no more I see—
   O! *then* my heart is breaking!
But when I think that thou
   An angel art in glory,
Again to sleep I go,
   And dreams repeat the story.

'Though thou hast gone above,
   And left this world for ever,
''Tis true, 'tis true, my love,
   I can forget thee never!
Then come in robes of light,
   Thy face with rapture beaming,
And let me, every night,
   Behold thee when I'm dreaming!

GARDENING.

BY CHARLES FRASER.

It is said that a Chinese map of the world is covered
with China. How delightful the idea of unfolding one
covered with a garden! And is it not possible for man, in

gratitude to that being who has made all nature "beauty to his eye," to realize this charming illusion, so that " every drop of rain which cometh from heaven and watereth the earth, shall make it bring forth and bud?" The Lord himself planted the first garden, and appointed Adam to dress and to keep it, as an employment meet for the purity and perfection in which he was created. Amidst the blossoms of Eden, and under the shade of its bowers, did woman receive the breath of life, full of joy and fragrance. Such an abode was deemed worthy of the few innocent days of yet unfallen man, and the first fruits of his disobedience was to be for ever banished from its goodly precincts. Milton represents as the first object of Eve's lament, on hearing the sentence pronounced by Michael, those flowers " which she had bred up with her tender hand;" and nothing can be more pathetic than the apostrophe with which she takes her last look of them.

Not only as spreading a mantle of beauty over the scenes of industry and cultivation, has a garden ever been the favorite resort of man, and its employments been sought both for duty and relaxation; but the luxuriancy it unfolds, the tranquillity it inspires, the odors it diffuses, the harmony it breathes, the diversity it embraces, the health it promotes, and, above all, its unceasing repetition of hopes and enjoyments, of promises and fulfilments, have made it in all ages the favorite of the poet, and afforded him an exhaustless field of imagery and illustration. Who has not read of the famed gardens of Alcinous, and the golden orchards of the Hesperides? Who, amidst the creations of mythology, has not beheld Dryads and Hamadryads guarding every walk and sporting in every shade? Flora lends her blushes to the blossoms of spring, Pomona and

Ceres display the golden treasures of autumn, and Faunus receives even the tribute of winter.

" Spargit agrestes tibi sylva frondes."

The prophets of old culled from a garden many of their most beautiful and striking allusions. The divine object of Isaiah's predictions was figuratively styled a "stem and a branch, and through him it was foretold" that the wilderness should rejoice, and the waste ground should be glad, and flourish as the rose. Solomon, in his prophetic inspirations, addresses the Saviour of the world as "the Rose of Sharon,—the lily of the valleys,—the fountain of the garden;" and again, in all the pomp of Eastern imagery, he describes "his cheeks as a bed of roses, and as sweet flowers;" and so in Ezekiel, "The land that was desolate is become like the garden of Eden."

It is remarkable that a garden was the scene of that Saviour's last solemn act of devotion, "whither," we are told, "he had ofttimes resorted with his disciples." And we know, that conformably to an ancient custom of the Israelites, the sepulchre in which he was laid was also in a garden. This is alluded to on account of the association it necessarily involves, that as a garden was the scene of man's first disobedience, so did it witness his triumph over the grave.

" Here mankind fell, and hence they rose again."

Now, if many of the pursuits, even of leisure and elegance, in which men are engaged, are the result of discoveries traceable to no very remote period, and recommen ded to their attention by successive improvements, in whic h their own ingenuity may perhaps have had a share, with what devoted zeal and unceasing delight ought they to ch erish that art whose foundations were laid coevally with creation itself! How ought they to love anoccupation endear ed and consecrated, as gardening is, by the most solemn and affecting associations!

Cert ain it is, as far as history informs us, that from the earliest ages it has been contemporary with national prosperity and popular refinement, and has always flourished together with other elegant arts, possessing this decided advantage over some of them, that, whilst they have obtained their acmé of improvement, and could advance no further, science is shedding on horticulture the rays of continued and progressive improvement, and encouraging its vota ries with a boundless field of research, and daily results of interest and delight.

In speaking of the antiquity of the art, as attested by history, we need not go beyond the days of Semiramis, who lived farther in time before the Christian era than we do after it. Amongst the embellishments of Babylon, were the celebrated hanging gardens (*pensiles horti*), constructed by her at immense expense, perhaps at the price of vanquished k ingdoms, and certainly, as we are told, with the labor of an entire population. These were raised in the style of an amphitheatre, on terraces of successive elevation, acces sible by flights of steps and supported by immense arches. On these terraces was a sufficient surface of soil for the roots of the largest trees, which flourished there in all the luxuriancy of their native forests, together with the richest variety of flowers and shrubs. The ancient E gyptians, who advanced the arts of civilized life to a degree of refinement which no one can venture to say has been surpassed or equalled in after times, bestowed great care upon their gardens, planning them upon a scale of magnificence, and irrigating them with canals and reservoirs, to ensure a continued luxuriance in their orchards and vineyards. Clarke, speaking of his passage up the Nile, says, "Upon each side of the river, as far as the eye could survey, were rich fields of corn and rice, with such beautiful groves, seeming to rise out of the watery plains, and to shade innumerable settlements in the Delta, amidst never-ending plantations of melons and all kinds of garden vegetables, that, from the abundance of its produce, Egypt may be deemed the richest country in the world." Their ancient taste for gardens still survives, for Cairo is said to embrace a prodigious number of them, and to be almost embosomed in trees. Hasselquist, a traveller of the last century, speaking of the roses of Egypt, and the water distilled from them, mentions an apothecary at Cairo, who annually purchased one hundred and eighty gallons of it. The poet Martial mentions a present of roses from the Pharian gardens to the Emperor, and those, too, of winter flowering roses.

"Ut nova dona tibi Cæsar, Nilotica tellus,
    Miserat hibernas ambitiosa rosas;" &c.

The early Romans cultivated their gardens with no other object than to supply them with vegetables and herbs, which induced that expression of Pliny, " ex horto enim plebei macellum;" for to them it was an abundant market, always at hand. Virgil's description of the old Corycian's garden, in his fourth Georgic, although brief, shows that even in his day, this important object was not neglected; for amongst the roses and lilies, the poppies, daffodils and myrtles,—onions and cucumbers, parsley and other pot-herbs, were not neglected. But in Virgil's day, it was not only *arbores and olera*, but aromatic plants, flowers and evergreens, the myrtle, the ivy, the laurel and the box, that exhibited the prominent beauties of the garden.

We know that agriculture was always considered an honorable employment among the Romans. Many distin-guished families took their names from the successful cultivation of particular grains, as Pliny informs us was the case with the Fabii, Lentuli and the Pisones, who were all distinguished husbandmen. The name of Cicero was derived from the vetch, or cicer, cultivated by one of his ancestors. So great was their love for gardening, that the Roman generals, on their return from foreign conquests, particularly in Asia, introduced and naturalized into their orchards and vineyards, many valuable fruits from the countries they had subdued, and of which they were the native product. Cherries were brought from the borders of the Euxine, and varieties of apples from Greece, Syria and other parts. Pears were brought from Alexandria, and also from Syria—"Syriisve pyris;"—peaches from Persia, apricots from Epirus and Armenia, plums from Damascus and Syria, pomegranates from Cyprus and Carthage, and olives and figs from Greece. And we further read, that many of these fruits were distinguished by the names either of those who had introduced or successfully cultivated them. The very Corycian of whom we have spoken, it is said, was brought by Pompey into Italy, from Corycus, a city of Cilicia, which he had conquered. All these facts show that the Romans, even amidst the successful career of conquest and victory, did not neglect the "cura colendi," nor, indeed, anything that might promote the glory and happiness of their country. We cannot here forget the story of an orchard of ripe fruit, within the limits of a Romish camp, that was left untouched by the soldiers.

Pliny, in his chapter on gardens, speaking of the encroachments of wealth upon the rights of plebeian industry, in monopolisingr are herbs and vegetables for its own luxurious enjoyments, complains of it as inconsistent with the impartial bounty of nature. Adverting to the change, both at Athens and Rome, in the ancient purposes of a garden, which were altogether those of utility, he remarks that it is no longer cultivated for the support of an industrious owner, but had become the ornament of cities, and under the name of *Hortus*, was converted, as he emphatically says, into " delicias, agros, villasque ;" and it is well known that the gardens in and about Rome, were adorned with the utmost magnificence.

Horace, in one of his Epistles, alludes to the custom of ornamenting their palaces with shady trees :

> " Nempe inter varias nutritur silva columnas ;"

and again,—

> "———— nemus
> Inter pulchra situm tecta."

Tibullus, in one of his elegies, also alludes to it :

> " Et nemore in domibus sacros imitantia lucos."

Hence, also, that beautiful expression of Martial, which has become so trite from repetition, " Rus in urbe." Indeed, the gardens of Rome have quite a classical character, and are identified with its history and its poetry. Those of Lucullus, Cæsar and Sallust, will live in unfading verdure.

The poet Martial beautifully describes the garden-like appearance of Rome to a stranger, on his first visit to it,—

> " Urbis ut intravit limina,
> Sic, quacumque vagus, gressumque oculosque ferebat,
> Textilibus sertis omne rubebat iter."

This fondness of blending the beauty and luxuriancy of nature, with the uniformity and regularity of art, has prevailed in every city where climate and situation have favored it. Man longs, amidst the lines and angles, and the artificial ornaments of even a palace, to behold the unmeasured variety of nature. And it is to that particular taste or propensity, to which Horace so aptly and forcibly applies that well-known observation :

> " Naturam si expellas furca,
> Tamen usque recurret."

How proud the distinction, even amongst comparative barbarians, is that attributed to one of the cities of India, " the city of one hundred thousand gardens,"—the city of the rose and the nightingale !

A recent English periodical styles the residences of some of the great nobility in London, city parks ; and mentions that even a part of one of their gardens would let for sixteen or eighteen thousand pounds a year.

The royal gardens of Aranjuez, in Spain, if they still retain their former grandeur, must be the most delightful in the world. Situated on the banks of the Tagus, with every advantage of natural beauty, they were originally laid out with much of the formality of art ; but nature, asserting her sway, has been allowed to intrude and break in upon that formality, advancing on the walks in some places, and receding in others, thus blending her luxuriancy with the regularity of art, and producing an effect altogether magical.

Thus, we see that wealth and luxury have always claimed a garden as the favorite object of prodigal expense. But instead of imitating the simplicity of nature, they have too often disfigured her with the motley inventions of art, and loaded her with ornaments which she abhors ; and which, " without speech or language," she is constantly reproving, even in the humblest of her productions. It is not in straight walks, clipped hedges, cones and labyrinths, or such caprices, that wealth may successfully employ itself in gardening ; but in collecting and naturalizing the kindred productions of various countries and climates, and bringing together, as it were, into one family circle, the scattered members of the same species,—in beholding their blended hues, and inhaling their mingled fragrance. In this respect, modern horticulture has a decided advantage over that of antiquity. No one can be a skilful horticulturist, that is unacquainted with botany and other kindred sciences, all of which were unknown to the ancients. Their efforts were practical and experimental ; those of the moderns are founded on principle, and directed by a knowledge of the properties and affinities of plants. The modern horticulturist does not merely regard the ornamental part of gardening, which is very much a matter of taste and observation,—but without neglecting that, he has higher objects. He calls Botany and Chemistry to his aid. By means of the former, he is able to ascertain the particular family to which every plant belongs, to know its peculiar properties and the purposes for which nature has designed it,—whether for ornament or use—whether esculent or otherwise—whether nutritious or poisonous. The latter, by its practical developments, informs him of the best means of manuring his grounds and increasing their productiveness ; of experimenting on his soil and finding out its peculiar nature, and employing it for that cultivation for which it is best adapted; what soils furnish the best aliment for particular plants, and the constitution of those plants, as determined by the nature of their roots, which are various,—some being fibrous, others bulbous or tuberose, others hard and woody. Professor Liebig, in his work on the application of Organic Chemistry to Agriculture, has done much to elevate the character of horticulture; for all that relates to the nutrition of vegetables, and the action of manure upon them, is equally important to both.

In addition to these, Entomology may be enlisted to give effect to his labors. It will acquaint him with the nature of those insects, which are so great an enemy to the garden,—from the grub and cut-worm that destroy in the dark, to those that are winged, and attack the tallest trees,—and direct his attention to the best means of destroying them, or of lessening their depredations. On this subject, there is yet a wide range of observation and experiment to stimulate the exertions of the horticulturist.

The ravages of insects have at all times been the subject of complaint with gardeners ; and all who have either labored or written have united their regrets. Whilst we are improving our gardens by the importation of foreign plants and shrubs, and habituating them to our climate and cultivation, we run the risk of introducing destructive insects, hitherto unknown. Some of the most fatal of these insects are exotics ; one, peculiar to the pear-tree, is said to be of foreign importation, as it was never observed in the United States until the introduction of fruit trees became common. And we all remember with mournful experience, the blighting effects of that little white insect, so fatal to our orange trees, which a few years ago visited our gardens, carrying with them a desolation as deadly as that which follows the march of the locust.

Sir William Temple, in his essay on Gardening, speaks of a disease known amongst orange trees, which he pronounces a most pestilent one. He describes it as proceeding from an insect which fastens on the bark of the tree, dark brown and figured like a shield. He quotes Pausanias as saying that they were much noticed in Greece. He is of opinion that they proceed from the roots ; but those to which we allude, cover and encrust the tree so entirely, not excepting even the smallest twigs or shoots, as to induce the belief that they are not generated in the root, but are winged. The excessive cold of the winter of 1837, which hastened, or rather completed, the destruction of our orange trees, still leaves us in doubt whether this disease was a transient or permanent one. We have not heard of their re-appearance.

What are the results of the scientific character which

Horticulture has of late years acquired (and here let me observe that the very term, " Horticulture," has grown into use from the more literal character it has assumed in modern times) ? " Gardening " has been the only word always used by the best English writers,—Swift, Addison, Cowley in his beautiful poem addressed to Mr. Evelyn, Sir William Temple, Horace Walpole and Cowper. For, in their day, it was altogether an art,—practical, and based on experience,—directed by taste, rather than science,—and considered the appendage of wealth, and used for the ornament of villas and palaces.

But a garden has now become a field of scientific research, displaying a knowledge of Botany, Chemistry and Vegetable Physiology, without any restraint or limitation on the exercise of taste. Those sciences entering into, and directing its employments, have elevated both its character and its name. They seem to have established a higher class, that requires a distinguishing name ; whilst the mere plodding gardener is left to his humble, though useful occupation, of supplying our tables with the best fruit and vegetables and herbs,—adding the experience of one year to the labors of another. The horticulturist is employed in the more liberal and enlarged sphere of the pursuit, aiming at higher objects,—to soften the asperities of climate,—to subdue the stubbornness of soils,—to obliterate the line between barrenness and fertility,—in a word, to bring the whole vegetable kingdom under subjection to the uniform government of science. He knows that in the ordinary course of nature, everything proceeds from established and regular principles,—that there are no phenomena that may not be accounted for,—no secret processes that may not be dis-

covered,—and no operations which may not be satisfacto-
rily explained.

But to return. One of the results, we might say one
of the triumphs of modern horticulture, is the introduction
and naturalisation, even the domestication, of foreign
plants and flowers, greatly diversifying the beauty of our
gardens, and enlarging the enjoyments of taste. Our
vegetable population is thus greatly increased, and like
that of our municipal and political communities, is fast
rivalling the number of natives. The extension of commerce, and the growing civilisation of the world, have
very much contributed to this. We may all remember
when our gardens produced a comparative meagre display,
when our roses were few, and those the descendants of
the Huguenot* stock : and our flower-beds confined to
anemonies and stock gillyflowers—pinks, jonquils, and
a few blue hyacinths (other colors being very rarely
seen), as prescribed by the old-fashioned vocabulary.
Whereas they now exhibit a splendid array of flowers
and shrubs; contributed by every part of the globe—
roses from China and Bengal, dahlias from Mexico,
jessamines from Arabia, verbenas and astremerias from
South America ; the gardenia florida, ixia sparaxis and
gladiolus from the Cape of Good Hope ; mignonette from
Egypt ; the ice-plant (mysembryanthemum crystallinum)
from Athens ; the various japonicas, including the lorni-
cera, the Italian honeysuckle ; the lagerstremia from
China, with its varieties, and that splendid shrub, the
pittosporum, also from China. These, with many other

* Several beautiful roses are found in those parts of the country
where the Huguenots settled, " to tell where a garden had been."

exotics, are now familiar to us, and may be fairly enrolled in the American Flora.

But all is not yet accomplished. New fields are to be explored and their beauties culled. It is said that there are dispersed on the surface of the globe forty thousand distinct species of plants bearing flowers, and this is thought but a moderate estimate. Of these there are thirteen thousand flowering plants in the intertropical parts of America, whilst Europe, which lies wholly within the temperate zone, contains seven thousand. It is to be hoped that the recent political changes which have taken place in China, enlarging its trade with other nations, and particularly with the United States, will give us still further insight into its botanical treasures, and add to what we already possess of them.

Amongst the foreign contributions by which our gardens have been enriched, is the rose, with its splendid varieties. But this paragon of flowers claims at least the tribute of a separate paragraph. It is asserted by naturalists, that all the diversities of form, color, size and fragrance, which now distinguish the rose, have proceeded from care and cultivation, there being but one native original. If this be true, what elements of beauty must there have been in that original, to develope themselves so luxuriantly and profusely! How like its prototype of Eden, in whom all that was "lovely—fair" was summed up, "in her contained." Transplanted from the wilderness, where its sweetness was wasted, it has become the pride and ornament of man's habitation ; it has spread its progeny over every clime, and is the inseparable companion of civilisation and refinement. The harbinger of spring, and emblem of youth,

"Celestial rosy-red—love's proper hue;"

it has received the homage of the poet in every age. The
offerings of taste and genius, of beauty and innocence,
have diffused an atmosphere of joy around it, and made it
the object of universal but harmless idolatry. Pliny places
the rose at the head of flowers, investing it, as it were,
with royal precedence. "Lilium rosæ nobilitate proxi-
mum est." He mentions many varieties in the gardens of
Rome, the names of which show that several had been introduced from abroad. Some of these varieties are beautifully alluded to by the poet, Martial, in one of his epi-
grams addressed to a chaplet of roses :

> " Seu tu Paestinis genita es, seu Tiburis arvis:
> Seu rubuit tellus Tuscula flore tuo;
> Seu Prænestino te villica legit in horto;
> Seu modo Campani gloria ruris eras," &c.

No doubt the celebrated rose of Pæstum, which always
had the word " bifera" prefixed to it, is to be found among
the varieties that adorn our own gardens, many of them having that peculiarity. Indeed, our gardens, which were formerly sterile in this branch of cultivation, now exhibit the
fruits of a most liberal taste. Of the white rose there were
but two varieties, the common white and the musk ; of the
red, the centifolia or common May rose, the damask, the
cabbage rose, and a few other varieties, were the only ornaments of the rosarium : whereas now the enterprise of
the American horticulturist has overspread our country
with one blush of beauty, almost realizing the visionary
hope before expressed.

That an enlightened interest is awakened throughout the
United States on the subject of horticulture, is not only

evident from the facts above stated, but from the active efforts of societies established for its encouragement. By these, information is sought, experiments encouraged, improvements rewarded, papers illustrating its various scientific relations and practical developments, read and published, and an intercommunication made on the result of individual effort; thus elevating the pursuit, imparting to it a more liberal character, and multiplying and enhancing the conscious enjoyments of him that practises it. And where is there a happier man than the horticulturist? Nature is his constant companion. His daily study is to improve his acquaintance with her, and to cultivate that intercourse whose delights are exhaustless. The alternate succession of expectation and reality, of labor and repose, of retirement and society, fill up the day and the year. He labors to brighten every hue in the mantle of beauty which she has spread over the fields, and to make her bounties even more worthy of gratitude. In investigating the phenomena of vegetable life, and exhibiting in his labors and improvements those results which minister to the enjoyments of taste, and to the more substantial comforts of man, he entitles himself, without any ambition for the distinction, to be called a benefactor of his race. Nor are his pursuits without moral benefit to himself. Decay and re-production are constantly before him as emblematic monitors. He is the steward of mysteries which no human science can unfold, and which, in the humblest flower of the valley, are daily declaring the unfathomable wisdom of the great Author of creation. The seeds that decay and germinate, have undergone the same alternate process as when they fell from the hand of him who planted the first garden. Hence he learns that it is the right and the privilege of the virtuous man who has been employed through life in cultivating its charities, to enjoy, in their richest display, the fruits of his labors, and to know that the seed that he reaps is to spring up and flourish after him.

THE OCEAN SPIRIT.

BY JAMES S. RHETT.

"There is a low and feeble sound which frequently precedes it, more sublime in reality than all the uproar of the storm itself. ' Did you never observe,' says Mr. Gray, in a letter to a friend, "while rocking winds are piping loud," that pause as the gust is re-collecting itself, and rising upon the ear like the swell of the Æolean Harp? I do assure you there is nothing in the world *so like the voice of a spirit.*' "—*Alison on Taste.*

WHILE the tempest was rising, O! heard ye the sound,
Like the groan of the waters it murmur'd around—
The deep breathing winds all whispering stole,
As the voice of a Spirit o'er the ocean did roll.

"I rule the rough ocean, I pillow the wave,
My cradle is rocking when hurricanes rave—
Like the mane of the war-horse when chaf'd in his pride,
Is the crest of the billow, the foam of the tide.

" Wild is the wail of the loon* from afar,
When the loud winds are must'ring to wrath and to war ;
And fearful the lightning that startles the deep,
Ere the shout of the whirlwind hath waken'd its sleep.

" I bid the lone minstrel of waters to wail,
When the vans† of the thunder around him do sail ;
And the glance of mine eye is the glitter of light,
That shaketh the pillars‡ of darkness and night.

" I sway the broad billow that breaketh in clouds,
When the tall ships are heaving, and rattle the shrouds ;
I roll the deep thunder that shakes the firm world,
When my banner of clouds o'er the gale is unfurled.

" Oh ! loud is the roar of the wave in his might,
When the storm-driven navies are shiver'd in flight,
When the whirlwind is moving in his dark curling shroud,
And the silver-wing'd sea-bird is cleaving the cloud.

" Then wide rage the waters, and streaming on high
Like a vision of terror the tempest rolls by,—
And the broad rushing surge like the pale sheet doth seem,
That robes the grim phantoms of horror and dream."

---

* The note of this sea-bird is beautifully soft and plaintive ; rising, as it were, from the bosom of the waves. The seamen say, it never is heard but when a storm is rising.

† His sail-broad vans he spreads for flight, and in the surging
     smoke
Uplifted, spurned the ground.—*Paradise Lost.*

‡ " And the Lord went before them in the pillar of a cloud."—
Exodus xiii., 21.

Such was the voice o'er the lone sea that came,
When the thunder mov'd onward in darkness and flame ;
But sweet was the strain when the high winds were still,
And faint as the light-pinioned breeze of the hill.

So breath'd the still voice when the æther was blue,
And the eye of the evening star trembling through ;
Soft o'er the heart in its beauty it stole,
And made the deep waters in melody roll :

" Now the sun is descending, and the purpling of night
Sheds over the scene a shadowy light ;
The waves breathing in slumber are sinking and swelling,
And the low gale the dirge of the evening is knelling.

" Oh ! where is the canopy lovely as mine ?
The stars are my tapers,—how purely they shine !
The lamp of the morn lights the hall of my home,
And tips with her splendor the crest of the foam.

" Far o'er the lone billows the light-house is beaming,
Wide, wide o'er the waters deep glories are streaming ;
And the moon, and the stars, and the ocean combine,
In one flood of effulgence they liquidly shine.

" At the birth of young morning how bright are the beams,
When the far flowing cloud like a wild mantle streams,
When the rose of the East is unfolding her smile,
And gilds the broad ocean with blushes the while.

" When the sun hath awak'd and the wild waves are
    dancing,
And in the gay beam the high sea-birds are glancing—
My voice is the whisper that thrills on thine ear,
And bids thee remember a *spirit is here !* "

———

PURSUIT OF HAPPINESS.

BY MAYNARD D. RICHARDSON.

Not to draw too much of our mood and its philosophy,
wise or unwise, from the Psalmist, still less to indulge in
those stale truisms which make up the burden of complaint in most essays, we are hourly compelled, nevertheless, as an unavoidable result of our experience, to
muse upon the vicissitudes, the uncertainties, or, rather,
we should say, the too serious *certainties* of life. " Man
that is born of woman," &c. This is the pitch note of
all moral meditation, and we say to ourselves, a thousand
times a day, with something of the gloomy fatality of
Mohammed, " it is decreed ;" sorrow, complaint, misgiv-
ing, pain and many regrets, fill and disfigure each page in
the life of man. And if his difficulties be neither
oppressive nor positive, the *negative pregnant*, as the
lawyers barbarously phrase it, is at hand, and something is always wanting to the completion of his happiness. There is always some step untaken, and which he
cannot take, towards his attainment of that vision of

promises, that proposed elevation, from which he may look down, with untroubled spirit, upon those clouds and that tempest, with which he may once have struggled, but from the assaults of which he has made his escape. The ideal is unattainable, and he feels it the illusion is still such, and not for him, until the "coming of that perfect day." He learns that " all is vanity," and gives up the pursuit. In doing so, he either becomes happier or less happy; he certainly does not remain where he was.

But though idle to look and hope for perfect felicity, as a condition of the human lot, it is something worse than idle to yield up to the despondency which comes with this conviction. Though unalloyed bliss belonged not to the angels, it does not follow that unalloyed misery, or misery in any degree, must, unless we so will it, be the destiny of man! We believe—who does not?—that we were intended by the Creator for happiness, as well here as hereafter; in a degree, at least, if not unqualifiedly. There can be little doubt that the means of such an acquisition are chiefly in our own hands ; still less should there exist a doubt as to the propriety of employing them.

Youth is the season for luxuriant hopes, triumphant anticipations, and all that gay company of warm desires, and fruitful and flower-invested fancies. These are blighted, baffled, set at naught, and defrauded of their promise, less by the decree—the stern and stubborn fate— than by ourselves. Were our views directed aright, did we send our hopes on the proper path, and check their frequent extravagances, would this be the case? Would our life be the long lesson of regret, of madness, of misery, that we sometimes find it—that we almost invariably make it? No; it would not. The *Creator* has been too much the *Creature* of the *Creature;* has been too mindful of man to leave us in doubt as to the fitting answer. In youth we are too prone to couple our ideas of happiness with dreams of glory, ambition, and the great name —the attainment of which, we at the same time forget, depends quite as much upon the disposition of our neighbors as upon the doings of ourselves. Apart from this fact, the desire itself is that of the boy-bauble, the gold and the glitter, and—but why speak at all of this strong panting for the breath, the uproar and huzza of the populace!

The ambitious man is the merest slave, and does his drudgery under the lash of a most tyrannical anxiety. Now scourged and now caressed, his existence is always divided, and he alternates between the two extremes of pampering promises and the deepest prostration. He rises, it is true; but then he falls as certainly. He wins the fruit, perhaps, for which he has been all his life climbing busily, heedless of the thorny branches which tear and torment him;—and like those of the Dead Sea, it turns to ashes on his lips.

Wealth is the key to happiness in the imaginings of another, and, perhaps, a much larger class. The *auri sacra fames* is the true jewel, the *sine quâ non* in the search after the imperial mistress, whose cheeks are flowers of perennial bloom. They overlook another text, or more, which the sacred volume furnishes. That melancholy morality —

> " Man wants but little here below,
> Nor wants that little long,"

is entirely disregarded, and they go on laying up the grain in mountain masses, unconscious that the worm is all the while making fearful havoc in the granary.

There is another place in which treasures are to be laid, where, it is said, the worm comes not, and through the security of which thieves never break. The instability and insecurity of earthly possessions is, however, a lesson of human wisdom—common, dull, matter-of-fact daily experience, and needs not holy writ for its enforcement. The same experience would speak of content, if men would hear ; but this personage has too little in her appearance that is attractive :

> " She comes too meanly dressed to win our smile,
> And calls herself content ; an humble name !
> Our flame is transport, and content our scorn."

It is not merely the privilege, it is the distinguishing characteristic of man, to look forward into futurity, and consider his actions in relation not only to their immediate but to their remote consequences. If, therefore, we desire to retain the rights of the rational creature, we must use them in reference to this survey, and take due note of its teachings. This will have a wonderful effect in taking off the thousand scales which obscure and impair the mental vision. We shall then, possibly, be able to ascertain the genuine from the deceptive happiness, the substance from the shadow, the chaste from the impure. It sometimes occurs, in matters of reason as in those of sense, that, what to the superficial examination would seem wise and valuable, a closer inspection makes out to be vain and worthless. To the eye, some fruits wear the most deli-

cious semblance, which are sour to the taste ; and, in the
pursuit of happiness, many have learned, with Cowper, to
exclaim—

> " I have sought thee in splendor and dress
> In the regions of pleasure and taste ;
> I have sought thee and seem'd to possess,
> But have found thee a vision at last."

" Defend me, therefore," says the same amiable moralist,
" from reveries so airy ; from the toil of dropping buckets
into empty wells, and growing old in drawing nothing up."
Well might he pray in this manner, and yet not touch the
subject. Because he was unsuccessful, because he sought
for water where water was none, because he was disappointed in his search for flowers in a desert, we are not to
infer the utter and final departure of happiness from the
earth. It is not because she is unattainable that she has
not been found, but she is so liable to be mistaken for her
neighbors, or rather, they for her, that no one need wonder that thousands perish in the wilderness, lamenting that
she is as far off as ever. We scarcely concur with the
poet of the " Task," who thus gives up the *task :*

> " No longer I follow a sound,
> No longer a dream I pursue ;
> Oh ! happiness, not to be found,
> Unattainable treasure, adieu !"

DU SAYE.

A LEGEND OF THE CONGAREE.

BY JAMES M. LEGARÉ.

PART FIRST.

Fades in the west, the latest flush
Of summer's gorgeous eve ;
With ceaseless moan, of Congaree
The dusky waters heave :
For one unknown the nightly bird
Commenceth now to grieve.

And twilight deepens to a night
In every forest glade,
Save one, wherein the soldiers' care
A blazing heap has made,
And in the circle of its light
Their toil-worn limbs are laid.

Their arms propped round the rugged trunks,
Or glitter from the ground :
Their steeds the scanty herbage crop,
Within the tether's bound :
Nor watch without the camp is there,
Nor wary sentry's round.

Some feed the flame, or seeking bring
Snapt twigs of sun-dried pine :
Tend well the haunch of buck, whereon
At once to sup and dine.
Or lazily, half blanket-wrapt,
With nodding brows recline.

While others sing wild songs, and pass
The cup from hand to hand ;
Recount how none of rebel breed
Fierce Tarleton's arm withstand ;
And boast of bloody laurels won
From outlawed Marion's band.

And here and there, in dizzy flight
The merry sparkles dart :
To mirthful life on every side
Old forest's echoes start.
One only, sad, with drooping head,
Sits from the rest apart.

As weeping days in budding May,
More lovely in their tears,
Is she who, warm and soft as they,
A captive's fetters wears.
A simple tale of love is hers,
And on my subject bears.

Of gentle blood ; her sire's sire,
A Refugee from France,
Had in the noble Condé's cause
Unfailing couched his lance.

His son now, sword in hand, beheld
St. George's flag advance.

One came ; brave, generous, fair of form,
Strong armed to aid the weak ;
They loved, bright Laura, brave Du Saye.
Love learneth soon to speak !
Why need I say she blushing gave
The hand none else might seek ?

The day is set, the friends are met,
The priest in surplice stands ;
The oaths are said, the prayers are read,
He joins their willing hands.
Lo ! through the open portals swarm
The ruthless tory bands !

Unarmed, beset, with frantic rage,
These struggle toward the door ;
Borne in their midst, the bride.   Their blood
Streams redly down the floor
In vain ; across their faltering path,
The others furious pour.

Fast ebbs their strength—back, back they reel
The dripping blades before.
Oh, for a rank of Rebel steel !
One volley—all is o'er :
Fast bleeds Du Saye at Laura's side ;
He fell,—she knew no more.

And now comes one with breathless haste,
And looks that fear denote.
"The Swamp-fox scents our trail," he cries,
"Fly!—man with speed the boat."
While yet he speaks, sounds from afar
A bugle's lengthen'd note.

Unconscious all, with lagging gait,
The rescuing squadron nears;
On flight intent the others throng
The wide piazza's stairs;
They gain the water's verge, their chief
The lifeless Laura bears.

But keen-eyed Marion marked the crew,
And bid his men divide.
With fierce Horry in hot pursuit,
A score of troopers ride;
Too late they win the beach; the bark
Shoots swiftly down the tide.

*   *   *   *   *   *

Broad shines the blaze; with noisy mirth
Old forest rings around.
And all save grief is loud of tongue
Within the covert's bound.
Nor watch without the camp is there,
Nor wary sentry's round.

PART SECOND.

Beyond the forest's giant growth
Soft smiles the morning sky ;
Deep in the shade, the embers round,
The slumbering warriors lie :
Chafes in its banks the stream, as if
Its comrade old to fly.

And forest leaf, and soldier's cloak,
And bank of russet hue ;
And stately bough of cypress grey
The wave that seems to woo ;
All sleep beneath the mantle fresh
Of summer's night-shed dew.

Up darts a startled bird with wheel
Of wing, and warning note :
Beneath the nest-hung branch soft glides
A lightly rocking boat ;
Close to the shore, the oar-man's grasp
Essays the skiff to float.

And steppeth to the beach Du Saye,
Whom Marion's troop had found,
Stretched in his hall, and with rude skill
His recent wound had bound :
But love is aye the surest leech,
Revenge, the staunchest hound.

A fox-skin cap, and huntsman's frock
Of grey, the other wore ;
A hunter stout, whose swarthy cheek
The Indian's knife-scar bore :
With care he scanned the turf, as one
Well skilled in forest lore.

" Hard by this swamp (he said) last eve
Their oozy footpath lay :
Nor far from here their camp.—Yet long
Is Marion's toilsome way.
Thy heart is stout, thy arm is strong,
What need of longer stay !"

" Now," cried Du Saye, and led the way,
" Thou well hast spoke my mind."
Old forest's dusky mazes through
With noiseless step they wind.
They mark—they skirt the camp ; apart
The heart-sick maid they find.

Lightly the captive sleeps,—she wakes,
Du Saye kneels by her side :
" Arise," he whispered soft, " and fly
With me, my own sweet bride."
His stalwart arm supports her form,
Back to the grove they glide.

Lo ! from the ground a sleeper springs—
Loud to each comrade calls :
Ere well the words are said, beneath
The hunter's knife he falls.

Huzza! thou gallant Eagle, who
The Lion's lair despoils!

As arméd men where Jason sowed,
Sprang up, so at the blow,
They wake—they shout—they arm in haste;
Fast in pursuit they go!
What may avail the Eagle, when
The woodsman bends his bow!

Yet, blade to blade, and foot to foot,
They sell the pathway dear:
On either hand the matted vines
Their stubborn bulwark rear:
Behind, the river lifts his voice
Inviting still more near.

And foot to foot, and blade to blade,
The river's verge they gain,
As sudden from the swoll'n cloud
Down bursts the furious rain;
The straitened stream of baffled men
Outpoureth from the lane.

The few behold the many now
Exulting round them wheel,
Straight to the bark, a gap they seek
To open with their steel;
But faint from loss of blood and toil,
With failing steps they reel.

Well had the night-dew served their cause
In drowning out the spark
Which slumbered, powder-cased, within
The rifle's chamber dark ;
For hostile steel and flint in vain
Their latent light impart.

And now a blow the hunter stout
Hath dashed upon his knee ;
His weeping bride pressed to his side,
His back against a tree,
Fierce stands Du Saye, at bay : a rock
Against a stormy sea !

The hunter falls.   No hope survives
In Laura's bosom now ;
Her arm around her lover cast,
Her hot lips press his brow.
Faint not in heart, brave partizan ;
Who would not die as thou !

He feels the kiss : a hundred lives
'Throb in each bursting vein ;
He lifts—he bears—the river's marge
His flying footsteps stain ;
Aghast the Riders shrink, or brave
The love-nerved arm in vain.

Close to the bank, the fragile skiff
That dances on the tide,
With last convulsive bound he wins ;
The straightened cords divide !

Far out upon the water's breast
With meteor's speed they glide.

The gunwale dips—the boat drinks deep,
The currents chafe and roar,
Above their fair devoted heads
Ere yet the waters pour,
They see their kinsmen gallantly
Come spurring to the shore.

Crash—crash, the shrubs are trampled down,
The boughs are bent aside ;
Forth from the dreary forest's frown
A rank of horsemen ride.
Tall, dauntless, dark, his restless steed,
Each trooper sits astride.

Their chief commands ; the horsemen wheel,
At once in circle wide,
Around the foe : on either hand
The rapid waters glide ;
Nor space is there for flight, nor yet
Dark coppice where to hide.

But Marion, in whose manly breast
All kindly virtues were,
Would fain the lives within his grasp
And wasteful bloodshed spare ;
When from their line a bullet-shot
Close hisseth past his ear.

10

With unmoved eye the chieftain glanced
Along his circling band;
Impatient paws the steed beneath
Each trooper's swarthy hand.
He spoke; like tempest-breath they sweep
Athwart the narrow strand!

And all is rage, revenge, and fear,
And shout and answering groan;
Down trampling hoof, and flash and shout,
And shot at random thrown:
Till to the river's blood-tracked beach
The remnant faint is borne.

Some cry for quarter, and receive
The mercy which they gave;
Or, struggling with the stream awhile,
But find a slower grave.
A few are Britons, and these die
As soldiers trained and brave.

The skirmish past; two troopers swim
Near to the shore their steeds,
And launch the fatal bark that lies
Embedded in the reeds;
Nor bride nor groom of yester morn
The other's pressure heeds.

Apart from where the charge had been,
They lay them gently down;
Above their heads the cypress dark,
Sun-lit, unbends his frown:

Dew weeps the stilly morn afar ;
The river's plaintive sound.

The soft young cheek, the silken curl
That on the bosom lies ;
The chill, damp brow of him who was
To her life's dearest prize ;
The chieftain looks upon, and tears
Stand in the soldier's eyes.

(Extract from " the Visit of Atticus to Rome.")

TRIAL OF MILO—ORATION OF CICERO.

BY BENJAMIN F. PORTER.

THE populace of Rome were crowding towards the Forum. It was the day fixed for the trial of Milo ; and Cicero was to speak. Anxious to hear this celebrated orator, I hastened to join Publius, who gave me a conspicuous stand. The occasion was this. T. Annius Milo had solicited the consulship, and was opposed with violence by P. Clodius, at the same time a candidate for the office of Prætor. Milo, previous to the election, on his way to Lanuvium, a municipal town twelve miles from Rome, accompanied by his wife and servants, encountered Clodius in the Appian way, attended by a party of friends and domestics, fully armed. A dispute commenced with the retainers. Milo and Clodius sustained the domestics, and a general conflict ensued. Clodius receiving a dangerous wound, retreated to an adjacent mansion, whither he was pursued by Milo, and, with eleven of his domestics, slain.

The expectation of this trial caused all Rome to tremble with commotion; and, when I arrived, an immense throng of centurions, soldiers and citizens, filled the arena and porticos of the Forum.

I could not look around me without humiliating emotions. A thousand statues, the work of Grecian art, seemed to frown indignantly upon me. Where, I thought, slumbered the patriotism of Greece, when these were torn from her soil to glut the insatiate ambition of Rome?

The judges were already in their stations. Near them I beheld a man attended by twelve lictors, each bearing fasces. He wore a white robe striped with purple, and held an ivory sceptre in his hand. A noble stature, and venerable and princely air, appeared to destine him to command the love and obedience of men. His features were engaging. His eyes were moist and brilliant, and of quick expression. His forehead fair and large, and covered with hair slightly curled. "That," said Publius, seeing my attention was fixed, "is Pompey. The Senate have elected him sole consul, and he attends this trial with a strong guard. In the Prætor's seat sits L. Domitius, appointed to preside. The judges are composed of senators, equites, and tribuni ærarii. The first used to be selected from the patricians; they are now often self-made, from any class. The equites are chosen from the middle, and the tribuni ærarii from the lower order of citizens."

At this moment we saw a covered litter brought into the midst of the assembly, from which descended a man apparently near the age of sixty. His person was slender and tall. He would be remarked for the length of his neck, and the manliness and regularity of his features. His forehead was ample, without hair; his mouth expressive; and his eyes lustrous and animated. Had Milo not before been shown to me, I might have supposed this the accused person. He was greatly agitated; and walked with trembling steps to a position below the judges. He looked anxiously around the assembly, and particularly at the armed men. " You see," continued Publius, " Cicero. You observe his emotion. He is naturally timid. Milo, fearing the effect of Pompey's guards upon him, has resorted to the expedient of the litter to convey him hither."

I was impatient to listen to an orator whose fame had filled the Roman world, and who was said to have carried eloquence and erudition from Greece. I noticed with uneasiness the preliminaries of the trial, though struck with the novelty of the ceremonies with which it proceeded. The trial began with the selection of judges. The names of these were placed in an urn, and, as drawn, the accused was called upon to make his objections. Thirty, of the eighty-one present, were rejected by Milo. The accusers, young Appius, M. Antonius and P. Valerius, now approached; and making oath that they did not accuse from malice, declared the charge. The witnesses of both parties sat on benches; and, when called to testify, each one holding a flint stone in his hand, pronounced the following words: " If knowingly I deceive, may the immortal Jove hurl me, with my goods, from the safe city and citadel, as I now cast this stone."

At last Cicero's time to speak arrived. He ascended

the rostrum amidst the clamors of the Clodian party. I
was concerned at the trepidation of an orator of his age
and fame. He was palsied with terror. His words
trembled on his tongue, and his almost inarticulate commencement betrayed his fears of Pompey. He concluded
his oration, pronounced by many the most declamatory of
his efforts ; but to me, who heard him for the first time, a
rich feast of rhetoric and composition. In the division of
a discourse he has improved upon the rules of Aristotle,
who recognizes only the Introduction, the Proposition, the
Argument and Peroration. Cicero has added the Narration and Digression. I sketched, while he proceeded, a
brief analysis of his oration, that my young countrymen
might learn the division of a speech, and perceive the art
which this wonderful orator displays in the arrangement
of his discourses.

The *Introduction*. The whole purpose of this was to
propitiate the judges, and render them kind, attentive, and
tractable. This was effected by allusions to the prosecutor,
the accused, the judges, and the orator. It was neither
argumentative, sentimental, nor explanatory ; neither elaborate, nor yet restrained. It was elegantly simple—not
uttered with pompous words, nor presumptuous looks. He
affected the want of affectation admirably ; and though this
prooemium was long, its length was justified by the complicated, dubious, and discreditable nature of the cause.

He spoke of his fears, but excused them by reference
to the unusual manner of conducting the trial. He com-
plimented the wisdom and justice of Pompey, and attributed
his presence to his regard to the State ; and not love of
the memory of Clodius. He urged the judges to consider

that the armed men were present not to awe them, but
to preserve order in the administration of justice.

He especially attempted to conciliate L. Domitius, by
alluding to his contempt of popular rage. He roused the
indignation of the judges and the assembly against Clodius,
by referring to his murder of M. Papirius, a Roman knight,
and his attempt, through his slave, to assassinate Pompey
in the temple of Castor. Cicero, taking advantage of the
moment, endeavored to excite sympathy for himself, by
calling upon the multitude to remember how often he had
escaped the threatening dagger and bloody hands of
Clodius. He urged, with much art, proofs of the justice,
disinterestedness, and equity of Pompey, who is suspected
of not only rejoicing at the death of Clodius, but of desir-
ing to be rid of Milo.

With this commencement, rendered delightful by the
grace of his action, and the fine modulation of his clear,
sweet, and sonorous, but embarrassed voice, he proceeded
to the narration.

The *Narration* was rather an explanation of the circumstances relating to the cause, than an opening of the cause
itself. It was concise, perspicuous, and probable. He
seemed to desire to make his hearers remember, comprehend, and believe ; to clothe truth with probability. His
expressions, in this, were neither common, nice, nor
unusual. He did not appear to commit the error of some
orators who make their narrations too fanciful for their
audience ; but while not confining himself to a bare, dry
statement, he joined elegance to conciseness. He scattered
over his narration a few proofs ; and with an appearance of
simplicity, as not intending it, while narrating Milo's conduct, insinuated everything unfavorable to Clodius.

The *Digression*. In this deviation from the main body
of his discourse, he took a view of the right of self-defence,
implanted by nature even in brutes; and alluded to the
conduct of Sextus Clodius, who, to gratify his revenge,
exposed his brother's body in the streets, naked, deprived
of the usual rites and funeral pomp.

The *Proposition*. This was brief, and raised the point
to be discussed, which Cicero said, was that a man who
lies in wait for another may lawfully be killed. That, in
this case, Clodius lay in wait for Milo and was slain by him
in self-defence. That the traitor was conquered, force
repelled by force, audaciousness overcome by courage;
and therefore the only question was, not whether Clodius
was killed, but whether justly or unjustly.

The *Argument* covered a large space, and considered
minutely all that happened before the occurrence, what at
the time, and what after; took into consideration the place,
the character and prospects of the parties, and what was
the interest of either in seeking the other's life. He compared the proofs and presumptions; and used many con-
jectural cases. The facts most dwelt upon were, that Milo
was compelled, by the law, to leave Rome to assist at the
sacrifices at Lanuvium, while Clodius had no pretence in
being absent from the city. That if Milo had cherished a
murderous design, he would not have chosen a public, but
rather a secluded spot. That it was Milo's interest that
Clodius should live, while Milo's death was a desirable
event to Clodius. That no violence was used by Milo.
That he was in his chariot with his wife and her women,
wrapped in his cloak. That Clodius sallied from his
house in the evening, unattended by his wife, as usual, and
on horseback. That the proof had shown that Clodius

contemplated Milo's death, in saying, that Milo should not live three days. He alluded to the ingenuousness of Milo's conduct in returning immediately to Rome; and spoke with bitterness of the calumnies uttered against him. He adverted to proofs that Clodius had ever shown himself a tyrant, opposed to the interests of the people; a violator of their wives and daughters: and compared his life with that of Milo, which he declared was identified with the fortune and preservation of Rome, her senators, and people. That he deserved the gratitude of all men, and that this would be denied by none who acknowledged an over-ruling power. He here indulged in a beautiful digression upon the nature of providence. He asserted that such a power did exist; that the grand fabric of nature surely had an animating principle, when man's feeble body possessed life and perception. Thence he rose to a sublime invocation of the Gods; supplicated the Alban groves, and Jupiter, most venerable, from the lofty Latian mount, to assert the innocence of the accused.

The *Peroration* was brief, and often interrupted by the tears of the orator. He implored the judges for compassion toward a brave man, who disdained to supplicate for mercy. He spoke of the efforts which Milo had used to recal him from banishment, and declared he was yet banished, if Milo, his friend, were taken from him. He besought the judges not to condemn the man, born to save his country, to die, but on her bosom—not to deny a grave to Milo, in Italy, which must for ever continue to exhibit splendid memorials of his services.

No sooner had the tumult subsided which followed the conclusion, than the ballots were distributed to the judges. Each was presented with three tablets, severally marked, *condemno, absolvo,* and *non liquet.* One of these was cast by each of the judges into an urn provided for the three orders, from which they were taken by L. Domitius, and counted. Milo was condemned. For acquitting him, there were Senators, six; Equites, four; tribuni œrarii, three. For his condemnation, Senators, twelve; Equites, thirteen; and tribuni œrarii, thirteen.

I afterwards saw Milo in banishment at Massilia. He gave me the oration, written out and corrected by Cicero himself. On remarking the superiority of the written over the spoken defence, Milo playfully said: "If this discourse had been pronounced on my trial, we would not now be feasting on the delicious mullets of Massilia."

THE SILENT GIRL.

BY SAMUEL GILMAN.

SHE seldom spake; yet she imparted
  Far more than language could;
So bird-like, bright, and tender-hearted,
  So natural and good!
Her air, her look, her rest, her actions,
  Were voice enough for her;
What needs a tongue, when *those* attractions
  Our inmost hearts could stir?

She seldom talked; but, uninvited,
  Would cheer us with a song;

And oft her hands our ears delighted,
  Sweeping the keys along ;
And oft, when converse round would languish,
  Ask'd or unask'd, she read
Some tale of gladness or of anguish,
  And so our evenings sped.

She seldom spake ; but she would *listen*,
  With all the signs of soul ;
Her cheek would change, her eye would glisten ;
  The sigh, the smile, upstole.
Who did not understand and love her,
  With meaning thus o'erfraught ?
Though silent as the sky above her,
  Like that, she kindled thought.

Little she spake ; but dear attentions
  From her would ceaseless rise ;
She check'd our wants by kind preventions,
  She hush'd the children's cries.
And, twining, she would give her mother
  A long and loving kiss ;
The same to father, sister, brother,
  All round, nor one would miss.

She seldom spake ; she speaks no longer ;
  She sleeps beneath yon rose ;
'Tis well for us that ties no stronger
  Awaken memory's woes.
For oh ! our hearts would sure be broken,
  Already drain'd of tears,
If frequent tones, by her outspoken,
  Still linger'd in our ears.

SONG.

BY GEORGE S. BRYAN.

On, on, thy gladsome way—
   I may not stem the tide
Which strong as death and dark as fate
   Still bears thee from my side.

Thy heart is full of glee,
   Thy step is strung to pride ;
Too joyous bright for me,
   Thou can'st not be my bride.

On, on, thy gladsome way
   With breath of vain desire,
I would not check thy spirit's play,
   Nor dim thy morning fire.

Still keep thee in the sky,
   Still mounting, soaring, sing—
Leave not thy home on high,
   Till *love shall* fold thy wing.

Yet will I trace with fond delight
   Thy sparkling gay career,
And hang upon thy upward flight
   With joy and trembling fear.

But could I fix that wayward heart,
  Win softness from that kindling eye ;
And claim thee for my holier part,
  For thee I'd live, for thee I'd die.

———

THE PARCHMENT EATER.

BY ALBERT G. MACKEY.

" The predominance of custom is everywhere visible, insomuch
as a man would wonder to hear men profess, protest, engage, give
great words, and then do just as they have done before, as if they
were dead images and engines, moved only by the wheels of custom."
—*Bacon.*

HABIT, says an old proverb, is second nature ; and some
of our psychologists have, as they suppose, amended the
adage by declaring that it is nature itself; " for of what
does our nature consist," say they, " if it is not made up
of our habits ?" It is a difficult question to decide, for, go
where we will, among the opium-eaters of Turkey, the
pipe-smokers of Holland, or the tobacco-chewers of
America, we shall everywhere have abundant reason to
exclaim—

" How use doth breed a habit in a man !"

The ancients have recorded an anecdote that strikingly
exemplifies the invincible control of habit. The Tyrin-

thians were a people so inveterately given to joyousness
and gaiety, that they were unable to enter upon the most
serious and important deliberations with anything like
solemnity. In their public assemblies the orators, when
they attempted to speak, were convulsed with laughter,
and the chairman's hammer lay idle upon his desk while
his hands were engaged in holding both his sides ; the
ambassadors of the neighboring kingdoms were received
with ridiculous grimaces, and the gravest senators were
neither more nor less than mere buffoons. In short, so
far had this spirit of levity extended, that a rational word
or action had become a prodigy among them. In this
deplorable state of things, they consulted the Oracle, at
Delphos, for a cure of their folly. The reply of the god
was, that if they succeeded in offering a bull to Neptune
without laughing during the ceremony, they might hope
thereafter for a greater share of wisdom.

A sacrifice is in itself by no means a capital joke, but
yet, well aware of their propensity, they took every pre-
caution to avoid the provocation even of a smile. The
youths of the city were debarred the privilege of assisting
at the ceremony, and not only they, but all others were
excluded, who had not some cause of melancholy within
themselves—such, for instance, as were afflicted with
painful and incurable diseases—such as were over head
and ears in debt—and such as were wedded to scolding
wives. When all these collected on the beach to immolate
the victim, they prepared to perform their office with looks
composed to seriousness, their eyes being cast down and
their lips compressed together. Just at this moment, a
boy, who had glided in unperceived, and whom some of
the attendants were endeavoring to drive out, exclaimed, in

a comico-serious tone of voice, "What! are you afraid that I will swallow your bull?" This was too much for them; their counterfeit solemnity was disconcerted; habit overcame their resolution; they burst into roars of laughter; the sacrifice was abandoned; and gravity never returned to the Tyrinthians.

Thus far by way of preface, and now to our narrative, the moral of which is, that a bad habit may sometimes lead to preferment. For proof of which,

> " I shall tell you
> A pretty tale : it may be that you have heard it,
> But since it serves my purpose, I will venture
> To scale 't a little more."

JOHN ERNEST DE BIRON was the son of a goldsmith, and his father had destined him for the profession of a notary, for the duties of which he had been properly qualified by his education, and more than fitted by his natural talents. During his residence in the obscure town of * * * * in Sweden, the Baron de Goertz, Secretary of State to Charles XII., was detained there some time by the unexpected illness and death of his private secretary. Having become acquainted with the talents of Biron, he bestowed upon him the vacant office. Biron followed the Baron to Stockholm. There the knowledge which he displayed of various languages, and his facility in decyphering all sorts of chirographs, together with his amiable disposition, soon rendered him the favorite of his master. But he was the slave of a vile habit which he had acquired in his childhood, when employed in the office of the notary to whom he had been apprenticed, and which was as sin-

gular in its character as it was about to be injurious in its
results. This was a habit of unconsciously chewing pieces
of parchment while he was engaged in writing. Like the
chewers of tobacco, Biron had so made himself a slave to
this indulgence, that he was wholly unable to overcome the
propensity; and his occupation placing him continually in
the midst of musty sheets, he found no difficulty in gratifying his appetite.

One day, while engaged on business of importance in
the cabinet of the minister, he picked, carelessly and unconsciously, from the corner of the table at which he was
writing, a piece of parchment; which, as usual, in a moment, found its way to his mouth.

After three or four hours of application to writing, he
was astonished to find that while his mind had been ab-
sorbed in his occupation, he had completely disfigured a
very important paper, being no less than a treaty on the
subject of Livonia, between the Czar of Muscovy and the
King of Sweden. He felt that, by this act of folly, his
hopes of preferment and of reward were at once dashed to
the ground. His utmost ingenuity could suggest no plausible excuse, and to make the matter still worse, while he
stood holding the disfigured parchment in his hand, his
eyes cast despairingly upon the almost obliterated letters,
and his whole countenance betraying the embarrassment
under which he labored, the Baron entered the room.

The minister was not long at a loss for an explanation;
for, looking upon the parchment, he discovered, by a few
scarcely legible words, its importance and value. The
first emotions of rage gave him neither time nor inclination
to examine into causes, and, not doubting for a moment
that his traitorous secretary had suffered himself to be

corrupted by the Muscovite minister, he ordered him to be conducted to prison.

Here, with full leisure to reflect upon his misfortune, he could not long doubt its result ; for, though he was really guiltless, appearances were so much against him, that he could expect nothing but a speedy condemnation. He, therefore, began to prepare himself, with all the resignation in his power, for the sentence of death which was impending over him. Nevertheless, as the frank avowal of the circumstances of his fault could add nothing to his danger, he determined to relate them, even at the risk of receiving no credit for sincerity from his judges. The opportunity of putting this resolution into action was not long wanting. He was summoned into the presence of the Senatorial Council of Stockholm, and after being severely reproached with the magnitude and baseness of his crime, he was called upon to confess the extent and nature of his communications with the Court of Muscovy. To all this Biron only answered with " a plain, unvarnished tale," of the habit which he had acquired in his youth, and of the unfortunate predicament into which its indulgence had plunged him.

The grave senators were too well acquainted with the human heart, not to be able to distinguish the unadorned truth of innocence from the cunning apology of guilt ; and their impressions in his favor were not a little augmented, when they remarked that he was even then indulging, to all appearance without any consciousness of the act, in the very habit to which he was indebted for the unenviable situation in which he was placed. This, with the fact that several fragments of parchment were found in his pockets, whose peculiar form and odor gave undeniable evidence of the uses to which they had been applied, speedily obtained his acquittal; and the Baron de Goertz, his master and accuser, was the first to solicit the restoration of his liberty. But his unfortunate masticatory habits rendered him somewhat unfit for the office of secretary to a prime minister, and he was accordingly discharged from his employment.

Biron was now compelled to seek support among strangers, to whom his habit and his misfortunes were unknown. Fortune did not desert him, and passing over to Courland, he soon obtained employment with the receiver-general of Mitau.

KASTELHORN, the receiver-general, was a man devoted to pleasure, and whose employment in the state sadly interfered with his indulgence in more genial propensities. He had been long looking for an honest and capable secretary on whom he might thrust the burden of his official cares and duties, and the appointment was, therefore, without delay, bestowed upon our hero. His talents and assiduity soon enabled his patron to deliver himself up wholly to the enjoyments which he so dearly loved, and Biron became as much the favorite of the receiver as he had formerly been of the Secretary of State. But his unlucky habit still pursued him like a vindictive demon, and plunged him anew into difficulties and dangers.

Kastelhorn had one day closed his accounts for the current year, and had just obtained a receipt in full signed by the Duke of Courland. The preservation of this paper he regarded as a matter of great importance, since his enemies, well aware of his dissipated habits, had long sought an opportunity of accusing him of embezzlement. He, therefore, delivered it to his Secretary, and charged him to take especial care of it. Now there was nothing in this paper to tickle the appetite of Biron, who had heretofore confined himself to the mastication of parchment. Yet the force of habit, a fit of absence, and the lapse of years having weakened the impression of his former disgrace, all combining, he inadvertently put it between his lips. It was no sooner there than the papyrivorous propensities of his teeth soon destroyed all traces of the duke's name, and when the fit of chewing was over, the injury was found to be irreparable. All the consequences of his first error now came strongly before him, without the hope a second time of escaping so easily. But remembering that, in that instance, the suspicion of infidelity which had attached to him was the cause of most of the hardships that he had suffered before his trial and acquittal, he determined to avoid their recurrence by a candid statement not only of the present error, but also of the one which he had committed at Stockholm.

The receiver-general fortunately looked upon the occurrence as a matter of pleasantry, and since the loss of the receipt could easily be replaced, he diverted himself for some time with the terrors of his frightened secretary. At length he restored him to confidence, and repaired to court to take proper measures for the replacement of the lost paper. The recital of the circumstances excited in the Duke of Courland a desire to see the young chewer of parchment ; and on his introduction at court, his good conduct and talents, together, perhaps, with one of those whims in which sovereigns are permitted to indulge, speedily secured to him the affections of the monarch, and he gradually arrived at the highest offices of the State.

But little more is known of the private history of Biron,

but it is scarcely to be supposed that his success in life, arising, as it originally did, from the indulgence of an idle habit,
would have had much influence in curing him of his pen-
chant for parchment.   At all events, whether he abandoned it or continued to cultivate it, it did not interfere with
his progress towards honor and celebrity.   The old Duke
in the course of time died, and our hero was transferred to
the service of the Empress Anne Ivanowna, to whose
kindness and partiality he was indebted for still greater
favors ; for in the annals of Courland we find encomiastic
mention of JOHN ERNEST DE BIRON, DUKE OF COURLAND.

———

CHILDHOOD AMONG THE TOMBS.

BY ALBERT G. MACKEY.

[These lines were suggested to the author by his seeing a troop
of children playing in the grave-yard of the German Lutheran
Church in this city.]

YOUNG ones, what do ye here 'mid awe and gloom ?
   Why have your footsteps hitherward been led ?
Let age alone hold converse with the tomb,
   And fell disease commingle with the dead.

But youth should seek some other spot for sport,
   Where gentle zephyrs round the rose-buds play,
Nor beard the monarch, Death, in his own court,
   And, heedless, trample on his destined prey.

Youth is the promise and the spring of life,
  Ere budding hope its blossom yet has blown,
When wanton malice and envenom'd strife,
  Still to the guileless bosom are unknown.

Then say! with you should Death communion hold?
  Ye're simple yet—let Death go seek the sage;
Ye're timid too—then let him face the bold;
  Ye're young—and Death should deal alone with age.

Then go not to the graves, or if you go,
  Go with your hearts more fitting for their gloom,
And whilst ye seek the homes of men laid low,
  Shock not by mirth, the silence of the tomb.

———

(From the "Times of Captain Willick.")

THE BOAT CHASE.

BY JOHN A. STUART.

"STRANGE!" said the captain, sweeping the horizon
with his spyglass, "that we see nothing of Trunkard and
Hilton. Raise that pine sapling at the head, that they
may be sure of us if they see us."

A few minutes after making this signal, we saw a boat,
also carrying a pine sapling at her head, outside the Bay
Point surf, on the side next the sea. It came nearly

opposite the point, and then rowed swiftly back and out of sight around the beach eastward. Two men, a short time after, walked down to the point, raised a sapling, planted it in the sand, and retired among the sandhills.

"Something wrong! They see us and answer our signal: but cannot venture out. We must break off fishing, and go to them at once. In with your lines, and up with the anchor!"

When this order was given, the whole aspect of the wide panorama, in the centre of which we floated, was undergoing a rapid change: and the deep noontide silence of nature, long unbroken except by the noise in our boat, was lost in the mingling of many sounds. First, a shoal of porpoises came plunging and puffing in from the sea, with antic leaps, turning head downward, and showing their flukes, as they went frolicking past us in the bay: then, an immense flock of sea-birds rose in a black oblique line from the bank to the south-east; gathered into a dense cloud; ranged themselves wedgewise into detachments, and wended landward: then a brisk breeze from the south-west swept its invisible mantle across the face of the watery mirror, tracking its march with blue, and waking the sleeping waves to rock us merrily with clamorous motion. The wind came in puffs; the clouds, which had been gradually marshalling in the south, were extending their columns; the frigate in the offing was scudding under shortened sail before the force of the gust, which had only brushed us with its passing skirts; and alluding to the white caps of the general mob of waves, and to the breakers on the banks now rearing their giant crests frantic and foaming, old Sam, not having the dread of the bathos before his eyes, said, quaintly enough, that

" Broad River was going to show himself, and had put on his *ruffle-shirt*." Cloud after cloud passed rapidly across the sun, throwing broad belts of indigo shadow athwart the bay, while between these the flashing billows gleamed like emerald chased with pearl in the narrow strips of sunlight that streaked the brine at intervals less and less frequent, until the whole landscape darkened into one sombre tone under the frown of the gathering storm.

Our anchor was shipped, and the boat trimmed, when, as he was balancing his oar for the first stroke, Old Sam pointed astern, and said, " Trouble comin'! Free Tony in de starn o' dat boat, mak sign to me."

We looked back: the canoe boat, which had been anchored above, just out of hailing distance, was laboring against the flood tide, and bearing down to us. The negro at the helm pointed rapidly and covertly to the marsh back of Bay Point, then to Paris Island, and, lastly, to the bottom of the boat; and, while he signalled to us with his opened palm. to hasten onward, I saw a white face, for an instant, above the gunwale near him. The discharge of a cannon boomed heavily from the schooner to the north ; and, simultaneously, as she attracted our attention, and we saw her with sails unfurled, beating down the river, a long dark boat shot rapidly out from the creek behind Bay Point Island, another from around the point of Paris's bank, and, in the canoe boat, now within musket range, about twenty men started up from their concealment; five or six sailors sprang to the thwarts, and ran out oars ; the rest were armed British soldiers.

" We must make for Bay Point or out to sea, as our only chance," said the captain, in a low voice to himself; and then cheerfully to the hands, " Stretch to your oars, boys !

there's no danger! Nothing this side of St. Helena can row with Devilfish. Put it to her lustily, and give the rascals a wide wake of dead water."

A volley of musketry rattled sharply from our pursuers, most of the bullets singing wide over head, a few splashing among our oars, or pattering against the side of the boat, and one carrying Maurice's new beaver by the board, and twirling it along the water.

"Shall we get our guns?" said William, eagerly.

"No! not yet. Uncase mine—but keep yours dry till we *must* use them."

The enemy had chosen a first-rate plantation-boat, and were evidently nearing us, although we seemed to flash through the waves, as, with a rolling sound, the oars rattled and rung upon our gunwales, in rapid but regular strokes.

"Sit down, Massa, for God sake!" cried Sam, as the captain raised himself, and stood to his full height. Without knowing his motive, the rest of us on the platform imitated him, and rose also.

"Down with you, boys! You'll spoil the trim of the boat. Silence, Sam! and pull," thundered the captain; and then, lowering his voice, said to me, "Our danger, James, is that the negroes may take a panic, and be good for nothing. Do all you can to cheer them."

Shot after shot now followed in quick irregular succession.

"Sit down, sir! you are hurt!" said I.

"Only skin deep," replied the captain, showing his arm, which was grazed and bleeding a little. "Cut loose those fish from the side! Maurice and William, throw the rest overboard; mind your oars, boys, and nothing else: row deep and don't catch crabs. You'll not be hit—they're firing at me, and over your heads. We hold way with them as the boat lightens: they don't gain on us now. Hand my gun. James! you put ball in one barrel?"

" Yes! the left!"

" Now, stop rowing a minute"—and he knelt on the seat and drew his aim. Old Thunder spoke! and the brawny sailor at the leading oar of the pursuing boat, bounced from his seat; his oar flew from the tholepins, and was swept away: he stood erect a moment, and fell backwards, with a crash, across the oar of the man next him.

" Now, Sam, make ready to raise the foresail, while they are getting to rights again. Load my gun with ball again, James, and cover the lock with your handkerchief."

" Trow away *all* de fish?" asked Sam beseechingly, as the proofs of our good luck were rapidly diminishing.

" No, save six: they'll about ballast us."

The captain was always considerate; for, with a pity more profound than from the bottom of my heart, I commiserate the man who never ate a fresh drum steak done crisp and brown to a turn.

" Foot the mast there! spreet the sail higher! Take the sheet rope, William! and now good bye to them."

But we had to do with salt water veterans. Their sail was rigged almost as soon as ours, and the distance did not widen between us, as both boats, under oar and sail, bounded across the mouth of the bay, in the direction of the sand bank on the bar. One of the other boats, cutting us off from the Bay Point shore, was approaching obliquely and rapidly on the left, while the other, taking no part in the chase, placed itself so as to intercept our return up Broad River or towards Hilton Head. Our case was

11

growing desperate: for, as the boat to the left compelled our round-bottomed canoe to steer more to the south, we ran too much in the eye of the wind to continue carrying sail, while they, enabled by their keel to run sharp on the wind, had both sails filled, and were rushing down upon us like a rocket. The canoe boat, immediately behind us, would, to be sure, be obliged to take in sail too, but even with the loss of one oar, she seemed to have the advantage of us in rowing ; and we had only to depend upon the ne-groes on board of her being our friends, and doing their best, and upon our guns.

" Take the helm, James, and give me my gun again !" said the captain, as striking our mast, which we were the first to do, retarded our progress, and brought the hos-tile canoe boat within range. He fired, and the soldier who held their sheet rope, after a short convulsion, was drawn overboard by the sail, and dragged in the water alongside, until the rope, which was twisted round his wrist, uncoiled, and he went down. The sail swung loose ; their boat gave a violent lurch to windward, took in water, and nearly upset. As she righted and struck her mast, the soldiers levelled their muskets ; but the cap-tain sent them the buck-shot from his right-hand barrel, which, if it did no serious execution, at least spoiled their aim, for they fired at random, and all their bullets went over us, except one, which gave William Dalton a smart flesh-wound in the shoulder.

" What are you about, William ?" said the captain, re-suming the helm, as the other, in a rage, was uncasing his gun. " We have had some revenge already ; save your shot for the tug ! Here, case up ' Thunder,' quickly ; look yonder !" and he pointed over the head of our boat. The clouds were arching up into a dark bow from the horizon, and moving rapidly in. The frigate, now entering the bar, vanished in the white mist beneath. A squall was at hand.

In a moment, with a stunning roar, and sweeping a sheet of spray from the short waves, which its violence would not suffer to swell into billows, it was upon us! Everything beyond the end of our oar-blades was wrapped in the dense cloud of rain and spray with which we were hurled backward; the useless oars drawn in, and the boat, which had been whirled round like a straw, steered right before the gust. We were about half a mile seaward of the bank, when the blast struck us, and, in the five minutes which it lasted, we were driven to about a quarter of a mile to the north-west of it. As it cleared, the waves began to rear themselves higher than ever ; the frigate, which had passed us unobserved in the driving haze, was seen making up the bay to the north, under reefed top-sails, having lost some of her upper spars. The more distant boat had vanished; but the other two occupied almost the same relative position to us, and re-commenced the chase. The wind shifted to south-east, dead ahead ; and all depended on rowing, as we again made for the outer edge of the bank. After a severe struggle, we had regained our lost ground, had passed the extreme part of the uncovered bank, and were almost on the long line of breakers that extended out for miles beyond. Both boats were now opening their fire upon us, at a distance uncom-fortably short, when the captain again arose. " Now, boys, for your last chance. The sand can't have shifted much since last month, when I was here. If we strike, ship your oars instantly, jump out, and shoulder her over the shoal, before the next wave fills her. They will scarcely follow here !" and he steered at right angles to our former course, and directly for the terrific reef. I have been among breakers before and since, and will not forget their sharp, biting, metallic dash, so different from the full pro-longed roar of the surge upon the level beach ; but never did I hear such a bewildering din as on that occasion.

Captain Willick's voice, however, rung clear above the crashing tumult. "Bend to her with all your strength !—three good strokes !—again ! again ! again ! now in with your oars !" We were lifted upon a surge so steep and high, that, to have come fairly upon the shoal from its summit, would have shivered our frail bark to atoms—"and the boldest held his breath for a time." Down we dashed ! but ere the rocking prow dipped again, it had been swept beyond the shallow, while the stern grated on the edge of the hard sand, with a shock so harsh as to demolish the rudder, and make the boat crack, shuddering through all her timbers. The cool eye of our pilot had hit the only and narrow strait through the lengthened shoal; and battered, and almost water-logged, we rode heavily on the comparatively smooth and deep basin that heaved within the swash.

Our oarsmen were at work again in an instant ; Maurice, William and myself labored as strenuously in baling out the water the boat had shipped, and which had increased rapidly as she had sprung a leak; while Captain Willick required all his skill and coolness to steer, with a broken oar in place of the lost rudder, through the still perilous though less desperate navigation of the numerous detached shoals, that yet frothed and grinned savagely across our course to the Bay Point shore.

The British keel boat necessarily abandoned the chase; her destruction must have been inevitable, had she approached the breakers nearer by a single oar's length: but, much to our alarm, and more to our astonishment, the other boat, finding that we had safely gauged the height of the tide, dashed through the same precarious channel, and came out, with seemingly less damage than ourselves.

"My life on it! there's an Islander in that boat!" said our gallant commander, as she burst forth from the jaws of the yeasty cataract of foam: "None other would have dared it! See now that our guns are dry. We shall need them. Only keep at long shot until we gain the beach, and we can land and let them do what they please with our shattered canoe."

After zig-zagging some time between the banks, we were describing the chord of an arc of breakers, which, connected with those we had crossed, curved on our right in the shape of a horse-shoe, to the Bay Point beach. Our chance of escape had brightened: only a single enemy was now in our wake; one of the keel boats we had safely fenced out by putting the breakers between us; and the other had disappeared,—wrecked, as we afterwards learned, on Paris's bank, in the squall. Our boatmen were the choice of three plantations; and, instead of flagging under their late arduous efforts, warmed and invigorated by the exercise and excitement, and fresh as when the pursuit began, bore themselves bravely and lustily. Their spirits, depressed at the first alarm, soon rebounded; and frequently, during the chase, throwing their right arms saucily into the air as they bent forward to give the oars their full sweep, they had whooped and jeered at the enemy. But the pursuing boat now pressed us harder than ever, sending us shot after shot, while her gliding prow flashed beautifully fierce, and her level lines of oars, like the wings of a kingfisher, dipped and rose, and dipped again, with a seeming ease and elasticity that was provoking. We were the first, however, to reach and shoot through the shallow channel between the shoal and the beach. It was so narrow, that the spray of the breakers, on the right hand, and of the surf along shore, on the other, mingled above our heads as we passed ; but, mauled as Devil-fish was, we thought nothing of this lesser peril, after our late escape.

"Now, stop rowing. As they come through, we'll give them a point blank salute of buckshot, and land through the surf. See to your flints and priming."

Sam drew from its concealment his long musket, which he had wrapped in his great-coat, and tied up in the sail which had not been in use.

"Mr. Willick," asked Maurice, "shall I shoot at the oarsmen ?"

"No! not at them. You, and William, and Sam, aim into the crowd astern. James and I will pay our respects to the three red-coats in her bows. Wait for the word! But see there !—see on the beach!" and our whole crew shouted a hearty cheer, as three white men and as many negroes rushed down the sands, from along the dead pines at high water mark, and wading waist-deep, fired into the British boat, while she was laboring midway in the strait behind us.

"It is Hilton and Trunkard! Nobly done !" shouted the captain, waving his hat to them. " Now for it! Back water, larboard oars! round with her, starboard oars! Now, pull away, all hands, and upon them! That will do! Steady her so! Aim well, boys, and fire!"—and we gave the hostile boat half the benefit of our double barrels, Sam winding up the volley with a hail-storm of slugs from his musket, followed by another cross-fire from our allies on shore.

The enemy were not passive, as I was made to feel by a sort of galvanic shock in my right side, that drove me, reeling, against the main thwart, with a goodly trench along my ribs; but they were too much disconcerted by the unexpected assault from the land, to return our fire with much effect. To increase their embarrassment, their four black oarsmen, swearing they could "stan' dis no longer," leaped overboard, and swam for the land; and the utmost labor and skill of the sailors remaining, could hardly keep their boat from being swamped in the surf. They put back, and were retreating when they received our second fire; and before the party on shore could re-load their pieces, they were out of the reach of our shot, and rowing, with the tide, toward Broad River.

HERE ARE ROSES.

BY EDWARD CARROLL.

Here are roses, fresh and blooming,
  Sprinkled with the morning dew;
Think, oh! think it not presuming,
  That I offer them to you.

Fresh, I found them, sweetly sleeping,
  At the balmy morning's rise ;
When Aurora just was peeping
  From beneath the eastern skies.

Soft, I stole them, without waking,
  From their slumber sweet and meek ;
And I culled them without shaking
  Dew-drops from each damask cheek !

Now awake, alas, they're weeping—
  Pearly tears are in their eyes—
For the friends which they left sleeping,
  Underneath the morning skies.

Kindly take them, and while pressing
  To your lips, a soft kiss lend ;
They will smile, and feel the blessing
  Of so pure and fair a friend.

STANZAS

BY WILLIAM ALLEN.

WHEN flowers are blooming fairest,
When gems are richest, rarest,
When every sound thou hearest,
  Hath music in its tone :

When joy is circling o'er thee,
When every form before thee
Beholds, but to adore thee,
    And make thy wish his own ;
Think, that those tones will grieve thee
Those gems, those flowers, will leave thee,
Those friends will yet deceive thee,
    And thou wilt be—alone.

But when sad hours are nigh thee,
When summer friends pass by thee,
When every joy shall fly thee,
    That late thy footsteps led ;
When memory, in sadness,
Reverts to days of gladness,
And stings thee even to madness,
    By whispering—they are fled ;
When thy soul's night hath no morrow—
From a thought that *now* is sorrow,
A balm thou then may'st borrow—
    " These are not with the dead."

THE WRECKERS: A TALE OF THE SEA.

BY J. A. HURLBUT.

THE fair blue waves of the Gulf of Mexico gently heaved in long rolls before the western breeze; the steamer

11*

cast loose from the various vessels she had brought down, and soon disappeared within the Balize. The different craft shaped out their respective courses, and gradually diverged from each other. Two, the American ship and the British brig, stood on the same course. Both were bound for Europe, and though the Milo far outsailed the Nimrod, yet they kept pretty much together, for the passes of the south of Florida bore no very good character then. Days passed, and still the favorable gale urged them on. Gradually it increased ; and ere long the American ship, under treble reefed topsails and storm jib, flew before it into the Florida stream. The wind blew fiercely, broad on the beam, as she hauled round the Tortugas ; and her experienced and kind-hearted captain hove to in that tremendous sea to wait for the Nimrod. In the course of the afternoon, the clouds rose heavy, dark and thick, crowding on each other from the eastward ; but still the wind hung in its old quarter, and flying before the gale, the stout English brig rushed madly into the stream.

The captain of the Milo wished to speak him, and reducing sail on his vessel, kept slowly on ; and as the Nimrod ranged up, gave his helm a sheer a-weather, and came into hailing distance. His clear voice rang through the howling of the tempest—"We shall have a heavy gale, and if you don't know this place well, you had better follow me ; keep just in my wake, and I'll try to lead you safe."

In a few minutes the Milo took the lead again, and with everything made fast and ready for the gale, pressed on in her dangerous track. The strong current of the Gulf, favored and increased by the wind, rolled in long mountain billows, which, though large and high, were not steep, but rose and fell in huge regular slopes. Up and down these the noble vessels rushed. No longer on the same elegant and taper rig in which she entered on the Gulf, the Milo was reduced to working masts only, her royals and light sails on deck, and her to'-gallant masts standing bare and stripped of the yards.

Under the little of her storm-sails that was shown, she flew on, bounding down the liquid mountain side like the freed and proud deer, while the showers of foam that rose high in air as her bows surged into the element, whitened the grim surface of the deep. Not far behind, plunged heavily on the English brig; collier-built, she could not compete in speed with the American packet ship, but still her black mass was urged through the waters with great rapidity. The piling clouds were black as night above, but skirted with a dull, dead, coppery hue, which was reflected on the raging waters. You might hear the distant growl of the muttering thunder as it rolled, gathering strength, through the unbounded arch of heaven,—dull and low in its first intonations, but rising in force of sound as it drew nearer, till it burst over head like the crash of a world. There was yet no lightning; but the hot, stifling, sulphurous atmosphere told of its presence, though invisible. The wind increased as the day fell; and before dark, both vessels, under bare poles, scudded before the gale. Suddenly the wind lulled away, and the huge waves ran rioting on, bearing the helpless vessels upon their foaming crests. The experienced captain of the Milo, well aware of the manner in which the storm would return, contrived to lay his ship, as much as possible, in the contrary direction from that they had hitherto pursued. There was a short breathing space, in which the elements girded

themselves up for their work. After a pause of a few minutes, a keen, dazzling flash sprang from the murky bosom
of the cloud, and was again swallowed up in the darkness.
The rattling shock of thunder instantly followed, and
with a rushing sound as of mighty waters, and enveloped
in a cloud of spray, the tempest burst out from the north-
east. So sudden and violent was the blast as to quell and
almost stop the roll of the billows, which, stirred by the
south-wester, and moving with the stream, had attained a
prodigious height. It fell upon the two vessels with equal
fury, and though the Milo was nearly before it, yet it poured upon her quarter with such force as to career her gunwale down, and away she went with the very smallest
piece of her storm try-sail set, and with three men lashed
to the wheel to keep her from broaching to.

The Nimrod was taken broad on the beam, and though
there was not a rag of canvass on her, she was pressed
bodily down ; but, fortunately, the succeeding wave struck
her on the quarter, with such force as to stave in her bulwarks, and heave her stern up into the wind. More
heavily built than the American, she was unable to keep
her in sight ; for as neither could show more than a yard
or two of canvas under the hurricane, it was impossible
for the captain of the Milo to reduce his fearful speed.
Still he hung out a light from the mizen-top ; though the
dashing of the rain, which now descended in torrents, and
the rolling and pitching of the vessel, soon extinguished
it. He hugged the wind as much as possible, and lay up
the channel from about Orange Key, where the wind first
shifted towards Cape Florida. The good ship was still
under command, and though she dashed with great violence into the precipitous trough of the cross sea, and there

strained up the unsteady ascent, still nothing had given
way; the cordage was strung like wire, but no rope had
failed, no bolt started. The wind hauled round more and
more to the north, and still more difficult was it to hold the
gallant ship up to her course; the strong undertow of the
gulf bore her on beyond the Cape, and she stood directly
in for the New Inlet. The clouds lifted far to the west,
and the low green shore of Florida appeared distinctly
right ahead. Still the fated vessel sped on, and a few
minutes would have seen her shivered and crushed upon
the beach. But at the critical period, when the foam of
the breakers might be seen from the deck, the wind hauled
again to the north-west, and the voice of the captain was
heard, as he ordered the head of the jib raised to pay her
off. The fierce wind seized it, and spite of lashings and
boltropes, blew it clear from the stay; but the head of the
ship was canted round, and she gradually gathered way
upon the other tack, the raging sea making a clear breach
over her. She plunged deep into the broad black breast
of the succeeding billow, and, when she emerged, from
stem to stern, the decks were clear of everything that
was not lashed down; the long-boat had broken from the
chocks, and, riven into fragments, disappeared in the boiling wave; and as the huge foam crest rolled away, the
convulsed and despairing motion of more than one arm
was seen amid the " yesty" froth, and the scream of the
drowning men heard above the triumphant shouting of the
tempest.

But the gallant ship was safe now,—the wind, though
still violent, was subsiding, and ere long she dashed by
the Great Isaac, through Providence channel, and under

reefed topsails and courses, came out upon the broad
Atlantic.

But where was her consort? After he lost sight of the
Milo in the distance, the English captain was thrown upon
himself; and, putting the brig before the wind, retraced
his course toward the Florida reef—and, running by that
dangerous ledge of rocks, stood on, till the change of wind
from the west and north compelled him to alter his course.
He ordered his helm down, and, calculating on the strength
of his vessel, risked the chance of injury to his spars from
the heavy roll, and wore her round. Unfortunately, as she
whirled rapidly round, she rose with her broadside on the
peak of a wave, and the full force of the gale striking her
in that position, she seemed to roll over to the trough
below. For a few moments she lay helpless and log-like,
tossed upon the billows, until her mainmast went by the
board, carrying with it the fore-topmast, and head of the
foremast. Slowly she righted—binnacle and everything
else, even to the caboose, swept from the deck, and the
wreck of the foremast still hanging on her lee. This,
however, answered a good purpose, for the resistance
caused by it threw her head farther round. The Englishmen, true tars, soon cleared her of this, and the dismasted
vessel rushed once more madly on. None of the hands
were lost; their time was not yet come. The compass
had gone with the binnacle, and the helpless vessel drove
on before the wind, unguided, and the sport of the storm.
At that fearful rate, they were not long in again traversing
the stream, and soon the long, low, sandy beach of Dog
Key lay just before them. The breakers ran in a long
career upon the shelving shore, gradually swelling till their
full bosoms burst in a sheet of foam. Then despair seized

on the seamen; but the captain, a man of iron nerve, took the helm, and, shouting to the men to hold on for their lives, put her bows on. She took the ground with a crash that shook every timber in her, and the foremast flew quivering like a reed far over the bow. The men, prepared for the shock, held on, though severely bruised and shaken; and again the groaning vessel was raised, and rudely set down upon the sand. Yet, violent as were the shocks, the English oak held its own; and the well compacted frame quivered and trembled, but did not part. The brig was laden with cotton, which, as usual, was packed with great tightness under the deck beam, and contributed materially to hold her together.

That long, long weary night did those ill-fated men cling to their vessel; and as the slow minutes passed, prayers from fainting souls went up in vain. Some, in the rage of despair, maddened by contemplating the horrors of their situation, threw themselves with frantic laugh into the boiling breakers. Others still clung to the shattered bulwarks until their energies were gone; when the fainting arms relaxed their grasp, and they sank quiet and without a struggle. When the red dawn beamed across the now cloudless east and tinged with roses the subsiding sea, but two were left upon the deck. The captain who, though a man of weak frame, had supported the terrors of the night, and one old weather-beaten seaman, inured to hardship in forty years' of exposure, remained sole tenants of the crewless vessel.

As the bright orb of day leaped up rejoicing from his stormy couch, they rose from the deck where involuntary devotion had prostrated them, and sadly grasped each other's hands. The rough cheek of the old tar was

channelled with tears, which all the danger he had undergone could not extort, as he looked in the withering countenance of his commander and saw his features, usually
so stern and composed, convulsed as he gazed upon his
shattered craft, and the formless and crushed bodies of his
crew dashed high upon the shore. For some moments
neither spoke; but at last the old seaman broke the
painful silence,—

"Bear a good heart, captain; what though we be laid
up high and dry on this here piece of shingle, the good
old Nimrod is under us yet, and sound from keels-on to
gunnel. My poor messmates is gone, to be sure; but
they've cast anchor in the port of Heaven, though their
passage there were summut rough." Here the old man
lifted his hands to his grey hairs in reverence, and his
eyes filled, and his strong deep voice trembled as he went
on. "Poor Bill Jones! did ye see him, sir, when he
slipped his cable? D'ye see, I made myself fast with a
double hitch to the stump of the mainmast; and Bill, he
comes and makes fast to the starboard head of the companion, but, poor fellow, he cast a slippery hitch over the
timber, and when the breaker came in, it carried him off
like a cork. He struck out manfully, but it pitched him
right bows on to the windlass, and smashed all his forward
timbers; and there was—Jol, too."

"For God's sake, Richards," interrupted the captain,
"say no more about it. Oh! it has been a night of horror;
but come, let us see what is to be done: the sea has gone
down, and we must try something."

"Why, your honor, it's all one to Bill Richards; but so
be as how it seems to me, that we is got nothing to do
but to rig a signal pole and put a distress flag on it; for,

d'ye see, the boats is all smash'd, clean entirely stove. See, there's a piece of the jolly hanging to the davits now ; but never mind, y'ur honor ; them wreckers 'll be here in the twisting of a marlinspike ; they scent out a wreck like a gull on a dead whale."

They soon raised a pole, and placed on it the union-jack reversed, as a signal of distress. The scorching sun rode high in Heaven, and yet no sail appeared. Thirst began to fix its hot fangs upon the shipwrecked men. But ere long, far in the blue horizon, gleamed a snowy speck. Was it the dipping wing of the tropic bird ? Again it rises, and nearer than before, and soon the large lateen sails of a felucca are distinctly to be made out, sloping backwards to the extremity of the taper yard. She comes down before the breeze ; but will she see the wreck ? A short time will decide. See ! she shifts her course a point or two away. " She sees us not, Richards ; but look again, she is brought up and comes down full upon us."

Gracefully riding over the swell, the low black craft came on ; her sharp bow dividing the waves, which sprinkled their spray upon the cane-work that raised her bulwarks. Into the very edge of the surf the light vessel came, and furling her sails, dropped anchor and hoisted out her boat. It was manned by a motley crew,— Spaniards, Indian and French. As they neared the wreck, the survivors raised a faint shout of welcome, which remained unanswered. The captain of the felucca, a swarthy and mustachioed Spaniard, called by his men Don José, spoke a few words in his own language to the crew, and they rapidly ran alongside and ascended the shroud ladder. The Englishmen ran to assist them up, and eagerly poured out thanks for their aid. The Spaniard asked them, " Are you all ?" The English captain replied, " We are the only two saved." Don José muttered awhile with his men, then asked again, " What is the cargo ?" To this the captain answered, "That there was a large amount of specie on board, and seven hundred and fifty bales of cotton." After another short consultation, the Spaniard called to his men, " Mata los, digo," and, coolly advancing to the Englishman, stabbed him to the heart as he reached out his hand to welcome him; while the crew rushed upon Richards, who vainly endeavored to resist, and striking him down with the boat-hook, tossed him overboard, and deliberately proceeded to rifle the brig of the specie and such other articles as they could stow. In the course of two hours they had carried off all that was portable, and setting fire to the brig, stood off to the southward. But their infernal plan failed; Richards, whose head was too hard to be easily broken, stunned and senseless, was borne by the tide to the beach; and when he recovered his reason, perceived the brig in flames, and the felucca standing off. Deeply did the despairing man curse the fiends, and earnestly did he cry to heaven not to suffer such crime to pass unpunished. Surrounded by the mutilated and tainted corses of his messmates, he sat anxiously looking out upon the horizon. Nor were his hopes disappointed. The American schooner-of-war Alligator was then cruizing in the vicinity, and the look-out reported that there was a vessel on fire, near, as he saw a huge column of smoke in the direction of Dog Key. In a moment, all the canvass she could bear was set upon the schooner, and in a beautifully tapering pile of snow-white sail, she passed

rapidly on ; the water ran in a sheet from the forecastle
aft to the quarter-deck, the scuppers were buried on the
lee, and the vessel sprang like a steed pricked by the
spur. In a short time she reached the burning brig ; and
the boat speedily lowered, rowed twice round her, but
found no one, and was about returning to the schooner,
when they heard the faint and husky halloo of Richards
from the beach. With parched and baking lips the
exhausted man vainly tried to speak, and the young mid-
shipman in charge of the boat, rightly interpreting his
signs, handed him a breaker of water. After a long
draught, he called hastily, " on board—on board ;" and, as
the boat returned to the schooner, repeated the tale. The
boat was instantly hoisted in, and the schooner's course
altered to the south-west. Far away in the distance was
the felucca. In vain did she press on to escape ; the full
breeze freshened as on purpose to aid the avenger, and
the noble schooner came up, hand-over-hand, bringing the
breeze down with her. The sun was setting as they ran
alongside, and at the crash of the meeting bulwarks,
thirty athletic seamen sprang on the low deck. A few
seconds of close and desperate struggle ensued, and Richards, cutlass in hand, led the way aft to the captain. At
sight of him, the miscreant trembled, for he thought the
dead had returned ; but taking courage from despair, he
fired, and the left arm of the brave seaman fell broken
above the elbow. With a loud and deep execration, the
undaunted Richards replied with the full sweep of his
weapon ; and the keen blade, vengeful and hissing, clove
him from shoulder to waist, and prostrated the ghastly
and withering corpse upon the deck. The struggle was
over, and the felucca taken in tow. The specie was

transferred, and the pirates committed to irons until their
arrival in Havana, where the last judgment of the law
passed upon them. Richards still lives, upon a pension
given him by the owners, and frequently whiles away
the tedious time by stories or rather " yarns" of past perils,
among which the above makes no inconsiderable figure.

MELODY.

BY WILLIAM WRAGG SMITH.

Ah ! when, in fancy dreaming,
   I gaze on thee, dear maid,
All nature's holy seeming
   Appears in thee portray'd !

The stars of heaven shine not
   More brightly than those eyes ;
While Love and Hope divine not
   Their tender mysteries.

The music of the forest
   Is glad when thou art glad ;
But, sweetest, when thou sorrow'st,
   The trees, they, too, are sad !

These flowers around us springing,
   Will die—will die, I'm sure ;

These birds all gaily singing,
   Will sing—will sing no more,

Whenever, dearest maiden,
   Those accents cease to speak,
And Beauty's blossoms fade in
   That fresh and rosy cheek.

THE VOLUNTEER.

BY ELIZA MURDEN.

Go, gallant youth, at honor's call,
   The glorious path to fame pursue ;
If in the conflict doom'd to fall,
   Your urn shall virtue's tears bedew.

And precious is the tear she sheds,
   To soothe the wounds which fortune gave ;
Or falling on the unburied heads,
   Which ruthless war denies a grave.

But oh ! as on the ensanguin'd plain,
   You victory's banner proudly rear,
With conquest flush'd, of prowess vain,
   Be yours the noble pride *to spare.*

O ! rather raise the bending reed,
   Than crush it rudely to the ground ;
Humanely close the veins which bleed,
   Not deeper urge the ghastly wound.

So shall the wreath, the fair entwine,
   The hero's generous brow to grace,
Unfading bloom with tints divine,
   Which envy never shall efface.

THE BEAUTIFUL.

BY J. D. B. DEBOW.

> Beautiful!
> How beautiful is all this visible world !
>   MANFRED.

THE truths of philosophy are the sober revelations of
the intellect; the truths of poetry are the lights of the soul,
the rapt visions of ideal glory, which shadow forth the high
destinies of the immortal. There is a head and a heart to
humanity; in the one originates the philosopher, in the
other the poet. With his abstraction, and his metaphysics,
dim thought sits upon the philosopher's brow ; but the
fervor, the devotion, and the enthusiasm light up the poet's
world. With man, the philosopher, we have no sympathy
now ; in the midnight, the taper and the closet, comes man,
the philosopher, with his diograms and his tomes : the

Bacon, the Locke, the Des Cartes, the Kant—a gloomy array. Our thoughts are rebellious under the restraint; they would wanton amid other prospects, they pant for the plenitude of freedom with man, the poet.

The Beautiful! how often have our souls been ravished with its contemplation! The Religious! has it not inter-woven itself with every fibre of our constitution! Can we say no more? Are the ideas independent and isolated, or do they harmonize and blend? Who has not sought for and realized the beautiful in the religious? The beautiful in the religious, does not the religious live and breathe in the beautiful? Search the heart, heedless mortal; there is more there than the loftiest flight of your philosophy has revealed; let the heart not repine at its ignorance, the heart will understand us.

The Beautiful speaks, and the soul answers from its depths; what if the sage only can reach the philosophy of its language, the whole world is possessed of its alphabet and its grammar. Go, sage, and in the sublime regions of thought and mathematics, build for yourself a world, and find a God; humble yourself before that God. Come, peasant, you have never heard of abstraction and mathe-matics—savage, leave your cave; is there need for a God to you—a God portrayed in the lineaments of mildness and of love? Take courage, the sensibility plays as im-portant a part as the intellect; poetry is as true as prose: both harmonize and work, both play their grand parts in the constitution of nature.

The Beautiful! Oh God! what a field have we to roam over here, what a miracle is this world to us; this world, with its features of loveliness, chiselled, and softened, and glowing! Plato, who can wonder that these fea-

tures had a soul within for thee, the soul of Beauty—
pierce through the eternal crust and reach it—the concen-
tration and the essence—God! God in nature, hear him,
see him, Θεος εν εμιν.* The thunders and the lightning,
the earthquake; the sky shakes and the heavens are convulsed. How dreadfully the flame darts! Splintered,
riven, how yon sturdy oak stretches forth its old arms from
the sapless trunk! Where have fled the vigor and the life
of yon fearful, blackened corpse? but a moment since, and
those livid lips were fair and warm to discourse of love.
Shrink back, Son of Earth, trembling, sinking; there is no
beauty here for you—there is fear. Nature makes other
revelations than those of the terrible, or man had never
yielded to the soft impulses of love; man had never been
religious.

The little infant—watch the gradual opening and development of mind. Does the darkness delight, or does it turn
to seek the light? Shut out the day's radiance and its gaze
is fastened upon the taper, it follows it; how its little arms
are outstretched to reach the moon! Man, watch that
infant—it smiles, the innocent smiles, those scarce developed features are not dumb, that infant already feels the
mysterious agency of the beautiful. Oh! who can tell in
the ignorance and darkness which surrounds us, and baf-
fles our inquiries, who can tell, but in that first thought is
fixed the incipiency of the idea, which, developing and

* We have no favor for the pantheism which exists in Plato.
Divinity may be found in nature without being confounded with it.
Plato's language is plain, ours figurative; he looked *into*, we
" *through* nature up to nature's God." Nor have we much sympathy for the transcendental philosophy which seeks to confuse all
things in its idealisms.

perfecting itself in after times, arrives, at last, on the con-
fines of thought, to acknowledge the Eternal—the Omnipotent—the God.

Throw away your books, philosopher, leave your closet
and your speculations ; the peasant has a lesson for you,
and will teach it cheerfully ; the poor Indian cares nothing
for your books and your closets. He has a book—it is
nature ; he has a closet—it is the world. See him bow to
the East, on Persia's shore, to greet the chariot of the
sun as it rolls along the sky. Is there error in that poor
Indian, to see

> " God in clouds, and hear him in the wind ?"

The worshippers of the Sun are the worshippers of the
Beautiful ; even the error, rather than the ignorance : " I
had rather believe," says Bacon, " in all the fables of the
Alcoran and the Talmud than that this universal frame is
without mind."

How touching, how exquisitely touching, the conception
of Magna Græcia's sage !* Was it not enough that the
old philosopher found all nature vocal here—the songsters
of the grove, the forest's dirge, the sublime ocean's roar,
the harp of Æolus !

> " Wild nature, warbling all beyond the reach of art."

* Pythagoras, who—
> ———— " the full consenting choir beheld ;
> And first discerned the sacred band of love,
> The kind attraction that to central suns
> Binds circling earths."—Thomson.

Is there even music beyond this empire of clay? Is it the characteristic of æsthetics to be terrestrial? Mount the sky, philosopher, upward, through the ethereal vault; softly, gently. What touch was that that swept the strings? Distant melody, scarce audible, like angels' whispers; rising, swelling, it breaks upon the ear—entrancing! ecstacy! Eternal strains of melody and song! harp strung with worlds, and swept by the minstrelsy of God! Do we dream how much we are indebted to music, when the soul feels its imperishable essence—when the bonds gall it, the crime disgusts it, the fetters break and the spirit soars, revelling amid worlds, and suns, and systems, on the bosom of eternity?

> " Music religious hearts inspires,
>   It wakes the soul, it lifts it high;
> It wings it with sublime desires,
>   And fits it to bespeak the Deity."—ADDISON.

What sermons, too, the fragile flowers of the field preach! Is the language of the flower but the fiction of the poet? Is the primrose " the primrose, and no more?" Heartless man! Have you never conversed with the flowers of the field when the dew-drop glistened on them, and they turned their heads to Heaven? Go, dwell at the pole, where the ice congeals into the mountain, and the snows never thaw; you have not known love, you have not known religion. These flowers have been painted to mirror forth the beautiful; and why the beautiful? God has not made them—

> —————— " to blush unseen,
> And waste their sweetness on the desert air."

Let us be instructed by their touching lessons ; and when the heart is breaking, and every hope and prospect seems withered and crushed, seek the garden and converse with the flowers.

Woman, too—fair, beautiful woman ! how she transports us, bewildered, to heaven !—how she breaks the ice that congealed at the heart ! The crime flies at the rebuke of her presence. Encircled by the fiery swords of the cherubim which waved around Eden, she is protected for ever from the advance of impurity ; a soft, steady, exhaustless lamp, to guide the virtuous to safety and to God !

> " Your lover is little better than a pagan ;
> On the heart's shrine he rears a human idol,
> Imagination heightens every charm—
> Brings down celestial attributes to clothe it,
> And dupes the willing soul, until at length
> He kneels unto a creature of the brain—
> A bright abstraction."

But where are the mountains and the valleys—the fountains, the cascades, and the Niagaras—the rainbow—the borealis—the deep sky, studded with suns—the pebbles—the shells—the grottos ? Are these voiceless—or have they their revelations too ? Ah, yes ! man feels among them, as one has eloquently expressed it, " that he is surrounded with holiness "—that " nature is holy." Amid such holiness, can impiety and vice hold up their heads, and live ? Must man be the only exception, and introduce deformity into the world ? He cannot, dares not mar this picture ; even the savage confesses it, when he turns and stays the pointed shaft, to apologize and obtain the pardon of the variegated serpent he is about to slay.

From how many thousand forms of matter did Milton cull the loveliness which his fancy threw around the garden of Paradise? The garden lived in the poet's mind; but he had gathered its elements amid

> " Beautiful forms, and eyes that are made
> Of sunbeams—with softest dew-drops arrayed."

" The mountains are my altars," exclaimed one of the brightest and most gifted of the sons of men, when accused of irreligion—

> " Creation's heir!
> The world—the world is mine!"

Was the enthusiastic exclamation of another, when impoverished, and without any of this world's distinctions, he stood upon the mountain's brow, to reach the distant vision. What a crime were it for such men to sin! Here, amid these scenes, the heart glows and enlarges; here the inspiration and the fire descends, which, touching the lips, transforms the meanest of us into a poet—our littleness and our greatness rushing, in their overwhelming might, upon the soul. Happy man! with the universe for a college, and every atom for a preceptor!

Oh God! we thank thee for this feeling that thou hast implanted within us, and the thousand modifications of the universe which call it into exercise. Let our souls be ever alive to the contemplation of the beautiful; let us feel its holiness and its religion; and, rising from the forms on which thou hast implanted it here, let the heart, purified from the dross of mortality, break the glass which dims its vision, and ascend to the divine contemplation of HIM, who combines within himself every lineament and every element of the beautiful!

———

THE NIGHT STORM.

BY THOMAS RADCLIFFE SHEPHERD.

Now gloomy night outspreads her sable wings,
　And a deep silence o'er the vale is cast,
Save where some solitary sheep-bell rings,
　Or dry leaves rustle in the boisterous blast.

Save that from yonder mournful aged yew,
　The moping owl just rais'd her boding screech,
Or the shrill whistle of the lone curlew,
　Sounds o'er the windings of the sandy beach.

See! the pale Cynthia darts her silver beams,
　The envious mists disperse, her orb unshrouds;
Then on the whit'ning surge uncertain gleams
　Through the dark covert of surrounding clouds.

Now horror broods upon the troubled main!
　Fierce swelling waves roll to the pebbly shore;
Thick dark'ning clouds pour down the driving rain,
　And angry winds like solemn thunders roar.

The spirit of the tempest shouts aloud!
　Starting I see the foaming breakers near,

That o'er fell shoals in wild disorder crowd,
  Whilst peals of thunder rumble through the air.

The storm increases, fiercer winds arise :
  And lo ! the moon withdraws her wonted ray,
Whilst vivid lightning streaks the flashing skies,
  And adds more horror to the dreadful fray.

GERMAN GRAVE-YARDS.

BY THOMAS CANTE REYNOLDS.

To a casual observer the Germans do not appear to be
a people of very deep feeling : but one has only to become
more closely acquainted with their habits and usages, to
see that quite the contrary is the case.   In nothing is this
more apparent than in the manner in which they " bury
their dead out of their sight."   A neglected grave-yard is
a thing unknown in the father-land of the German.   Order
reigns in the gravelled walks and well-trimmed shrubbery
of the " city of the dead," and each grave, even the low-
liest, bears traces of the care of the living, whose hearts
have not ceased to yearn after those who have preceded
them on the way to the bourne from which no traveller
returneth.   Green turf is carefully laid over the newly-
made mound which covers the remains of a cherished one ;
nor does the unsightly clay, as with us, offend the eye, by
breaking the soul-soothing continuity of the green sward.

Rose-bushes and other shrubs, planted near or on the grave, are so many monuments of the first gushes of grief, while the fresh garlands which lie on the mound, or are hung on the tomb-stone, evince the continuance of that feeling when the last mortal remains of its object are no longer to be distinguished from the surrounding dust. Even distant ancestors are not forgotten in this touching and poetic usage by descendants on whom, even in infancy, their eyes have never rested. The pious offering is laid by the German on the graves of forefathers whom he knows but by name.

But it is on All Saints' Day that this national custom assumes its most striking form. The emptiness of the streets, the hushed hum of the quarters where business is wont to draw the eager and active crowd, announce that the population has left its accustomed occupations to join in some general rite. On the highways to the cemeteries (always out of the city), the slow and measured tread, the sombre dress, and mourning air of the pedestrian, disclose its religious and melancholy nature. In the grave-yard itself may be seen the rich and the poor, the lowly and the proud, the monarch himself and the humblest menial of the peasant's household, bending alike before the majesty of the Destroying Angel, and confessing the truth in holy writ, that dust they are and unto dust shall they return. The grey-locked sire mourns there over the flower which was plucked from him when just budding into womanly beauty; the manly figure of youth there renews the grief which overwhelmed his soul, as the guide of his infant footsteps was laid in her last resting-place; there, over the grave of him who won her in her youth, and guided and protected her as time fled on in Hymen's silken bonds, the widow recalls the memory of a husband's love, and bids her offspring join her in thanks to the God of the widow and the orphan, who has guided their footsteps in peace and smoothed for them the rugged paths of adversity. Nor is the spirit of him who has perished a stranger in a strange land, and been borne to a tomb afar from the resting-places of his kindred, forgotten in the orisons of the pious : for him does holy mother church offer up her prayer, and on his grave do her ministers lay the emblems* of that eternal bliss which she has in store for all her children, while she seizes on the solemn occasion to admonish the living that—

> " All the souls that are were perfect once ;
> And He, that might the vantage best have took,
> Found out the remedy."

Sobered and bettered do they return from the silent home of the dead to the busy mansions of the living, while hope and religion whisper to them, with a still small voice, that all is not gloom beyond the grave. Truly, aye truly, the house of mourning is better than the house of feasting !

* Garlands, called *immortelles*.

THE SISTERS.

BY WILLIAM J. RIVERS.

" Omnes eodem cogimur ; omnium
Versatur urna ; serius ocius
Sors exitura."

HORACE.

ON earth, an angel robed in power appears,
To call the happy few whom heaven ordains,
In tender youth to change their mortal birth,
And all its woes, for an eternal bliss.

Two gentle sisters, fresh in innocence,
At life's fair, flowery entrance gates, were seen
To walk in sweet embrace ; and love had placed
A smile on both their cheeks.   Like gentlest birds,
From grove to grove with blithesome steps they roved ;
And twining rose-bud garlands in their curls,
They wandered joyous on, o'er hill and dale,
In thoughtlessness of bliss ; or bending o'er
The minor surface of the sleeping lake,
They watch'd the passing summer-clouds beneath.
And when the breezes rustled near, they drew,
With simple hearts, each other from the brink ;
As though the pool were deep as it appear'd,
And filled with clouds, far down, below the earth.

Alas! I knew those tuneful sisters well,
And loved the bloom upon their smiling cheeks!
Nor yet the first green leaf had droop'd and died,
And fallen into its grave,—'ere they were called,
And heaven's glad inmates bade them welcome home.
As when the moon, at mid-day, seeks the west,
Serene amid the troubling clouds,—they moved
In melancholy meekness to the tomb.
And lilies with the modest violets joined,
And daisies pure, and fragrant jasmine vines,
In sweet memorial, sprang spontaneous there.

THOUGHTS ON SPRING.

BY JAMES W. SIMMONS.

Spontaneous and involuntary is the gratulation with
which we welcome, always, the return of Spring! The
aspect and the voice of Nature, at this, the most auspicious period of the year,—when winter has furled his icy
banners and retired to his chambers in the north; and
gentle airs and odorous blooms, which " whisper whence
they stole their balmy sweets,"—give token of a milder
and benigner influence, shed by the ever-merciful hand of
Him who

   " ————— paints the lily,
  And throws a perfume o'er the violet,"—

appeals touchingly and irresistibly to the mind of man.
He who is not dead to the better sympathies of his being,
must feel pleasurable emotions, then, when at this season
of paradise, he casts his eyes over the visible creation.
No " petty griefs or evils of a day" should have the effect
of shutting his heart upon the scene—it were almost sin,
it were certainly selfishness to do so—unless, indeed, he
have cause to exclaim, in the affecting language of the
inspired volume,—" the foxes have holes, and the birds of
the air their nests, but the son of man hath not where to
lay his head." But even if he have such cause, there is
something beautiful in the thought, and touching in the
fact, that grief loses a portion of its asperity when the
light of Heaven is permitted to visit it, and the glorious
company of stars to keep, as it were, vigil over it; and
the blessed air, with healing on its wing, comes to bathe
its brow and breathe a balm into its breast! It is only
the damp dungeon and the clanking chain, that shut out
hope!—it is only *there*, " where hope comes not, that
comes to all,"—that the immortal spirit droops and forgets
its destination! Let it take the wings of the morning,
and be free to commerce with the broad heaven, the
boundless ocean, or the wilderness ; or, if its aspirations
be less lofty and more gentle, let it wander amidst the
beautiful mounds and terraces of nature—its verdant
walks and mild acclivities, and at "dewy morn," within
the " horizontal shadow of its woods,"—and there will
come a voice, and there will be a presence with power to
soothe, and, as it were, to disembody its then emancipated
energies ; and in that momentary but blissful sublimation
of the better part of the Creator's work, the more earthy
and transient portion of the creature will be forgot! The

most affecting trait in the character of Rousseau was
developed by virtue of influences like these. In the
crowd, the crush and hum of Paris, the man of genius
became merged—if not in the man of pleasure—at least
in the circumstances of *place*—its vain passions and vile
irritations—the petty triumph, and the paltry prize !—but
(and the circumstance is recorded by Mad. de Staël) once
alone with nature—enshrined, as it were, within her
sacred temple ! with all her glorious emblems and magnificent forms around him, appealing silently but irresistibly to his better and unchecked sympathies—and the
mere, miserable world he had left behind him, was in that
precious moment forgot ! He cast it from him, as the
fabled warrior would have done the poisoned garment
that preyed upon his vitals ; and, lifting his spirit up to
heaven, soaring through nature up to nature's God ! he
was no longer the poor citizen of Geneva, contending
with low wants—mixing, constrained with coxcombs,
knaves and fools—obnoxious to those missiles of malice,
which the base, the brutal, the envious and the ignorant,
were ever ready to launch from their petty quivers at his
fame ; but the emancipated man of genius ! released from
the trammels of the world at Paris, to commune, free and
unfettered, with the great world of the Universe around
him.*

* Rousseau's " Confessions" have been triumphantly appealed to,
as furnishing conclusive evidence, that the most abject moral little-
nesses may sometimes be allied to the highest gifts of the understanding ; but, I apprehend, with very little success. In that
singular work, we detect the waywardness, the irritability and the
absorbing pride and sensitiveness of the " Apostle of Liberty ;"
we are there led to sympathize with the moral infirmities of the

Thus it was, that when having attained the summit of a hill, whence the eye wandered over wood and vale, Rousseau's friend and companion was preparing himself either for some flight of fancy, or for some profound moral reflection, such as he thought the scene around them was most likely to elicit from the inspired genius beside him,—the latter took up a piece of straw, and began playing it between his fingers—apparently unconscious of what he was doing; and unmindful of the presence of his astonished and disappointed friend! His companion, with a perhaps pardonable vanity, incident to men of ordinary minds, who, when accidentally thrown into temporary fellowship with genius, on rare occasions, indulge in the weakness of anticipating, always, what is called a "scene," had, as usual, prepared himself to be regaled with some of those "Memorabilia," which generally find a place in the portfolios of tourists; something to be set down; no matter what; a word, a gesture, or a look; and was thus not a little chagrined at having to record nothing beyond the simple fact of Rousseau playing with a piece of straw!

Such is the wholesome influence, such the divine

man of genius; there is much to condemn; a great deal to regret and deplore—but nothing to despise. Instead of commencing his career as a needy and obscure adventurer in letters, emanating from the shop of a poor watchmaker at Geneva, had Rousseau's genius suddenly and brilliantly burst upon the world, aided and advanced by the imposing auxiliaries of rank and fortune—together with the stirring and stimulating recollections of a distinguished ancestry; there is, perhaps, no predicting how nearly parallel might have been his career, both as a man and a writer, with that of the gifted and not less unhappy author of " Childe Harold."

efficacy exercised by nature over the hearts of those who
have an eye for the charms, and a soul for the language,
which she addresses to them. The tendency of both is
to meliorate and simplify the elements within us ; to make
us the children of her love !—a love which, unlike that of
the world, or its fashion, "passeth not away ;" a love
which misfortune cannot chill, distance estrange, nor
time abate. There is no moral so touching as that which
nature seems to inculcate when she puts on the livery of
Spring. The pyramids—the haughtiest monuments of the
genius and pride of man—will have crumbled, and been
levelled with the dust, whilst the grass, which now grows
at their base, is destined to be renewed from day to day,
"unto the last syllable of recorded time !" There is no
moral like mortality ! and yet, in the most secret nook of
nature, in the most humble flower, those who are not
"slow of faith," may detect some type, some living
emblem, of the soul's immortality ! Nothing dies that is
not destined to live again. The little modest violet, nipt
by the frost, or rudely shaken from its stem, and rifled by
the hand of man,—puts forth its innocent head again in
May, "stealing and giving odor ;"—

> " But when shall Spring visit the mould'ring urn,
> O when shall day dawn on the night of the grave ?"

ODE TO FANCY.

BY GEORGE HEARTWELL SPIERIN.

[Who died at sixteen.]

AIRY, magic-sceptred maid,
In what consecrated shade,
Through what unfrequented grove,
Tell me, dost thou deign to rove ?
Say, what lonely valley most,
May thy heavenly presence boast ?
From what mountain's awful height,
Dost thou view the realms of light ?
On what solitary shore,
Pausest thou to hear the roar
Of old ocean's briny waves,
Dashing through their gloomy caves ?
Nature's daughter, free as air,
In what happy fav'rite sphere,
Sorrow-soothing Fancy, tell,
Dost thou most delight to dwell ?
Parent of each tuneful muse,
O'er my soul thy sway diffuse ;
Thou who taught'st so long to please,
Epic Melisigenes,
Thou who Pindar didst inspire,
Who wokest to love Anacreon's lyre,
By whose influence Maro stole
Great Octavia's tender soul ;

Teach the lay that praises thee,
Eloquence and Poesy :
Thou whose shadowy awful form
Ne'er shuns the fervid heat nor storm,
With bosom bare, and zone untied,
Whose tresses Nature's beauties hide,
Enraptur'd maiden, tell me why
So wildly rolls thy lucid eye ?
Ah ! why that sudden start, that stare,
Delirious burst of wild despair ?
Heart-rending sighs, the throb of bliss,
Those tears of wo, or happiness—
O ! show the visions that control
This sensibility of soul !
Drawn by winged delusions far,
Seated on thy airy car,
Thou, who soar'st sublime on high,
Over earth, and sea, and sky,
Where no mortal's humble sight
Can pursue thy rapid flight ;
Thou who in thy ceaseless course,
Searchest being to its source,
Say, from what first cause began
The mysterious soul of man ?
Did it e'er exist before ?
Shall't be after death no more ?
Is the wond'rous human mind
To nonentity consign'd ?
Is not perfection found afar,
In regions of some brighter star ?
Mysterious strange ! thought cannot dare
To follow further—Fancy, spare !

Plato alone could search with thee,
The realms of dark futurity.
Fearless maiden, let us haste
Through the battle's stormy waste,
Where destruction's terror spread
O'er the dying and the dead ;
Where ambition, glory ride,
Dreadful, through the purple tide ;
While from earth freed spirits rise,
And, groaning, seek their native skies ;
Let us seek, thou maid divine,
Melancholy's darkest shrine ;
Let us roam, at midnight hour,
Through some lonely, haunted tower,
From whose turrets, ivy-grown,
The owlet makes her fearful moan ;
Where now its low-laid owners lie,
The wild storms rage, the breezes sigh,
Its lofty domes repeat no more
The midnight bacchanal's loud roar :
Long unremember'd, in the dust,
That bourne they've sought, which all men must ;
Their mould'ring tombs now scarce appear,
And long has ceased the kindred tear ;
In gloomy silence all is drown'd,
While superstition reigns around.
Fancy, let us lightly tread
O'er the mansions of the dead,
Where departed spirits stray,
Till Aurora usher day ;
'Mong mould'ring tombs, whose only pride
Is, that some mortal lived and died,

Reflecting through the shades of night,
In polish'd rays, the moon's pale light,
We'll stray, or pensively reclin'd,
Oft listen to the passing wind,
Which wafts the solemn midnight knell
Of some lone ghost-toll'd abbey bell.
In thy airy skiff we'll glide
Down the Shenandoah's tide,
Where the blue ridge bending o'er,
Seems to threat us from the shore,
Till we meet Potomac's flood
Winding through the neighbor wood,
Where the confluent streams essay,
Roaring wide to force their way
Through the mountain's fractur'd base,
Almost tumbled from its place,
Where some dry rock affords a seat,
While pours the swift tide at our feet;
While the vast sheeted water spreads
A fearful gloom high o'er our heads;
Where Niagara's dashing spray
Wantons with the sportive ray,
We'll view the many-color'd bow,
Resplendent in the spray below;
We'll view the Indian, strong and brave,
Plunging down th' affrighted wave;
Or hunt the swift deer through the brake,
Or skim, in light canoe, the lake.
Lead me to those lonely shores
Where the vast Atlantic roars;
Where, against the rocky steep,
Groans the " many-sounding deep;"

While the moon, with silv'ry ray,
Emulates more fervid day ;
While each rock reflects her beam,
And surrounding billows gleam ;
While pure æther, clear, serene,
Beautifies, star-gemmed, the scene ;
While the music of the waves,
Rolling through their gloomy caves,
Soothes with exquisite control,
The passionless, creative soul.
How sweet, O maid ! with thee to try
Excursion through yon boundless sky ;
To leave this world's corruption here,
And spotless seek some happier sphere,
Where no unworthy passions bind
To ignorance, th' immortal mind ;
Where all perfective spirits rove
Through endless scenes of endless love ;
Where thou alone dost rule their will,
To seek perfection higher still.
How sweet to hear the wild notes swell
From the mermaid's plaintive shell,
Who in her scaly glitt'ring car,
Shines on the tumbling wave afar,
At midnight hour when toil-opprest,
Busy mortals sink to rest ;
Moments like these, more joys impart
To the grief-torn, afflicted heart,
Than all the pleasures pomp and pride
E'er to the sated sense supplied :
Say, what this splendor, balls and beaux,
The midnight masquerade and shows,

The flattering smile, the courtly air,
The silly titterings of the fair,
To that intellectual bliss,
Which alone is happiness?
Maid! from thee, what terrors rise,
To the guilty wretch's eyes,
How thy spells his bosom tear,
How thy dreams create despair;
Tho' no witness to the deed
Saw th' assassin's victim bleed,
Fancy still the scene portrays,
And the wretch himself betrays:
In ev'ry form a ghost he sees,
Groans oft he hears in ev'ry breeze;
When sleep his heavy eyelids close
In restless, painful, short repose,
In every dream he sees him die
With all the pangs of agony;
The last sad moan e'en still he hears,
The piteous prayer still racks his ears;
In vain amusement, pleasure vain,
Still fancy haunts his tortur'd brain!
O! thou, whose strange mysterious power
Rules the visionary hour,
Parent of dreams, whose magic sway,
Grief, and joy, and hope obey,
At thy command our sorrows fly,
And all the pangs of memory;
Thy blest delusions strife destroy,
And wretchedness convert to joy;
Mis'ry's victim, soothed by thee,
Is all his heart could wish to be.

When relaxing toil shall steep
In the balm, each sense of sleep,
To mine humble couch repair,
On thy flying car of air ;
Though far distant realms divide,
O ! place Eliza by my side ;
Then let her bless my longing sight
With ev'ry innocent delight,
Till morn's intruding beams destroy
The sweet futility of joy ;
I ask no more, one single kiss
Suffices for terrestrial bliss;
Were here too great a portion giv'n,
All claims were lost to joy in heav'n.
What pleasure from such visions springs,
Where kings are beggars—beggars kings !
The am'rous boy, whom love inspires,
Tastes ev'ry bliss his heart desires ;
The youthful untried hero there,
Learns to conquer, learns to spare ;
And I who tune the youthful song,
Claim honor in the Muses' throng,
Whilst immortality my name
Writes in the lasting book of fame !

MENTAL STRUCTURE OF HUGH S. LEGARÉ.

BY B. S. CARROLL.

Mr. LEGARÉ's ability as a scholar has been implied in what we have said of him as an orator. There were few languages, dead or living, with which he was unacquainted ; and of the modern, there were scarce any of them which he could not fluently speak. It was, however, to the classic literature of Greece and Rome he devoted most of his attention ; and how intimate he made himself with the learning of those countries, is best inferred from his magnificent disquisitions on subjects connected with it. His reviews will be found not only equal in ability to those of any living writer, but for the most part, abler. We say this, not at random. Take those for instance, on Roman literature, on the Roman orators, on Demosthenes, on the Democracy of Athens, on the Civil Law, in a word on all the various subjects of literature and jurisprudence upon which he has written, and there will be recognized in them, a fullness of material, an originality of thinking, a rigidness of reasoning, and a justness of conclusion, which no writer of his day has surpassed, and very few of them have equalled. In his published eloquence there is no one in this country, with whom a comparison of him might be instituted. William Pinckney possessed the same order of mind ; his argumentative and logical powers were perhaps more rigid ; but he wanted the full learning and suggestive memory, which permitted nothing it had once taken in, ever to escape, and which, on all occasions, not only supplied him with the proper thought and word, but the very best thought, and very properest word, the most fastidious critic could require. In copiousness of classical learning, though not in the mode of its application, Edward Everett is, in every respect, his equal. Whatever Mr. Legaré read, became his own by re-creation ; in which respect, his mind resembled the properties of a certain metal, we have sometimes seen, thrown into mineral liquids ; it at once possessed the power of taking from the solution its solid parts, and precipitating them in forms of dazzling beauty. His only prototype is to be found among the models of British eloquence and genius. And in looking for those combinations of qualities, which constitute his peculiar excellence,—for lofty genius, blended with exact knowledge,—for elegance of exposition, with depth of thought,—for acuteness to perceive, ingenuity to plan, and perseverance to mature,—for principles with facts,—philosophy with practical illustrations,—maxims of abstract wisdom with correct characterization of men,—for all these high attributes of genius and full acquirements of mind, Mr. Legaré, with less originality, though with finer taste,—with more beauty, but less splendor,—with not so much strength, but with greater dignity, can only find his superior in Edmund Burke.*

It would be a task of much delight, did our limits permit us to substantiate this apparently large assertion, by an analysis of some of the more striking merits of Mr. Legaré's writings. But we must content ourselves, while we invite the reader to examine their beauties for himself. They

* See Prior's Life of Burke, Chap. XV.

may be read over and over with profit and delight; and apart from the solid masses of learning the student will acquire in their perusal, he will be taught how the simplest words in our language may be dignified by a fit use of them; and how the most ornamental and showy will appear only proper, when used to finish, and not merely to embellish, discourse. In imitating his own classic model, he will learn the inappreciable advantages of being, as Mr. Legaré was, a perfect scholar; and, in studying as he studied, to use his own language, "the student will have his taste formed, his love of letters completely, perhaps enthusiastically awakened, his knowledge of the principles of universal grammar perfected, his memory stored with the history, the geography and the chronology of all antiquity, and with a vast fund of miscellaneous literature besides; his imagination kindled with the most beautiful and glowing passages of Greek and Roman poetry and eloquence; all the rules of criticism familiar to him; the sayings of sages, and the achievements of heroes indelibly impressed upon his heart. He will have his curiosity fired for further acquisitions, and find himself in possession of the golden keys, which open all the recesses where the stores of knowledge have ever been laid up by civilized man. The consciousness of strength will give him confidence, and he will go to the rich treasures themselves and take what he wants, instead of picking up eleëmosynary scraps from those whom, in spite of himself, he will regard as his betters in literature. He will be let into that great communion of scholars throughout all ages and all nations— like that more awful communion of saints in the holy church universal—and feel a sympathy with departed genius, and with the enlightened and the gifted minds of

other countries, as they appear before him, in the transports of a sort of vision beatific, bowing down at the same
shrines and glowing with the same holy love of whatever
is most pure and fair, and exalted and divine in human
nature. Above all, our American youth will learn that
liberty—which is sweet to all men, but which is the passion of proud minds that cannot stoop to less—has been
the nurse of all that is sublime in character and genius.
They will see her form and feel her influence in everything that antiquity has left for our admiration,—that bards
consecrated their harps to her,—that she spoke from the
lips of the mighty orators,—that she fought and conquered, acted and suffered with the heroes whom she had
formed and inspired; and after ages of glory and virtue,
fell with him—her all accomplished hope—him, the last of
Romans— the self-immolated martyr of Philippi. Our
young student will find his devotion to his country—his
free country—become at once more fervid and more enlightened, and think scorn of the wretched creatures who
have scoffed at the sublime simplicity of her institutions,
and ' esteem it,' as one expresses it, who learned to be a
republican in the schools of antiquity, ' much better to
imitate the old and elegant humanity of Greece, than the
barbaric pride of a Norwegian or Hunnish stateliness,'
and, let us add, will come much more to despise that
slavish and nauseating subserviency to rank and title,
with which all European literature is steeped through and
through."

*   *   *   *   *   *   *

His sensibility was acute to a fault—and at times so
much diseased, that he suffered himself to believe he was

designedly neglected, where the apparent slight might be traced to his being unknown. He forgot, that where every one is exhibiting his own wares, and huckstering them to the best possible advantage, he who shuts himself up in a closet ought not to complain that his superior value is not appreciated. This was Mr. Legaré's case; it is a great error, therefore, to charge upon his State the want of a just reward for his merits. All he aimed at, he attained. The first wish of Pericles was to make Athens the chief city of Greece, that he might become the most illustrious of her citizens; the same sentiment actuated Mr. Legaré. By line upon line, and precept upon precept, he labored to improve the literary taste and scholarship of his native State,—not, we confess, with the single gratification of seeing her the most polished and adorned, but, like Pericles, that he might enjoy the honor of being the first son of so excellent a parent. He wished to become the most distinguished orator, the best scholar, and the first jurist among his competitors; and, wherever he was known, he was appreciated as such. If the popular breath did not sound his praise when the less deserving were lauded, it was because he had never cared to court such favor. He labored for that fame which is built of more enduring materials. To borrow a fine passage of his, he knew " that sorrow is knowledge; that if in much wisdom there is much grief, the reverse is also true, and that adversity is the only school in which genius and virtue are permitted to take the highest degrees." His was that deep love of ideal beauty,—that passionate pursuit of excellence in the abstract,—that insatiable thirst after perfection in art for its own sake, without which no man ever produced a master work of genius.*

———

COGDELL'S BUST OF BISHOP DEHON.

BY EDWARD PHILLIPS.

ART did so well to fashion thee, pale bust,
Like him, still lov'd, who slumbers in the dust,
One dares to wish the chisel could but give
Promethean fire, and make the marble live.
Here are those features, calm and holy now,
As when life's ray gleam'd on that classic brow ;
The very face, as true as sculptur'd clod
Could imitate the workmanship of God.
Remembrance must its few defects supply,
The speaking smile, the mild expressive eye :
And more than these, what skill cannot impart,
The glory beaming from the good man's heart.
When thought like this appears, time stops his flight,
To travel back through childhood's life and light ;

* In the same letter alluded to, in a former note, Mr. Legaré says, " there is a saying, and, indeed, a true one, that sorrow is knowledge, *nocumenta documenta*, but commend me to the oppo- site experience for true wisdom. Byron has finely expressed it, 'pleasure is the sweetest of moralists,' and 'the preacher' would not have exclaimed that ' all is vanity,' had he not drank the cup of Comus to the dregs."

Amidst his rosy hours it then would stray,
And throw all care to unknown years away ;
But let them pass : sad memory does not crave
To linger round the Jordan's troubled wave ;
If it may see the last Elijah rise,
Or kiss his mantle falling from the skies.
Go, classic bust, to strangers' hearts commend,
The Christian Bishop and the poor man's friend ;
But let them know his epitaph is here,
Read in the widow's sob and orphan's tear.
Go, tell the Briton what our church has done
For fallen man, by her exalted son ;
Columbia wept beneath this heavy cross,
And Zion mourned with her the common loss.
But what of that ?   Dehon, thy sainted name
Triumphs in death, o'er human love and fame,
Angels rejoice, whilst men thy fate deplore,
And both to know, must love thee more and more.

(From "A Day on Cooper River.")

A GLIMPSE OF A GHOST.

BY JOHN B. IRVING, M.D.

WHEN the city surrendered to the enemy in 1780, the
then occupant, Henry, who had been long declining,
"turned his face to the wall," and yielded up his spirit
into the hands of Him who gave it. His widow finding

it lonely and sad, with only her four daughters about her, abandoned the upper part of the house entirely, and slept below. Some few months had passed away, when she received into her family an instructress for her girls, a young and gay widow, a Mrs. Latham, just arrived from the " Emerald Isle." Mrs. Latham having been but a few days on shore, knew nothing of the family she had entered; consequently, when she was informed that she was alone to occupy the upstairs, and a servant was offered to her to sleep in her chamber, she ridiculed the idea of being afraid, and declined accepting the offer of a companion. The next morning (being Sunday), the family, and the servants about the house, assembled in the back porch, to go through the church service. They had not progressed far, when a great tramping about was heard over head; after some time, Mrs. Latham came down stairs, and asked who had passed out that way. She was assured that no one could possibly have done so, without being seen, as the family were assembled at their devotions at the foot of the staircase. The household was now thrown into great confusion. The rooms up stairs were all thoroughly searched to no purpose. Mrs. Latham then explained, that whilst she sat reading a *Novel*, she heard a noise along the passage. She put her book down, and listened attentively, when she distinctly heard coming steps along the corridor. The door of her chamber was soon gently opened, when an old lady of benign countenance, dressed in a black silk gown, white muslin handkerchief pinned across, and wearing a close cap, stood before her. She rose, and gave her several invitations to enter, but finding her motionless, and that there " was no speculation in those eyes, that she did glare withal," went towards her, when, like Ajax's spectre, she moved slowly off to the large east room; from that she glided into the smaller rooms, which opened into it, and from which there was no outlet, and there she took the faintest part of nothing, and vanished into the air,—

> " Not a word she deign'd to say,
>   But like a spectre stalked away."

These were the rooms in which the old lady passed the last years of her life. She seldom joined the family down stairs in her latter days, but it was customary for the members of the family to gather around her with their work and books, in her own suite of apartments. In the closet of one of these rooms she left little partitions, which she directed to be put up as baby-houses, for her two eldest grand-daughters at home.

The Sunday following the one on which the above incident took place, Mr. B. Smith, a son said to resemble his mother in no slight degree, came to dine with the family. Mrs. Latham, on seeing him, became much agitated. He had a long conversation, however, with her, and at last succeeded in quieting her apprehensions, by hinting that his good old mother had no doubt been only sent to reprove her thoughtlessness, and to warn her not to set such a bad example to her family, now entrusted to her care, as by *reading a Novel on the Sabbath day*. This hint had a wonderful effect. Mrs. Latham became a faithful and pious instructress. Some of the most accomplished ladies, that now by their virtues and acquirements adorn society, derived their first lessons from her. Among the number of her pupils was Miss E. Scott, now

Mrs. Poyas, a descendant of the eldest branch of the
Landgrave; Elizabeth Read, now Mrs. Parker; and
Laura Carson, now Mrs. Brevoort. There are many
others living, but we need not enumerate them. Mrs.
Latham was married a second time, changing her name
to Brady. As she attained a good old age, having been
dead only about ten years, many of the present generation have often heard from her own lips the incidents I
have told above. I have been given to understand, that
many a time and oft, as her little flock would gather
around her, to hear the old lady's *phantom story*, although
she would frighten the little people half out of their
senses, and " make their hairs to stand on end, like quills
upon the fretful porcupine ;" yet, they would not, for the
wealth of worlds, have had her omit a single circumstance
recorded on her memory. Such startling things she told,
that, although for a while she chilled the hearts of her
little listeners, yet her tones were so soft, like flakes of
feathered snow upon the moistened ground, they melted
as they fell.

NATIONAL VIEWS.

BY WILLIAM HAYNE SIMMONS, M. D.

The sensation which appears to have been produced
throughout the land by the publication of Mrs. Butler's
" wicked book " (the term applied by Cardinal Wolsey to
one of Luther's publications), will, we apprehend, be regarded abroad rather as a proof of the truth and justness

of the lady's representations and satiric strictures, than as
an ebullition of that " virtuous indignation " at calumny
and ingratitude, for which it seems to be so lamentably
mistaken by ourselves ; for our sensibility to strictures of
this sort, to the coarse satire, and heavy attempts at wit,
of which we have so often been made the subject,
by the beef-headed John Bulls, who occasionally travel
among us, is, evidently, much more the result of wounded
vanity—of that childish vanity which courts and finds its
chief gratification in the admiration of foreigners—than of
a just self-respect, and a proper national pride. Of this
latter quality, indeed, the authoress of the " Journal" ac-
cuses us (and it forms, by far, the keenest home-thrust in
the book) of being wholly wanting ; and a writer in the
London Athenæum, in commenting upon our neglect of our
own writers, and the avidity with which the worst trash of
the British press is re-printed and circulated amongst us,
makes a similar charge, and, we fear, with too much justness. As it is, however, among the fantastic fashionables
of our commercial cities, and our travelled and travelling
countrymen, that the apery of foreign, or, rather, British
manners (the worst of all possible models), which renders
us so ridiculous in the eyes of the rest of the world, is
most observable, it is to these that the unsparing satires of
Mrs. Butler's book may be considered as chiefly directed,
and, we think, very fairly applying. When, indeed, shall
we have the grace to adopt, and the spirit to exhibit, the
independence of action, and unaffected dignity of manners,
becoming republicans, and appropriate to the simple, yet
sublime character, of our free and equal institutions ?
Travellers, who generally visit us with high raised notions
of our superior intelligence, national dignity, and political

wisdom, must be both disappointed and astonished to find us, in all our social ideas and practices, more strongly infected with European errors and prejudices, than even many of the more enlightened nations of the Old World itself; and copying, with close and servile imitation, the aristocratical manners and ostentatious habits of the upper orders of England, where the false distinctions, founded upon mere rank and wealth (the barbarous remnants of the feudal system), continue to be kept up with an absurd and ignorant perseverance ; while, in all other countries, they are fast giving place to the more just and liberal ideas of the age, and to more correct views of the objects of society, and the interests of governments. They must, in a word, be no less mortified, than astonished, to find us *mere second-chop English* in our manners, customs, and ideas ; and a century behind the rest of the world in all that relates to the higher improvements and refinements of social existence ; while in France, Germany, and Italy, the higher circles, and even the courts of princes, are enlivened by the wit, and entertained by the accomplishments of authors, artists, and men of talent, who are esteemed and caressed in proportion to their merits, their powers of pleasing, and of contributing to the refined and elegant enjoyments of life. In England, alone, mere upstart wealth, or superior titular rank, and often, even the poor notoriety derived from dandyism and extravagance in dress, form the readiest passports to notice and distinction, and to fashionable pre-eminence. Even John Bull himself would seem to be but little flattered, or pleased, at the close, yet clumsy, imitation of his worst follies and errors by his indefatigable American *Double* (for such we certainly deserved to be called) ; and vainly endeavors to

discountenance, and even to spurn him from him, by holding him up, and turning him round, before the world, for
its derision, laughter, and contempt; for, like the horse of
the equestrian Tailor, who had both a tough skin and a
short memory, his abused, ridiculed, and calumniated, but
still faithful follower and copyist, forgets his ill-treatment,
or, rather, seems to consider it less as a mark of the scorn
and fixed hatred of his beloved parent and great exemplar,
than as a humiliating proof of his own slow progress in his
studies, and the awkwardness of his efforts at improvement and imitation. He, therefore, only bestirs himself
the more diligently to mend his manners, and, if possible,
to do better for the future. The world, in the meantime,
cannot but sympathize with him in his distress and per-
plexity, under the *double* misfortune of the total failure of
all his efforts to mollify and conciliate his morose parent
and inexorable censor, and the publicity and severity of
the castigations which the latter, right or wrong, so punc-
tually and unsparingly inflicts upon him, whenever he has
an opportunity, or can spare time for the purpose. It is
evident, however, that the true source of the aversion and
hostility of John Bull toward his western descendants,
which he takes so little pains to conceal, is the strong
family resemblance to himself, which he instinctively recognizes in their leading faults, and their less amiable peculiarities, while their virtues and better qualities, and the
brighter traits of their character, are of indigenous growth,
underived, and, in a word, all their own. Their errors and
foibles, also, necessarily assume an exaggerated character
in his eyes, being divested of the veil and perstige thrown
around them, in his own case, by the aristocratic distinctions, the gewgaws of rank and title, to which he attaches

so high a value, and which form the chief criterions by which he estimates worth, and judges of the character and qualities of others. Deprived of this infallible standard of reference, he can see only faults where he might otherwise copy excellences ; and, to his eyes, even virtue itself, appearing thus without any meretricious aid, or extrinsic recommendation, "loses discountenanced, and like folly shows." Laughed at, as John Bull is himself, by his more polished neighbors in Europe, for the moroseness of his manners, the selfishness of his habits, and his want of native sense and refinement, he seems to find some consolation in being enabled to turn and vent the long-hoarded stores of his spleen against his unfortunate offspring in America, whose yet imperfect advancement, and youthful errors and defects, afford him an opportunity of being also able to make merry, in his turn, at the expense of others, and of setting up, for the first time—and among those whose habitual reverence for his better qualities and real virtues, renders them less sensible, or, rather, wholly blind, to the absurdity of his pretensions—as an *Arbiter Elegantiarum*, and oracle in matters of taste, fashion, and refinement. This character, nevertheless, we must do him the justice to say, we believe he would never have thought voluntarily of assuming, but for the blind respect and deference which he found paid to his opinions on all subjects ; and the resolute adoption of all his tastes, whims, and follies, by his cis-atlantic admirers, his sturdy and unalienable friends in America. The rough and even brutal manner, however, in which he set about his new task, and performed his "spiriting," betrayed, at once, both his natural character, and his unfitness for the office he assumed ; unless, indeed, he considered the mode of instruction adopted by the

Spartans, who sought to deter their youth from the vice of intoxication, by exhibiting a drunken Helot before them, more eligible than any other; and, therefore, undertook to teach politeness and good manners to his American pupils, by displaying " in his conduct and language, in the Professorial chair, the most flagrant violations of both ; and a disregard even of decency and common propriety—so as to afford them the benefit of the impression produced by *contrast*, and of the lessons to be derived from an *example in point* of the errors which it was desired and deemed necessary to cure or guard them against." For not only have English travellers, but the critics and scholars of that country, indulged in a strain of brutal insolence, and a " ruffian style of criticism," towards America, of which there is no parallel example in the literature of any other nation, and of which, indeed, none but Englishmen appear to be capable—the cultivation of letters and the advantages of education, which have so softening and refining an effect upon the minds of every other people, seeming, *with them*, to serve no other purpose than to supply new weapons to their ferocity, and the means of more envenomed abuse and diffusive calumny against their enemies and the objects of their hatred. By no other people have the press and the pen been made subservient to the purposes of " savage warfare," such as that which has been carried on by England against this country, its people, its reputation, and its institutions. It is time, for her own sake, at least, that this unworthy warfare should cease ; and it is time that we should appreciate her censure at its true worth, and perceive the very low grade which she really occupies in the scale of genuine civilisation ; and learn to separate her achievements in the industrious arts, her wealth, her power and her prosperity—which so much dazzle our vision and obtund our senses—from her boastful and empty pretensions to the higher attributes of virtue, of refinement, and of true national greatness. With respect to these pretensions, in no country have the fountains of justice been more shamefully polluted, or the laws more flagrantly perverted to the purposes of tyranny by judicial subserviency and corruption, than in England, through every stage of her history. By no country has the system of foreign conquest, spoliation and oppression, been carried further than by Great Britain, whose " roll-call," as a second Daniel in our Senate boastfully stated, is heard around the globe ; and whose navy, a scourge well known to many a wasted shore, now bears the thunders of her power to the farthest lands, and to climes where those of heaven are unheard and silent, as in awe at the desolation of nature. As respects her claim to refinement, the more candid among her writers admit their national incapacity for the higher achievements of civilisation, and their improficiency in the lighter graces and accomplishments which distinguish their French rivals and the politer nations of the continent. We yet seem wholly insensible to the disgrace of being ridiculed and made, in a manner, a standing jest of by the English, who are themselves the ridicule and amusement of the rest of the world ; and who are everywhere laughed at on the continent of Europe for their awkward imitation of the higher refinements of their neighbors, or the desperate attempts to render their own vulgar habits and native boorishness fashionable and the *ton*—by boxing at Paris, riding races at Rome, and feats of drinking and debauchery at Venice, or Vienna. It is

surely lamentable to behold the people of this great country, whose general enlightenment, whose natural advantages and political position, entitle them to take a lead in
the march of human improvement, and to rank among the
foremost nations of the earth, so little sensible of their
advantages, and so uninspired by anything like national
pride, or patriotic sentiment, as to turn aside from the
bright and alluring track of glory and greatness spread
open before them, and to follow in the rear, and copy with
creeping servility and childish eagerness, the fantastic
follies, the fashionable extravagances, and even the vices
of the old and corrupt nations of Europe, whose moral
degeneracy and political debasement should rather occasion
us to regard them as beacons to warn us, than as models
inviting our imitation.   On the contrary, however, we
rather console ourselves with the reflection that whatever
may be the present pre-eminence of Britain, and her
various and enviable advantages over us, we may yet
hope, in due time, to rival her in wealth and grandeur,
and in prosperity and renown,—seeming to consider this
as the highest point of greatness and glory at which we
could possibly arrive.   We seem not to reflect that what
we consider as proofs of our social advancement and
precocious civilisation, must be viewed in a wholly opposite light by all other nations ; that the nearer approach
we make to the models that we so sedulously imitate, the
more rapid must be our degeneracy and corruption of
manners, and the wider our departure from republican
habits, and from the principles and spirit of our free institutions.   When shall we properly appreciate the enviable
elevation and dignity of position which we enjoy, as the
only truly free nation of the earth, and thence be led to

cultivate that high feeling, those lofty patriotic sentiments, and that plain majesty of manners, which distinguished the upper, and characterized even the lowest orders of the free states of antiquity; and that imparted to Roman citizenship a dignity that caused it to be sought and contended for by kings. It is only by aiming at, and establishing a truly republican character, and conforming our manners, sentiments and *modes of education*, to the nature and objects of our free institutions, that we can acquire either dignity in the eyes of foreigners, or a proper respect and just value for ourselves.

We propose, Mr. Editor, to continue this subject in a series of " National Views," which extend to innovations in our modes of education, our systems of jurisprudence, and domestic habits; and which, however Utopian they may appear to many, we deem not unworthy the attention of a young and republican nation, whom the force of parental example has led widely astray; but to whom destiny and time point out the bright track that leads to the temple of glory and virtue, and to the summit of prosperity and true greatness.

TO HENRIETTA.

BY W. GARDNER BLACKWOOD.

Thy orb of blue, thy orb of blue,
Peeping the drooping eye-lash through,
How mild—how pure, its beam!

The bright intelligence, that keeps
A living watch, yet dream-like sleeps,
   Like star beneath the stream.

Thy golden hair, thy golden hair,
How clust'ring, o'er thy white neck bare,
   Its sunny ringlets flow ;
Or how they, dallying with the breeze,
Like love with pleasant memories,
   Play wanton round thy brow.

Thy dimpled cheek, thy dimpled cheek,
How does the warm flush o'er it break,
   Like summer's silent glow ;
Or hues, which at the twilight's hour,
The sun, from his Hesperian bower,
   Sheds o'er the spotless snow.

Thy dewy lip, thy dewy lip,
That tempts the very bee to sip,
   The breathing fragrance there ;
How sweeter far than Paphian rose,
Or any flower that sweetly blows,
   To bless the morning air.

Thy form of grace, thy form of grace,
How truly did a fairy trace
   Its outline in her shadow :
Such ne'er before companioned love,
O'er Lesbian steep, thro' Delian grove,
   Or o'er Aonian meadow.

Maiden, so beautiful thou art,
To earth, a shrine for poet's heart,
  I feel that thou wert given ;
And fear alone, lest while I sing,
Some zephyrs soft, with scented wing,
  May waft thee back to heaven.

———

THE KINDNESS OF CONTEMPORARY CRITICISM.

(An Extract from Monaldi.)

BY WASHINGTON ALLSTON.

THE poem was at length published. Alas! who that knows the heart of an author—of an aspiring one—will need be told what were the feelings of Maldura, when day after day, week after week, passed on, and still no tidings of his book. To think it had failed was wormwood to his soul. "No, that was impossible." Still the suspense, the uncertainty of its fate, were insupportable. At last, to relieve his distress, he fastened the blame on his unfortunate publisher ; though how he was in fault he knew not. Full of this thought he was just sallying forth to vent his spleen on him, when his servant announced the Count Piccini.

"Now," thought Maldura, "I shall hear my fate ;" and he was not mistaken ; for the count was a kind of talking gazette. The poem was soon introduced, and Piccini rattled on with all he had heard of it: he had lately been piqued by Maldura, and cared not to spare him.

After a few hollow professions of regard, and a careless remark about the pain it gave him to repeat unpleasant things, Piccini proceeded to pour them out one upon another, with ruthless volubility. Then, stopping as if to take breath, he continued, "I see you are surprised at all this; but indeed, my friend, I cannot help thinking it principally owing to your not having suppressed your name; for your high reputation, it seems, had raised such extravagant expectations as none but a first-rate genius could satisfy."

"By which," observed Maldura, "I am to conclude that my work has failed?"

"Why, no; not exactly that. It has only not been praised; that is, I mean in the way you might have wished. But do not be depressed; there's no knowing but the tide may yet turn in your favor."

"Then I suppose the book is hardly as yet known?"

"I beg your pardon; quite the contrary. When your friend, the marquis, introduced it at his last conversazione, every one present seemed quite *au fait* on it; at least, they all talked as if they had read it."

Maldura bit his lips. "Pray who were the company?"

"Oh! all your friends, I assure you: Guattani, Martello, Pessuti, the mathematician, Alfieri, Benuci, the Venetian Castelli, and the old Ferrarese Carnesecchi. These were the principal; but there were twenty others, who had each something to say."

Maldura could not but perceive the malice of this enumeration; but he checked his rising choler. "Well," said he, " if I understand you, there was but one opinion respecting my poem with all this company ?"

" Oh ! by no means. Their opinions were as various as their characters."

" Well, Pessuti ; what said he ?"

" Why, you know he's a mathematician, and should not regard him ; but yet, to do him justice, he is a very nice critic, and not unskilled in poetry."

" Go on, sir ; I can bear it."

" Why, then, it was Pessuti's opinion that the poem had more learning than genius."

" Proceed, sir."

" Martello denied it both ; but he, you know, is a disappointed author. Guattani differed but little from Pessuti as to its learning ; but contended, that you certainly showed great invention in your fable, which was like nothing that ever did or could happen. But I fear I annoy you."

" Go on, I beg, sir."

" The next who spoke was old Carnesecchi, who confessed that he had no doubt he should have been delighted with the poem, could he have taken hold of it ; but it was so *en regle*, and like a hundred others, that it put him in mind of what is called a polished gentleman, who talks and bows, and slips through a great crowd without leaving any impression. Another person, whose name I have forgotten, praised the versification, but objected to the thoughts."

" Because they were absurd ?"

" Oh ! no, for the opposite reason ; because they had all been long ago known to be good. Castelli thought that a bad reason ; for his part, he said, he liked them all the better for that ; it was like shaking hands with an old ac-

quaintance in every line.   Another observed, that at least
no critical court could lawfully condemn them, as they
could each prove an *alibi*.   Not an *alibi*, said a third, but
a *double ;* so they should be burnt for sorcery.   With all
my heart, said a fourth ; but not the poor author, for he
has certainly satisfied us that he is no conjuror.   Then,
Castelli ; but 'faith, I don't know how to proceed."

"You are over delicate, sir ; speak out, I pray you."

"Well, Benuci finished by the most extravagant eulogy
I ever heard."

Maldura took breath.

"For he compared your hero to the Apollo Belvidere,
your heroine to the Venus de Medicis, and your subordi-
nate characters to the Diana, the Hercules, the Antinous,
and twenty other celebrated antiques ; declared them all
equally well-wrought, and beautiful ; and like them, too,
equally cold, hard, and motionless.   In short, he maintained that you were the boldest and most original poet he
had ever known ; for none but a hardy genius, who consulted nobody's taste but his own, would have dared, like
you, to draw his animal life from a statue-gallery, and his
vegetable from a hortus siccus."

Maldura's heart stiffened within him, but his pride con-
trolled him, and he masked his thoughts with something
like composure.   Yet he dared not trust himself to speak,
but stood looking at Piccini, as if waiting for him to go on.
"I believe that's all," said the count, carelessly twirling
his hat, and rising to take leave.

Maldura roused himself, and, making an effort, said,
"No, sir ; there is one person whom you have only named
—Alfieri ; what did he say ?"

"Nothing !"   Piccini pronounced this word with a

graver tone than usual; it was his fiercest bolt, and he knew that a show of feeling would send it home. Then, after pausing a moment, he hurried out of the room.

M U S I C.

BY S. A. HURLBUT.

THERE's music in the air
That bathes in light the proudly rolling earth,
Among the stars she found her primal birth :
    Still dwells she there !

Throughout the mystic choirs
Pours forth the solemn harmony of night,
Expanding, swelling, with the spreading light
    Of heavenly fires.

In ocean's heaving breast,
Peals the wild chorus of the winds at play,
And music quivers on the glancing spray,
    The blue sea's crest.

Far in the sighing wood
That bows unto her voice, does music dwell,
And makes within the trees her airy cell
    In solitude.

But in the well-known voice,
There lies a deeper and more secret spell,
Bidding the heart in tones remembered well ;
    Once more rejoice !

She quells the stormy power,
Which bore the spirit madly from its sphere,
And bids the buried shapes of joy appear,
    As in the hour

When life was tinged with hue,
Fair as the tints on dying daylight set,
Or those which gleam in night's gemmed coronet,
    The spangled dew.

———

THE GREEK LANGUAGE.

BY HUGH S. LEGARÉ.

It is impossible to contemplate the annals of Greek literature and art, without being struck with them, as by far the most extraordinary and brilliant phenomenon in the history of the human mind. The very language, even in its primitive simplicity, as it came down from the rhapsodists who celebrated the exploits of Hercules and Theseus, was as great a wonder as any it records. All the other tongues that civilized men have spoken, are poor, and feeble, and barbarous, in comparison of it. Its compass and flexibility, its riches and its powers, are altogether unlimited. It not only expresses with precision, all that is thought or known at any given period, but it enlarges itself naturally, with the progress of science, and affords, as if without an effort, a new phrase, or a systematic nomenclature whenever one is called for. It is equally adapted to every variety of style and subject— to the most shadowy subtlety of distinction, and the utmost exactness of definition, as well as to the energy and pathos of popular eloquence—to the majesty, the elevation, the variety of the Epic, and the boldest license of the Dithyrambic, no less than to the sweetness of the Elegy, the simplicity of the Pastoral, or the heedless gaiety and delicate characterization of Comedy. Above all, what is an unspeakable charm—a sort of *naiveté* is peculiar to it, and appears in all these various styles, and is quite as becoming and agreeable in a historian or a philosopher—Xenophon, for instance—as in the light and jocund numbers of Anacreon. Indeed, were there no other object in the learning Greek, but to see to what perfection language is capable of being carried, not only as a medium of communication, but as an instrument of thought, we see not why the time of a young man would not be just as well bestowed in acquiring a knowledge of it—for all the purposes, at least, of a liberal or elementary education—as in learning Algebra, another specimen of a language or arrangement of signs, perfect in its kind. But this wonderful idiom happens to have been spoken, as was hinted in the preceding paragraph, by a race as wonderful. The very first monument of their genius, the most ancient relic of letters in the Western world, stands to this day altogether unrivalled in the exalted class to which it belongs.* What was the history of this immortal poem, and of its great fellow? Was it a single individual, and who was he, that composed them? Had he any master or model? What had been his education, and what was the state of society in which he lived? These questions are full of interest to a philosophic inquirer into the intellectual history of the species, but they are especially important with a view to the subject of the present discussion. Whatever causes for the matchless excellence of these primitive poems, and for that of the language in which they are written, will go far to explain the extraordinary circumstance, that the same favored people left nothing unattempted in philosophy, in letters and in arts, and attempted nothing without signal, and in some cases, unrivalled success. Winkel-

---

* Milton is, perhaps, more sublime than Homer, and, indeed, than all other poets, with the exception, as we incline to think, of Dante. But if we adopt his own division of poetry into three classes, viz., the Epic, the Dramatic, and the Lyrical, the Paradise Lost, like the Divina Commedia, is more remarkable for lyrical (and sometimes for dramatic), than for epic beauties; for splendid details, than an interesting whole; for prophetic raptures bursting forth at intervals, than for the animation, the fire, the engrossing and rapid narrative of a metrical romance. Who cares anything about the story or the plot, or feels any sympathy with the dramatis personæ, not even excepting Adam and Eve, whose insipid faultlessness reminds one of the Italian proverb, "*tanto buon che val niente.*" Besides, are not the preposterous vauntings and menaces of the Devil against the Omnipotent, like the swaggering insolence of a slave behind his master's back; or his conspiracy like that of Caliban with Trinculo and Stephano, against the magic powers of Prospero? Devoted, as we are proud to avow ourselves, to Milton, we have always felt there was something even savoring of the comic in his Rabbinical plot.

man undertakes to assign some reasons for this astonishing superiority of the Greeks, and talks very learnedly
about a fine climate, delicate organs, exquisite suscepti-
bility, the full development of the human form by gymnastic exercises, &c. For our own parts, we are content to
explain the phenomenon after the manner of the Scottish
school of metaphysicians, in which we learned the little
we profess to know of that department of philosophy, by
resolving it at once into an original law of nature; in
other words, by substantially, but decently, confessing it
to be inexplicable. But whatever it was—idiosyncrasy
or discipline—or whatever was the cause, it is enough for
the purposes of the present discussion, that the fact is
unquestionable.

THE MARRIAGE FEAST.

BY A. A. MULLER.

THE lamps are bright in Cana's halls,
And countless mirrors deck her walls;
A thousand faces beam with joy,
Unmixed with passion's base alloy;
The young have met at beauty's call,
To join the sacred festival,
And age comes there a peaceful guest,
To smile upon the Marriage Feast!

14

Judea's virgins foremost stand,
Like hills of snow on fairy land ;
Or like the mighty seraph train,
Revolving o'er the cloudless plain,
When naught is heard in earth or air,
Save sainted hymns that meet the ear,
And naught attracts the gazer's eye,
Save blessed orbs that light the sky !

Within each vestment's graceful fold,
Gleams the bright cinctur'd clasp of gold ;
And brighter still the diamond's crest,
That dazzling gleams of beauty's breast ;
That, with its far-illumined blaze,
Confuses the beholder's gaze ;
So to the raptur'd prophet seems a flight
Of purest angels robed in dazzling light.

Music has breathed her purest sigh,
To grace the thrilling harmony ;
And hallowed harps and hands are there,
Pouring their strains on beauty's ear ;
E'en Cana's chiefs and princes all
Have mingled in that festive hall,
Where wealth and rank their arts combine,
In mingled rays to warm and shine.

But comes there One to bless that scene—
Pure, spotless, holy, meek, serene ;
Whose presence sanctifies the place,
And lends to earth celestial grace ;

Whose look gives joy to those who share,
Such sinless mirth, such love sincere;
And sure that feast must splendid shine,
When Jesus makes its rites divine!

———

LOVE'S BENEDICTION.

BY WILLIAM CRAFTS.

Be as thou art, for ever young,
   Still on thy cheek the vernal bloom,
The honey's essence on thy tongue,
   And on thy lips the rose perfume.

Be as thou art, for ever fair,
   Still beam with love, those eyes of thine;
For ever wave thy yellow hair,
   And round thy graceful bosom twine.

Those coral lips, those teeth of pearl,
   Those smiles, those glances, and those sighs;
Heaven save them long, my charming girl,
   To bless this heart, to bless these eyes.

For all of thee, thank heaven, is mine;
   And I am happier made by thee;
As when the oak supports the vine,
   'Tis glad and looketh cheerfully.

THE NATIONAL SABBATH.

BY GEO. S. BRYAN.

It would seem impossible that man could forget his
Creator! When we regard his absolute dependance on
the Almighty, subsisting, day by day, upon the unmerited,
overflowing bounty of his hand;—his life, which at best
is but a hastening shadow,—held by a gossamer tenure,—
which a breath at any moment may destroy;—when we
consider the rich gifts which he has received from his
Heavenly Parent;—ennobled by conscience, crowned
with intellect, made but a little lower than the angels;—
when we view his position in this world, surrounded by
the stupendous wonders of the Universe;—himself, an
atom, standing upon a point, yet endowed with a mind
in which that Universe is reflected as in a mirror;—capable, through the divine quality of reason, of scanning the
immense systems which expand themselves in the infinity
of space; of comprehending the adamantine laws which
control their movements; of appreciating and enjoying the
everlasting harmonies which pervade the apparent discord,
and give a musical order to seeming confusion;—when
we behold man, the creature, thus dependant, so honored,
so enriched,—truly does it seem impossible that he could
forget his Creator and Benefactor. Surely, God will
reign in all his thoughts!—and his heart will be an altar,
from whence will unceasingly arise the incense of Gratitude. His life will bear a living and unbroken testimony
that he carries with him, in all his walks, an abiding con-

sciousness, a profound conviction, that he owes a debt he
never can repay! Alas! alas! it is not so! All these
remembrances; all these multiplied claims upon his affections; all these varied appeals to his understanding,—are
in themselves insufficient. And the infinitely Wise One,
who created the heart, and who, from the beginning, knew
all its weakness and waywardness, knew they would be
insufficient. He foresaw the fascinations of self—the
enchantments of pleasure—the spells of ambition—the ten
thousand magic voices of this world, which are continually
sounding in the ear of man, engrossing his spirit, and
calling him off from his highest duty. To silence these
magic voices—to break these spells--to dissolve these
enchantments—to tear self from its idols;—in pity to his
erring children—in aid of their feeble and uncertain
virtue, He established a day of Holiness to himself, to be
observed throughout all time, in which the tides of human
passion should stand still, the eager and reckless chase of
life be arrested, and the vexed and fevered spirit, disen-
thralled from its sordid bondage, should be lifted up into a
calm, purifying, invigorating communion with its celestial
Original!

And does our country need no Sabbath? And shall
not this day be holy? The sun, at his coming on this
day, saw his rays dim and pale in the dawn of a brighter
luminary. On this day, dejected humanity arose from the
ashes of her mourning; she put off her rags; her sorrowing heart was glad; it beat with a tumultuous joy, as
she greeted the illustrious Child who was to rescue her
name from its long abasement—place it on high, and shed
around it an undying glory! On this day, Liberty, sick
from many a sad defeat and sore discomfiture, lifted up

her drooping head, and as she gazed upon her Infant Hero, her proud form dilated, her sober eye brightened, kindled, blazed, as, in prophetic vision, she anticipated her own and her champion's dazzling triumphs! It is the birth-day of Washington! Shall it not be the Jubilee of Freedom, sacred to Patriotism,—a Sabbath to our Country!

THE CHARTER OAK.

BY JOSEPH H. DUKES.

LONE remnant of departed time!
Within thy spreading shade
I stood—while on thy outstretched arms
The light of morning played.
And while with bounding heart I gazed
Upon thy giant form,
Which, for a thousand vanished years,
Had battled with the storm,
I felt thee in thy towering strength
And loneliness—sublime!
Type of true virtue as thou art,
Unscathed by tide or time!

How many a wintry wind—that in
Its wild, dread fury came—
Hath madly shook with tempest power

Thy rude, unyielding frame!
Yet, bowed not, still thou standest here
As in thy youthful pride,
While gleams thy wide-extended crest
In spring's bright verdure dyed.
And, tho' clouds lower, and storms rage on,
Still may'st thou flourish here—
And put thy cheering blossoms forth
In many a coming year.

Long may'st thou rear thy shining crest,
Of not one beauty riven,
And steadfastly, as Faith herself,
Soar upwards still to heaven!
Since thou art lone and desolate,
Of every mate bereft;
Since time has kindly passed thee o'er,
And still thy beauties left.
Long! long beneath thy shelt'ring boughs
May happy thousands raise
The song—befitting Freedom's land—
Of gratitude and praise.

Long in thy branches may the birds
Of heav'n delight to rest!
And long the sun, at earliest morn,
Greet with its smile—thy crest;
And long as freemen love their land—
The land of fame and glory,
Still may thy praise illume the page
Of her undying story!
Farewell! upon thy honored head,

New blessings we invoke !
Pride of thy land ! the poet's theme !
Thou scathless—stern old oak !

———

THE INFLUENCE OF LETTERS UPON HAPPINESS.

BY SAMUEL HENRY DICKSON, M.D.

And what has been the influence of literature upon the happiness and moral well-being of mankind ? The delight of youth—the solace of old age—amusement in health, and consolation in sickness.—What would life be without letters ? One can scarcely believe the suggestion of danger from this quarter to be sincerely made. In all times, indeed, writers have been found to constitute what has been recently entitled a " Satanic School"—men who scoff at public and private virtue, and trample upon the social and domestic affections ;—who instruct the young in vice, and harden the old against repentance. But their power to do harm has always been limited. However reckless and malignant themselves, they dread, for their own sakes, to arouse the malignity and recklessness of others. They fear the recoil of their own doctrines. Experience teaches the extreme danger of exciting the passions of the many. " Even those who think themselves most capable of directing the storm, are apt to be swept away in its fury. The French revolution has been attributed to the influence of the philosophers, so called, of the previous age—Voltaire, Rousseau, D'Alembert, and the rest—and to the restless uneasiness of bad men under the restraints of law and religion. For my own part, I find in the memoirs of the time, and in the history of the French court for two or three generations, of the Regent d'Orleans, and of the *parc au cerf* in the reign of Louis XV., abundant materials for the explosion ;—nay, I cannot imagine by what human means it could have been avoided or suppressed. Yet, allowing the truth of the assumption for argument's sake, this would seem a single and remarkable instance in which an untoward influence had been exerted by literature and literary men upon the destinies of a people. According to the ordinary course of things, the knowledge of good which they diffuse, serves abundantly as corrective of the knowledge of evil. Since the invention of printing, the press is alike open to all. If, on the one hand, there issue from the vile cellars of the sensualist, the traitor, and the infidel, pamphlets and broadsheets, spreading corruption and filling the land with suggestions of crime ; we are sure, on the other, to see equal talent roused to the conflict, and exerted conservatively, to protect, maintain, and strengthen, all valuable institutions. If any particular course is found available and impressive by one party, it is resorted to by the other also ; and the result of free and untrammelled discussion need never be feared. Truth is mighty and will prevail. Let us remark, in passing, the increased and increasing republicanism of literature. Until recently, one would imagine that all the talents and all the virtues were circumscribed within the higher orders. Even in Shakspeare, loyalty appears to be almost the only excellent quality discoverable in the lower and middle ranks. But the people, properly so called, have gradually

14*

emerged from this feudal deluge of contempt. We honor Goldsmith as among the first who dared to select his subjects from his own condition, and to throw a purple light over the virtues of the poor. After him, Burns and Scott have followed, the latter with some degree of hesitation and much expressed deference to the noble and lofty; and now, the novelist raises from the farm-yard, the retail-shop, and the workhouse, some of our most exquisite examples of grace, gentleness, and of beauty.

It ought to be considered before we leave this topic, that the knowledge of evil is by no means and in no regard difficult of attainment; while the acquisition of good principles and correct views, of social relations and duties, must be made slowly and with effort. Suppose all, of impious and vile, that the ingenuity of man has ever committed to writing or passed through the press, to be at once obliterated and completely destroyed and forgotten; the world, I fear, would not long be more ignorant of evil, or more innocent than it is now. The least active mind is sufficiently fertile of dark and impure suggestions, to accumulate readily for itself an abundant stock of such lore. But what would be the effect of the loss of the opposite literature? Sweep away into oblivion the discourses of Socrates and Plato, of Confucius and Menu, of Milton and Taylor, and Fenelon and Paley, and ages upon ages would roll by without a reproduction of the thoughts and sentiments for which we are indebted to these illustrious sages.

It has been urged, indeed, as a serious subtraction from the benefits of knowledge, that it is fatal to cheerfulness and gaiety; that thought brings carefulness and gloom. It is assumed that intelligence prompts us to look for-

ward, and that the shadows of coming events are darken-
ing to the human spirit. " *Calamitosus est animus*," says
Seneca, "*futuri anxius*." " *Prévoyance*," exclaims Rousseau, "*prevoyance, la veritable source de toutes nos misères*."
But is forethought necessarily connected with despond-
ence ? Does knowledge essentially lead to the increase
of anxiety and care ? The answer to these questions
will, in every case, be determined by the constitution of
the individual mind, and as there is in the majority a
preponderance of hope over fear, so there will be in the
contemplation of the future, a sanguine anticipation of
good, for the most part, rather than any prevailing dread
of evil. And it does not seem likely that the latter shall
be at all increased by a reasonable calculation of proba-
bilities, not to speak of the possibility of applying preven-
tion, when the nature and source of any coming danger is
understood. It is a uniform fact, that persons who
purchase annuities, in the process of which transaction
they cannot help becoming pretty clearly informed as to
what are called " the chances of life" in their own cases,
become more at ease, live more tranquilly, and enjoy
better health than before.

THE MAY QUEEN—A SONNET.

BY WILLIAM H. TIMROD.

SARAH ! throbbed not thy young heart, on that day,
　With innocent triumph—when the youthful throng,
　With rites of ancient usage, and sweet song,
Had crowned thee Queen of verdant-mantled May ?
And not unmeet thy triumph—for the voice
　Of thy young peers, which singled thee from all,
　To circle with the rural coronal,
Spoke merit in the Queen of their free choice !
But still remember, Sarah, thou can'st find
　No lasting joy in earthly diadems,
Whether of flowers composed, or costly gems,—
Those fade, and these oft dazzle but to blind ;
And we must look to other worlds than this
For crowns of real and abiding bliss.

———

THE TUSCAN MAID.

BY WASHINGTON ALLSTON.

How pleasant and how sad the turning tide
Of human life, when side by side,
The child and youth begin to glide
　Along the vale of years ;

The pure twin-being for a little space,
With lightsome heart, and yet a graver face,
    Too young for wo, though not for tears.

This turning tide is Ursulina's now;
The time is mark'd upon her brow;
Now every thought and feeling throw
    Their shadows on her face;
And so are every thought and feeling join'd;
'Twere hard to answer whether heart or mind
    Of either were the native place.

The things that once she loved are still the same;
Yet now there needs another name
To give the feeling which they claim,
    While she the feeling gives;
She cannot call it gladness or delight;
And yet there seems a richer, lovelier light,
    On e'en the humblest thing that lives.

She sees the mottled moth come twinkling by,
And sees it sip the floweret nigh;
Yet not, as once, with eager cry,
    She grasps the pretty thing;
Her thoughts now mingle with its tranquil mood,
So poised in air, as if on air it stood
    To show its gold and purple wing.

She hears the bird, without a wish to snare,
But rather on the azure air,
To mount, and with it wander there,
    To some untrodden land;

As if it told her in its happy song
Of pleasures strange, that never can belong
    To aught of sight or touch of hand.

Now the young soul her mighty power shall prove,
And outward things around her move,
Pure ministers of purer love,
    And make the heart her home ;
Or to the meaner senses sink a slave,
To do their bidding, though they madly crave
    Through hateful scenes of vice to roam.

But, Ursulina, thine the better choice;
Thine eyes *so* speak, as with a voice ;
Thy heart may still in earth rejoice,
    And all its beauty love ;
But no, not all this fair, enchanting earth,
With all its spells, can give the rapture birth
    That waits thy conscious soul above.

———

LITERATURE AND THE FINE ARTS.

BY JOEL R. POINSETT.

THE importance of cultivating and using our utmost
efforts to improve the literature of our country, must be
apparent to all. It is the vehicle of science, and upon
its character the dignity and reputation of a nation

depend. It exercises a controlling influence on the public liberties. The patriotic citizen who would, either in the forum or through the press, warn his fellow-citizens of impending danger, or enlighten them on their interests—who would dissipate ignorance, correct error, or reform abuse—must borrow the tones and wield the energies of literature. Our freedom reposes on the guarantee of our political institutions ; and who can wrest them from our posterity, with a competent literature to inculcate and vindicate its doctrines and principles, and to proclaim its rights !

Literature and the fine arts go hand in hand. The flourishing condition of the first is a sure prelude to the advancement of the latter ; and their united influence adds, in a high degree, to the enjoyment of human existence. Their progress has everywhere kept pace with that of the moral and social condition of mankind, and their history marks, with unerring truth, the rise and fall of nations. In tracing that history, it is gratifying to perceive that, while literature and the arts contribute so largely to improve and refine mankind, they have flourished most in those countries where free institutions prevailed, and where liberty loved to dwell. In other countries, a taste for literature and the fine arts is confined to a favored few ; the aristocracy of birth, of wealth, or of talent ; and there, such a distinction is natural, and may be sufficient, because these classes alone govern those countries. *Here*, the people reign ; all power is centred in them ; and if we would have them not only maintain their ascendency, but use their power discreetly, no expense or pains should be spared to inspire them with a love of literature, and a taste for the fine arts. To effect this, the effort must be made here. It must originate at the seat of government, and spread from this place over the populous plains and fertile valleys of the land. Could a greater curse fall upon this country than that the sons of the intelligent, and enlightened, and virtuous men, who achieved our independence and secured our freedom, should become less intelligent, less enlightened, and less virtuous than their sires? That these valleys and plains, instead of teeming with a race burning with the love of freedom, and ever ready and able to vindicate their rights, should be filled by a people supine and ignorant, the fitting tools of demagogues and tyrants?

In a free country, *literature* may and will flourish by the well-directed efforts of individuals; but *the arts* require the protecting hand of government. They owe their origin, their progress, and present condition to that source, and to religious enthusiasm. Their first object was to personify the god-like forms of heathen idolatry, and to hand down to posterity the images of heroes to whom a nation owed its gratitude. They subsequently became the means of recording the miracles of the true faith, and of spreading the history of the Christian church over the world. In our favored land, they would commemorate the heroic deeds of our forefathers, their achievements and sacrifices in the cause of independence, their deep devotion to the freedom of their country. To a certain extent this has been effected by the liberality of government; statues have . been erected, paintings executed, and medals struck by order of Congress. Copies of such pictures, statues and medals, should be spread far and wide over the land, that they may penetrate into every hamlet, and inspire the people universally with gratitude and emulation. From the advancement of the fine arts, we may promise ourselves great improvements in the architecture of our private and public buildings; in the former, a better adaptation of the arrangements to the comforts and conveniences of life; in the latter, more suitable forms and arrangements for the purposes of business. We are led away by the imposing appearance of massive colonnades and splendid porticos, and apply them equally to temples and to buildings intended altogether for the transaction of public business. This is a mistake which the more chastened taste will correct.

A collection of models and paintings at Washington could not fail to be highly useful. It would aid the cultivation of the art of design, which cannot be too strongly recommended. It multiplies the resources and enjoyments of the professional man, and is an essential accomplishment to the architect, the machinist, the artizan, and the mechanic. It ought to be taught in our common schools; and every mechanic should be able to sketch with accuracy his own plans, and to copy those of others, so as to be able to profit by every improvement that comes under his observation.

The science of music, although not so manifestly useful, exercises great influence over the moral and social condition of society. It is taught in the common schools in Germany, and there music constitutes the chief amusement of the people. Instead of hearing in their streets the indistinct roaring of senseless rhymes, out of time and tune, the Germans may be seen assembled in groups, after the labors of the day, singing, in parts, the delightful music of their inspired composers, elevating their voices in grateful adoration of their Maker, or chanting some of the spirited patriotic songs for which the father-land of the Teutonic race is so celebrated. Whoever has witnessed this contrast; whoever has been startled with the discordant sounds of the one, and enraptured with the exquisite harmony of the other, will understand the advantages that are likely to accrue to the cause of temperance, of morality, and of religion, by cultivating the science of music, and making it a part of the education of the people.

THE TEMPLE OF JUPITER AT OLYMPIA.

BY JAMES W. SIMMONS.

BEHOLD the dome, which Greece, in happier hour,
Proud of the magic of her matchless skill,
An off'ring worthy of the Thund'rer's might,
Erected to her God! In that blest day
When arts and arms alike were in their prime,
And Glory's Sun unmenac'd with eclipse,
From envious shadows of a far-off world,—
High, in its fretted vault, supremely shone,
Ethereal Fane!—proud rival of the skies!
Unequall'd monument of human pow'r!
In solitary grandeur, towering o'er
The pigmy efforts of succeeding time!
Oh! who can dream of thee—of what thou wert,—

E'er Time's dark wing had mantled on thy flight—
Nor worship mem'ry of that god-like race,
Whom dark-revolving ages, in their lapse,
Have swept to the abyss, but cannot shroud
From mortal ken, the glories of their line.
The heritage of *feeling*, who can mar ?
Deep in the vault, in imag'd conflict, view
The human Centaur and fierce Lapith glare ;
While Herculean labors frown full front.
The massy portal gain'd—in softest guise,
See cherub Peace her civic garlands weave,
To grace the brow of beauty-breathing Art.
Lo ! In the centre of the Temple—look !
Behold the God of Phidias' mighty mind !
Sublime conception !   On his vaulted throne
A burning mass of breathing harmony,
That rears its starry summit into heav'n—
Rob'd in the terror of his awful state,
And cloth'd in thunder, Jove Olympian tow'rs.
The God ! the God ! majestic and alone,
Supremely mighty, bares his blasting hand,
Dark with the destinies of Gods and men ;
That iron arm, that, sweeping, rocks the vast
Of the eternal conclave, and from high
Hurls the live lightning—on his glitt'ring brow
The peaceful olive.   Victory, on the right,
Sits plum'd with Horror, and a Diadem
Of dazzling glory nods upon the left.
See—how he smiles to view the Theban babe
In torture writhe beneath the Sphynx's gripe,
With fiery fangs into his vitals wound,
And gorg'd with blood-drops of his blasted heart.

And orphan'd Niobe, with streaming eye
And supplicating hand, in vain implores,
From the unbending marble of his brow,
The pitying mercy that would deign to save
From vengeful Fate, the scions of a race
That flourish'd once, and once was beautiful.
Beside his throne, in full proportions, view
The immortal Heroes of Olympic fame!
The keen-eyed coursers of the Elian plain,
In all the lusty vigor of the race—
Speed in each nerve, and fire in every vein.
But who is He—with laurel-wreathed brow,
All radiant in youth, conspicuous there?
With eye of light, and cheek of roseate hue?
How firm his step! and how with manly grace
He rears his marble front to heaven!—lovely
The pride with which he spurning vaults from earth,
To tread th' impalpable of his spirit's home!
Beneath that glorious form, who near the God
Hath ta'en his seat, look down!—what fairy dream
Dawns to the eye—of bridal fruit—by Loves
And Graces guarded!—with their girdled zones—
In all the pride of maiden purity—
With tinsel-slipper'd feet, and braided hair?
They look like Heralds of Eternity—
Pure as Hesperian odors that they breathe,
And newly 'lighted from Elysian fields.
But sorrow's soft and melancholy tinge,
Doth sweetly mantle o'er the lines of light,
That blending, form an Iris of the cheek,
Where precious tears, like dew-drops of the rose,
Reflect the rich effulgence of its hues :

For, full in view, the agony of nerves,
And mighty muscles, wringing bloody sweat,
Is seen sustaining, pillar'd on the base
Of Atlantean shoulders, starry worlds,
That to their centre reel.—How, drop by drop,
That tortur'd spirit falters life away !
While Gods, malignant, triumph in his fate.
And there—Oh ! sight of painful loveliness !
The fair-hair'd daughter of a wond'rous race,
The bleeding Penthesilea reclines—
Pillow'd in arms that *slew*, but *lov'd* her still ;
Ilion's stern hero *vanquish'd*, yields to *grief*,
Whose potent power the Gods themselves confess.

THE NECESSITY OF A SOUTHERN LITERATURE.

BY DANIEL K. WHITTAKER.

It is time that we should make a vigorous movement in
behalf of Southern literature, and when we say *Southern*,
we mean nothing invidious. There is to be, if there be
not already, a Southern, as well as a Northern literature,
in our country, but not for that reason, in either case, less
an American literature. The South as well as the North,
belongs to the country, and the light of her genius and
scholarship is yet to shed its rays, like the sun in the firmament, over every part of our wide-spread Union. *Her
sons are to come from afar, and her daughters from the
ends of the earth*, and are to aid those who come from the

North, the East, and the West, in building up, and extending everywhere, the literary fame of our common country. Shall the South be deprived of her portion of this inheritance of glory, merely because she is the South, and glories in the title? Does she not look, with pride, upon the American Eagle as he soars upwards to the heavens and looks fixedly and without blenching at the sun, because it is the emblem of her country's fortunes? Does she feel indifferent to the stars and stripes of her country's flag, as it floats proudly to the breeze over every ocean and every sea? Is the South destitute of those national feelings of an instinctive reverence, which the name of the American Republic awakens in the breast of every native-born American citizen? Is she destitute of patriotism? Does she not love the Union, which our fathers purchased and established at such fearful odds? She does love it, and he who denies that she does, is a traitor to the truth, and belies her real character. But the South is still the South, if we have not mistaken the points of the compass; and in promoting the great cause of our country's literature, she must move towards her high calling, *as* the South, because she owes it to her own dignity to do so, and because the North, for similar reasons, has acted *as* the North, in promoting, with all her ability, the same object. The plantation States, bound together by common pursuits and common ties of interest, must co-operate and move together in this matter, and must exert all their strength for their own protection, for there are rumors of danger in the distance, coming even from the land of the Puritans. Does "the North American Review," by the mere force of its comprehensive title, represent and maintain the interests, social, civil, and literary, of all North America?

Does any one of its collaborators imagine that it does? Does it represent and sustain with good will, in good faith, or at all, the agricultural and slave-holding interests of the Southern States of the Union, guaranteed to them by the constitution? Will any one pretend that it does? Is it not—we will not say, extreme and violent in the opinions it expresses upon the latter topic—but is it not anti-slavery in its feelings, its sentiments, its whole position, and in all the language it employs in reference to it? Is not this the case with " The Boston Review," " The New York Review," and most of the Northern Periodicals? It is. Shall we be asked, in return, is the freedom of speech and of the press to be trammelled? Shall we not be permitted to write and publish what we think proper? Shall we be prevented from speaking out our thoughts freely on the subject of slavery, or any other subject? Not at all, gentlemen! Speak out your minds freely; absolve your consciences; discharge your duty, if you have a duty to discharge, like men; be not timid or backward in a matter which you seem to have so deeply at heart; the press is free, free as the winds of heaven; you know it is; use it freely; w rite, print, and publish what you please; it is your co nstitutional privilege; but while you do so, remember that the whole South, with the Constitution of the Union spread out before it, as a broad banner, reads your writings, and compares them with that great charter of its rights, and see to it, as you would when taking a solemn oath in a court of justice, that you utter *the truth, the whole truth, and nothing but the truth;* that you " extenuate nothing, nor set down aught in malice;" and let us have no concealments, no vacillation in expressing your views with a down-right honesty of purpose, no skulking behind hedges, no lying in ambush and aiming your arrows at us from a dark corner, when we would meet the enemies of our institutions upon the broad and open field of controversy, man to man, and face to face, and test our respective strength by an appeal to God and the right! All that the South wants, all that she has ever wanted, in reference to this matter, is a fair field, fair weapons on both sides, and an opportunity to defend herself. Will it be said that this is impossible, quite out of the question,—that the whole world is against the South, already, in reference to her slave institutions, and will be against her, however proudly she may assume an attitude of defence and defiance? We have heard of this before, and we do not believe it. But be it so; let it be taken for granted. The South, in that case, will take its ground against the world, and employing against it God's law, which is not of the world, and the everlasting principles of right, justice, and equity, which are not always uppermost in it, will obtain the victory in the contest! This " world's voice," and " world's opinion," so hostile to us, and which are used, on all occasions, as hobgoblins, to frighten weak minds and alarm timid consciences, will turn out in the end, however, we apprehend, to be very much like that *brutum fulmen*, that great bubble, " the world's convention," when the world begged to be excused from any participation in the wild schemes, in which a few madcap fanatics would involve it. Let the truth be spoken on this subject. It can never hurt the South, if it be spoken openly, honestly, without disguise, without concealment. It is only misrepresentation, falsehood, and slander, that do injury and provoke hostility. It is only because one party, the abolitionists, express their views in coarse, offensive, and inflammatory language, without caution, without reason, without forethought, without decency ; it is only because they misstate facts, and conceal, exaggerate, and misrepresent the truth, declaring that to be a great physical evil, a great moral wrong, an offence against religion and humanity, which is a great physical good, and a great moral and political right ; and because, in attempting to maintain the right, or what they conceive to be such, they confound the right and wrong together : it is only on these accounts they are to be regarded as dangerous and odious members of society. It is because another party, the anti-slavery men, among whom are to be placed the Northern Reviewers, are timid, through apprehension of being denounced as abolitionists, and, accordingly, express their opposition by remarks, hints, and inuendos, thrown out occasionally in the course of their speculations, striking deeply at the roots of our Southern policy, and which, by their silent and imperceptible operation, produce more extensive injury than would or could be effected by a bold, open, manly discussion, on its merits, of the entire question, that they are even still more dangerous enemies to the South than the abolition party, and are to be viewed with greater distrust. It is because the third party, who are neither abolitionists nor anti-slavery men, but simply office-seekers, place-hunters, would convert slavery into a political question, and break up the Union by their ambition, provided they may avail themselves of the disaster and ruin which ensue, to ride over the necks of Southern citizens to some post of honor or profit which tempts their aspirations and their efforts, that *their* course is to be cautiously and constantly watched by the whole South, and their designs detected and baffled. The South must defend herself, without looking for any protection from her brethren of the North and East, except it be " such protection as vultures give to lambs, covering, while they devour them !' She is able to do it. She has strong minds and stout hearts, which are faithful to her honor, and alive to their duty, and who stand ready to do battle for her ; and let them come up, and that right early, to the help of the South against the mighty.

WINTER SCENE.

BY MAYNARD D. RICHARDSON.

Look upon the winter hearth,
What a scene of careless mirth ;
Yonder goes a thoughtless round,
Wheeling at the viol's sound ;
There is many a wanton fairy,
With light heart and footsteps airy ;
With no thought upon the morrow,
Things that never yet knew sorrow.

There are some of riper years,
Taught, methinks, in human cares,
Yet they look with grateful sight,
On the whirling ring's delight—
Care has lesson'd to be kind,
And has mellow'd well each mind,

Till their very griefs become
Gentle teachers for their home.

These are small and humble joys,
But their presence never cloys—
Though they come with every night,
Still their presence brings delight.
Memory has not lost its pow'r,
And the old survey the hour,
When like those that wander by,
They, too, had their revelry.

'Tis a pleasant song and play,
Those who know them well may say,
Which the wrought and anxious ear,
Listens evermore to hear—
That same song by winter sung,
Uttered forth by childhood's tongue,
That same sport, when none would tire,
Round the good old winter fire.

Never may the open brow,
Or the heart that's joyous now,
Or the wild and wanton dream,
Or the gay, unflickering beam,
Or the footstep light and airy,
Find the future visionary—
'Twere a Poet's sweetest pray'r,
That their fortunes should be fair.

THE DELIGHTS OF KNOWLEDGE.

BY HENRY L. PINCKNEY.

How delightful is the pursuit of knowledge ? Who would not like to trace the progress of science, from its earliest dawn in Egypt or Chaldea, to the full splendor of the present age ; and the gradual advancement of society, from the origin of civil institutions, to the refinement and perfection that are now displayed in the civilized portions of the globe ? Who would not wish to be conversant with the prominent events of history, and with all those occurrences, at every epoch, that produced important effects upon the fortunes of mankind, and to be so thoroughly imbued with classic lore, as to be competent to appreciate the beauties, and adjudge the merits, of the ancients and the moderns ? Who would not desire to be well-skilled in politics, to comprehend the advantages and defects of every form of government, and particularly the complex structure, and peculiar operation of our own constitution ? Who would not desire to be acquainted with every system, and with every sect—to hold improving converse with the moralist, as he inculcates the lessons of wisdom, and the dignity of virtue—to listen to philosophy, as it explains the motions of the heavenly bodies, or the structure of the earth, and the various strata of which it is composed—or to walk humbly with religion, as it unfolds the relations between man and his Creator, and points out the only path which can lead through peace and pleasantness here, to unending felicity in a future life ?

Who would not like to travel with the traveller, accumulating information as he roams abroad, or to accompany the
adventurous explorer as he visits the utmost regions, and
inhospitable climes, cheerfully enduring hardships and
encountering hazards, for the exalted purpose of enlarging the boundaries of science, and enrolling his name
amongst the honored benefactors of his race ? Who
would not like to be familiar with the eminent men of every
age and nation—to sympathize with patriots who have
nobly suffered in their country's cause—to dwell upon the
achievements of warriors, who have erected the standard
of independence upon the ruins of a throne—to hang
upon the lips of orators, rousing their countrymen to the
assertion of their rights, and catch the inspiration of liberty from their burning words—or to revel in the charms
of poetry, whether it moves with the majesty of the epic
muse, or pours forth the plaintive softness of elegiac verse?
Who would not desire, in short, that new light should be
daily infused into his understanding, new accessions made
to his intellectual resources, and that he should grow in
knowledge as he grows in years, constantly perfecting his
nature and increasing his happiness, by multiplying his
literary attainments, and expanding the capacities of his
immortal mind ? *And how valuable is knowledge to the
fortunate* possessor ! What a sphere of usefulness does
it offer ! What a fund of enjoyment, of which nothing
can deprive him ! What a source of influence and power,
particularly in a country like ours, in which no distinctions
are recognized, but those that arise from superior intellect
and virtue. Who then would be ignorant, rather than
take the trouble to become enlightened ? Or contented
with obscurity, rather than strive for eminence ? Or

willingly forego a treasure, which no moth or rust can destroy, which will go with him wherever he goes, which confers pleasure at home and fame abroad, dignifies prosperity, and affords consolation in misfortune ? *And how all-important is knowledge to the welfare of society !* Who can tell the mischievous errors it has corrected, the false and dangerous theories it has exploded, the degrading superstitions it has banished, the ignorant fears it has dissipated, the cruelties it has repressed, the sufferings and labor it has mitigated or abolished, the comforts and luxuries it has introduced, the intelligence and happiness it has universally diffused ? Who can estimate the advantages that have resulted, in reference to war and commerce, from the invention of gunpowder and the discovery of the mariner's compass, or the beneficent influence which the Reformation, aided by the art of printing, has exerted in disseminating the blessings of religion, liberty, and learning, throughout the world? What indeed would society be, without the light of knowledge ? What is it that teaches us the properties of matter, and the laws of motion ; the nature of light, and the laws of vision ; the properties of air, and the nature and effects of heat and cold ; the causes of earthquakes and volcanoes, of winds and clouds; and, in a word, that elucidates the phenomena, and enables us to control the elements of nature ?

What is it that gives to geography its correctness, to navigation its security, to commerce its extension, to agriculture its productiveness, to architecture its strength and elegance, to machinery its diversified application and unbounded power? What is it that has made us acquainted with the inhabitants of the air, the ocean, and the earth—with the nature and properties of every animal or

vegetable that is fit for food, or that supplies an article of
commerce—of every plant that contributes to our clothing,
or alleviates disease—of every mineral or metal that is
indispensable to comfort, or that enters essentially into the
wealth of nations—of every insect that is either useful in
medicine, or that produces a delicacy for the taste, or a
luxurious material for manufacture, or a beautiful color to
adorn it? What is it that unfolds the structure of the
human frame, showing, indeed, how fearfully and wonderfully it is made—or has invested surgery with the admirable precision and dexterity which it now exhibits—or
that enables medicine to conquer all the maladies to which
mankind is subject, those plagues and pestilences alone
excepted, which seem destined by Providence to perform
the office of special judgments, and to remain incurable
scourges of the human race? What is it that disarms the
lightning of its power—elevates valleys and represses
hills—cleaves the ocean, and ascends the sky? What is
it that we behold in every elegant and useful art—in the
diversified hues that attract the eye—in the dresses and
decorations of our persons and our houses—in every im-
plement of husbandry or war—in the subterraneous aqueduct, or the heaven-kissing monument—in the animated
canvas, or speaking marble? What are all these, but the
varied triumphs of the human mind! And who can estimate their value! To say nothing of that absolute state
of barbarism, " when wild in woods, the noble savage
ran," who can measure the difference between the splendid illumination of the nineteenth century, and that glim-
mering condition of society, when astrology assumed to
regulate events, and alchemy to transmute all the other
metals into gold—when ignorance was affrighted by an

ignis fatuus, and comets and meteors were regarded
as the immediate precursors of the dissolution of the world
—when science was considered synonymous with magic,
and punished as the evidence of atrocious crime—when
superstition occupied the seat of justice, and guilt or innocence was established by the righteous decisions of fire
or water, or the infallible ordeal of military prowess?
Science is, indeed, to the moral, what the great orb of day
is to the natural world; and as the extinction of the latter
would necessarily be followed by universal darkness and
decay, so, were art and science lost, society would inevitably relapse into the savageism from which it is their
proud boast to have elevated and redeemed it.

But, advanced as knowledge is, it has by no means
attained the ultimate height to which it may be carried!
In medicine, for instance, the mastery still remains to be obtained over various diseases that deride its power, and the
gratitude of mankind is yet reserved for him who shall
achieve the victory. Indeed, every department of knowledge still affords room for improvement, and rewards for
genius. The sun of science knows no meridian. In fact,
scarely is one improvement in the full tide of successful
experiment, before it is superseded by another. Even
now, whilst steam is riding, like a sea-god, in his ocean
car, it is in contemplation to dethrone it, by the substitution, in its stead, of the novel power of electro-magnetism.
Such is the limitless nature and aspiring tendency of
genius. Every year will develope new principles, or the
applications of known ones to purposes to which, as yet,
they have never been directed; and thus, new inventions,
and new improvements, like newly discovered stars, will
be constantly increasing the light of science, and adding

to individual comfort and national wealth, by furnishing new instruments of power, and disclosing new sources of prosperity !

———

THE SCHOOL GIRL WATCHING THE STARS.

BY A. A. MULLER, D.D.

> Sacred the lawn, where many a cypress threw
> Its length of shadow, while he* watched the stars.
> ITALY—ROGERS.

'Tis said that when at eve the far off sky
  Hath spread o'er earth its glittering robes of light,
And stars look out from their bright canopy
  On flowers that breathe their fragrance to the night;
That then, thy gentle muse will eager turn
  Its eagle gaze, to where yon fires above
Shed o'er the countless orbs, that silent burn,
  Their light of beauty and their charm of love !

'Tis said that when, throughout the sleeping world,
  No sound is heard save the lone night-bird's strain,
And naught is seen save streams of light unfurl'd,
  From silvery banners of the starry plain ;
That thy young spirit leaves its bed of earth,
  To seek among those chroniclers of time,

* Galileo.

15*

The famed recital of their early birth,
    When, at creation's morn, they glowed in all their prime.

And thou hast thoughtful gazed o'er that high dome,
    On those bright orbs of beauty as they glowed,
Till thou hast made each star a seraph's home,
    And o'er the lost and gone thy love bestowed :
At this lone hour how many an eye like thine,
    Hopeless of sleep and freed from feverish dream,
Looks on the pale light as from Dian's shrine,
    It throws o'er rock, and lake, and woods, its lengthen'd
        beam !

Perhaps with Fancy's light thy mind hath traced
    Each classic legend of the starry heaven ;
And sought, amid those realms, the forms that graced
    Each fabled name by ancient sages given ;
Yes ! thou hast seen Pleone's daughters fair,
    And watch'd the quiv'ring lustre of those eyes,
Trembling with liquid light as from each sphere
    They look'd on earth from their own palace in the
        skies.

And thou hast seen the Virgin's golden zone
    Set with rich gems from heaven's own sainted shrine ;
While sister planets, round her azure throne,
    Hymn'd the soft music of their harps divine ;
And Leda's graceful curve of spangled beads,
    Crested in beauty o'er her wings of light ;
Orion's belt, and Mars, whose fiery steeds
    Bore his red banner o'er the fields of night !

But brighter far than all that meet thy view,
　　Was the long milky-way—that shining throng,
Where seraphs, with their white wings, swiftly flew
　　To swell o'er all this earth the Saviour's cradle song ;
That melody which breathed from harps of old,
　　The harmony of heaven,—the song of cherubim,
And from that spangled arch, sublimely told
　　" Peace and good will to man "—Creation's choral hymn.

Such hast thou seen, when thy uncovered head
　　And thy pale cheek have felt the falling dews,
While many a lonely star hath o'er thee shed
　　Its purest offerings to thy cherished muse :
Child of the Zodiac ! those bright gems are thine !
　　Still bid thy muse pursue its eagle flight ;
Still woo their loveliness—for thee they shine !
　　Types of thy maiden innocence—the soul's best light.

'Tis well that thou in loveliness and youth,
　　Flowers 'neath thy feet, and o'er thee, starry skies,
Canst bring thy young heart to this page of truth,
　　And learn o'er earth, and all its woes, to rise.
'Tis well thy spirit, clothed in darkness here,
　　Should seek the freedom of that light above :
Who would not leave this earth, for yon bright sphere,
　　Where sainted spirits dwell in light and heavenly love !

CAMPOS SANTOS.

BY F. WURDEMAN, M. D.

ONE of the chief objects of curiosity to the stranger, in every town in Cuba, is the Campos Santos; he visits it, propelled by the same feeling which prompts him to witness an execution, or any other sight that will chill his blood, and create a certain sense of sinking at the pit of his stomach, which those, ignorant of its position, have referred to the heart. Having hired a volante at the Plaza for seventy-five cents an hour, one-half of the price asked, I rode out at the gate del Punta, through a long street of mean-looking houses, built near the borders of the sea, to the common cemetery of Havana, where all the dead of the city and its large suburbs are interred. The entrance to it is through a pretty shrubbery of perpetual roses, papayas, pomegranates, and other tropical trees, irrigated by meandering rills from an aqueduct, which supplied several reservoirs placed about the garden; while two large majagnas over the gate, and several tall palms interspersed about the garden, threw a grateful shade over all, and added to the inviting freshness of the spot. Through the centre of an oblong building, used for a chapel and dwelling-house of the sexton, an arched passage led me into the cemetery, a level square divided into four equal parts by two transverse, flagged walks, each quarter being enclosed by a neat, low, iron railing, and having in one corner a receptacle for the bones disinterred in digging new graves. They were already more than filled, the pile of bleached skulls and

other bones being heaped up above the top of the walls
of each, while above them, to soothe the friends of the
deceased for the liberty thus taken with their remains, four
obelisks raised their tall forms, having inscribed on them
the comfortable assurance—" Exultabunt ossa humiliata."
About forty large pines of the country, resembling cedars,
threw a partial shade over the walks, while the ground,
bare of shrubbery, was covered by a luxuriant growth of
grass. At the extremity of the middle walk was a small, neat
chapel, containing a few fresco paintings, and a chaste
altar in the form of a sarcophagus, supporting a small
image of our Lord on the cross. Within, and over the
door and porch without, suitable inscriptions in Latin reminded those who read them of the final resurrection, and
gave encouragement to those who died the death of the
righteous. Near the chapel, the ground in the adjoining
squares contained numerous slabs of marble and other
stones, covering the entrance to the vaults beneath, and
having the names of the families to which they belonged on
them. On several were coats of arms in basso-relievo, but I
saw few individual names, and only one short epitaph. They
were very chaste, with no pretensions to style, and were
placed close to each other, forming a large and varied
pavement. At the other end of the same square, two
negroes were busily employed in digging graves, breaking
up the stiff clay with pickaxes, and throwing out with
each spadeful of earth numerous bones, some of which
were still connected by their ligaments, and were intermingled with portions of clothes and shoes. It was
evident, from the great number of these remains about the
graves, that the Campos Santos of Havana did not possess
those solvent powers which that of Pisa does; and which,

filled with soil brought from Palestine by a pious priest, destroys in twenty-four hours—as every visiter to it is told—all vestiges of the bodies buried in it. As this cemetery contains only four or five acres, and from ten to twelve bodies are daily interred, this deficiency is greatly felt, and quick-lime is often thrown in the graves to hasten their decomposition. There was little in the place to please the eye, and I was about to leave it, when a black covered cart drove to the gate, and a postilion with a gaily embroidered coat entered, and whistling to the two negroes, beckoned to them. They methodically took up a bier, and having approached the hearse, opened a door behind and drew out a kind of shallow tray containing two bodies— one a dark mulatto, the other a white man, both half-dressed in ragged clothes. On passing me I followed, the only attendant on their burial, and having reached the grave, looked on. There seemed, at first, to be some consultation between the two negroes, whether it was best to tumble them in together or singly; they decided on the latter, and taking them up by their hands and feet, laid them in their narrow cell on their backs, as they had been brought, their feet in opposite directions. While I gazed on their upturned features, exposed to the bright rays of a meridian sun, and almost fancied that their open eyes and half-parted lips showed signs of life, the negroes returned with another load from the hearse, a fine-looking, young black woman, dressed in a clean, gay-colored, calico frock, with neat slippers on her feet. She was covered with a blanket, probably her last bed, and beside her were some soiled clothes; these were first thrown in, and then the body deposited on those of the men. The sexton now approached, and measuring with his eye the depth of the grave, concluded that it was full enough, which I thought also; and the process of throwing in the earth and stamping it down commenced :—when the whole was completed, I am sure the soil was not two feet over the bodies. While this was enacting, two young ladies, with their caballero, were promenading the walk close by, totally unmoved by the scene; while a negro woman, who had been peeping through the cracks of the hearse when it arrived, gazed listlessly on, smoking her segar, in defiance of the notice placed at the entrance, which promised excommunication to all who in this place smoked, did any damage to the contents, or eat,—the latter being, in my opinion, quite superfluous. Familiar as I have long been to the sight of the mutilated contents of the dissecting-room, I confess that my feelings were somewhat shocked at the way in which these bodies were buried, and I walked slowly away, musing on the different manner in which I had seen the equally worthless remains of one of the great of the earth, consigned to its kindred dust. The whole spot had a look of desolation. Here were no flowers planted round the graves,—no garlands of immortals strewn over the tombs of departed friends,—not even the usual recital of the grief of the survivors engraved on the marble. All was cold and heartless. I never saw the separating line between the living and the dead more strongly marked than in this burial-ground; and I left its precincts with feelings far different from any I had ever before experienced in a similar place. The cessation of burials in the vaults of the Havana churches, was the work of one of the bishops, Juan de Espada, who laid out this cemetery, and was a perfect Tacon in his own line. Soon after he had consecrated the ground, a nobleman died; and although the bishop was strongly urged to let him be interred with his ancestors in the church vaults, he refused, and the body was sent to the Campos Santos. With all its defects, it is the best I have visited on the island. That of Matanzas is still more offensive to the eye. And those of country villages have, not unfrequently, broken temporary coffins lying about the gate, while over the grounds will be seen portions of the scalp with the hair attached, and other half-decomposed remains of the buried. It is well, therefore, that they are always there, situated on the west of the village, which, as the wind blows almost constantly from the eastward, is seldom on their leeward. The better classes are, as elsewhere, enclosed in coffins ; but very many have not this temporary protection from that common caterer, the grave-worm.

NATURE MADE FOR MAN.

BY CHARLES FRASER.

WHILE conscious reason for itself beholds
This plenteous banquet spread, what kindled joy
Shall man enraptured feel, or how express
His grateful love ?   For him, the morning smiles
And scatters fragrance from its balmy wings ;
For him, a thousand harmonizing lays
And choral hymns breathe joyful from the grove ;
For him, the stream slow murmurs in its course
To soothe the lonely hour of pensive rest.

The rushing tempest and the sighing breeze
Alike for him diversify the year.
In bright uncertainty his hopes repose,
Amidst the blushing promises of spring ;
And autumn, clad in golden mantle, crowns
With rich reality his happy dreams.
Perpetual change the varying seasons bring ;
Alternate gloom and gladness nature proves,
The summer's beauty and the winter's frown :
But man, unchanged, beholds the scene revolve
With ceaseless round,—whilst pleasures, ever new,
The ample page of nature's book affords.
On renovated wings the Phœnix mind,
Triumphant o'er decay, exalted soars
In every hallowed shade, 'midst every hue,
By nature's hand profuse, thrown graceful round,—
Or in the blazing noon's resplendent ray,—
Or darkly, in the fearful midnight hour,
On the blue-rolling wave, or hanging rock,—
To reason's eye unveil'd, ethereal beams
The seraph charm of heaven's immortal Love.

———

THE LOST MAIL.

BY CAROLINE GILMAN.

My cousin Lewis Walpole, from the earliest childhood, was remarkable for finding things. His companions

thought he enjoyed what is commonly called good luck,
but a closer philosophy might say he was particularly
observing. He once found two letters in a morning walk,
the reward for which filled his pocket with spending
money for a year; and as we were rambling together one
day, he brought up from the mud on his rattan a gold ring.
It was a plain ring with two initials; and though no immediate reward followed, it introduced him to a friendship
which was like golden apples for the rest of his days.
Once I stepped on a bit of dirty paper; Lewis followed me,
picked it up, and laid it in his little snug pocket-book.
Six weeks after, an advertisement appeared offering three
hundred dollars reward for that very bit of paper, which
was the half of a note worth as many thousands.

It seemed to me that pins sprang from the earth for
Lewis, for he was never without a row of them in his
waistcoat. If an old lady was in want of one, Lewis was
always ready; and then his head was patted, and he was
treated to tit-bits. If a pretty girl's shawl was to be fastened, behold, Lewis's pin came forth, and then such a
beautiful smile beamed upon him! If a child was in
danger of losing her bonnet, Lewis's offered pin was
seized, and he was caressed with lips and eyes, for her
preservation from a maternal chiding.

Cousin Lewis, some time since, removed to the far
West, and I, his senior by a dozen years (though he was
a stricken bachelor), went with him to darn his stockings,
and keep his hearth clean. We called our log house
Sparrownest, and in one way and another made it as cozy
as heart could wish. What could poor cousin Lewis find
now, in his wide fields and vast forests? Not pins, certainly! but one day, twenty miles from home, he did find

in the wild woods a strange thing—a pretty Irish girl, about sixteen years old, all alone, wringing her hands, and sobbing as if her heart would break. Cousin Lewis dismounted (he was a noble horseman), and offered her assistance. The poor child only wept the more, crying out—

"And isn't it alone in the wide world that I am?"

It was an awkward business; but cousin Lewis knew better than anybody how to do a kindness; so he wiped her eyes, soothed her, and bade her be of good cheer; then took her up on his saddle and brought her home. What big bundle has cousin Lewis brought home? thought I, as he rode up to the door in the twilight. And great was my astonishment to see a red-cheeked girl slip down from the saddle, with a shame-faced look. I bestirred myself and got supper, for the child was cold and hungry. When her appetite was appeased (she ate a whole chicken, poor thing!) she began to cry.

"What can I do for you, my child?" said I.

"And isn't it of my father I'm thinkin'," said she, sobbing and wringing her hands. "There were twenty of us, big and little, in the wagons, and him in the front one. It was with a clever old lady I was, in the after one, we to take the charge of one another, ye mind. And when the 'orses was stopped for walthering, I minded to go and gather some flowers I had never seen in my own counthry. So I sated myself down to pull some flowers, and a bit of weed thereabout looked like the shamrock, and I fell a thinkin'; a kind of thdream came upon me, and I was at play with Kathleen and the girls, and then we were for throwing peat at Dermot, and Dermot made as if to kiss me, the impudent ——, and I slapped him on the face, and then

I knew nothin' more until I started up and found myself
alone! The wagons were gone, the owls were hootin',
and the night comin' on. Then I shouted, and cried, and
raved, and ran till my feet failed me, and then my heart
was jist like to break in two, when the masther (here she
made a low curtsey to cousin Lewis) came along like the
light, on a dark night, and took compassion on the poor
girl; and she will love him all her days for his goodness,
she will."

With that cousin Lewis took out his pocket-handker-
chief, and I punched the fire.

So Dora became one of us, and she sung about Sparrownest like a young bird, with a natural sigh now and
then for her father.

Did cousin Lewis find anything else in the forest?
Listen. As he was riding on horseback, in his deliberate
way, on the far outskirts of his fields, he saw something
white scattered among the green herbage. He spurred
his horse toward the spot. It was strewed with letters,
which were dashed with mud and rain. Cousin Lewis
alighted, and quietly deposited them in his saddle-bags.

Dora and I had made a blazing fire, for the night was
chilly; and while I was knitting, she trod about with a
light step, laying the cloth for supper, and singing an old
Irish air about " Dermott, my dear." When cousin Lewis
came in, she sprang towards him with such joy, and
hung his hat on the peg, and put his heavy saddle-bags in
one corner, and brought him water to bathe his hands,
and helped to draw off his great boots. He looked very
fondly on her. You would not have thought he was so
much older than she, for his hair was curling and black
as the raven's; mine has been grey many years.

At supper, cousin Lewis told us about the letters. I
confess, old as I am, I could scarcely keep my hands
from the saddle-bags, and I thought Dora would have torn
them open.

"We shall have a rainy day to-morrow," said cousin
Lewis, in his quiet way, "and will want amusement;
besides, our Yankee clock points to bedtime."

"Masther, dear," said Dora imploringly, "the letthers
will not slape a wink for wanting to be read."

"We must keep them locked up, my love, as we do
restless children," said cousin Lewis, and I think I saw
him kiss the hand that struggled to take the key of the
saddle-bags away from him. No wonder he felt young,
for he was very straight and graceful. The next morning,
when we assembled at breakfast, the rain descended in
that determined style which announces a regular outpour-
ing for the day.

Dora and I glanced at the saddle-bags ; cousin Lewis
smiled.

"Have you settled it with your conscience," said he,
"whether those letters should be read? There has
evidently been a mail robbery."

"You wouldn't in rason be after sendin' the letthers
away, poor things," said Dora, "when they were left in
the forests. And it wasn't *that* ye did to me, any how!"

Cousin Lewis looked down and sighed and smiled. I
could not tell whether he was thinking of the letters or
Dora, but I noticed, when he smiled, how white and even
his teeth were.

After some discussion, we decided that no seal was to
be broken where the superscription was legible, but that it
was right and proper that we should constitute ourselves

a committee to decide which of them were in a state to
return to the post-office. Cousin Lewis was appointed
reader. While he gave us the contents of the following,
Dora amused herself by treading on Carlo's paw, who
looked up in her face and whimpered. The date was
erased :—

DEAR JUDGE,

"You will be surprised to learn that   *   *   *   has
taken the field against us. What will European cabinets
say when such addle-headed fellows form a part of our
government? B——, is up and doing. You must be on
the alert, and circumvent these movements if possible.
The Secretaryship may yet be secured by a general can-
vassing. T. and J. are fit tools to take care of S., and
give a sop to the old Cerberus on the Island. Keep the
date in mind as——"

The rest of the writing was obliterated. The next
letter made Dora stop playing with Carlo's paw.

Philadelphia, &c.

DEAR RUSSELL,

"I received the books and thank you. After looking
them over I had an odd dream, and was awoke with my
own excessive laughter. It was utterly preposterous that
a staid lawyer, half a century old, should be dreaming
such dreams.

"I dreamed that I was blowing soap bubbles out of a
clay pipe; a thing I have not done since you and I were
boys at Fishkill. One after another they floated off,
poetically enough; now rising gracefully in the sunbeams,
and now exploding softly on the turf at my feet. At

length one, the king of the rest, grew and grew at the end of my pipe, until it became as large as a wash-bason. It fell and lay rolling about, offering beautiful prismatic hues to the eye, when presently a little square-nosed pig came grunting towards it. Twice he smelt and tried to turn it, but retreated as it rolled towards him. Again he seemed to gather up his courage, and thrusting his square snout against it, it exploded with a noise like a pistol. Little square-nose ran as if for life and death, and I awoke in a positive perspiration with excess of laughter."

"interpretation of
" Your,
JAMES COL——."

Dora shouted with glee at this droll description, and her interest was kept awake by the following, written evidently by a relation of a certain popular character:

" Mrs Sippi
"<i>West end of A merry K.</i>

" Dear Veller,

"Wot with my see sickness and warious causes, its ben utterly onpossible for me to rite to you, tho it warnt for want of thinkin' on you, as thief said to the constable. Were you ever see sick, cousin Veller? If you was, you would say that you felt in the sitivation of a barrel of licker, that's rolled over and over agin its vill. A most mortifyin' thing happen'd a board the wessel. You know, my lovin' cozen, the jar of bake beans you put aboard for my private eatin'. Wot should the stewhard do, but set it a-top of three basins in my stateroom, and won day wen the ladies was eatin' lunch, there came an awful lurch of the

see, the which burstin' open my door, driv the whole concern into the cabin. The beans was mouldy beyond account, and smelt werry wilely, as the pig said wen he vent
to his neighbor's pen. The beans was awfully griddle
about the floor under the ladies' feet, who scrambled up
into cheers. I put my head out of my birth to explain,
and was taken with an awful qualm in the midst of a
pology.

"Give my love to Miss ——, and tell her the Merry-
cans have been quite shy of my letter of introduction from
her. I'm jealous she didn't move in sich respectable society as me, or else she made a mistake as the dissector
said wen he got hold of a live body. I ain't seen a drunk-
en lady, nor a young woman married to her grandfather,
nor a hypocriticle parson since I left the wessel.

"I vill write agin as ever I get to Mis Soreey e.

Your loven cozen
TIMOTHY."

It may well be imagined that Sparrownest rang with
our mirth, for little matters move one in the country. Dora
laughed until she cried, but her mood was soon changed
when cousin Lewis, in his pathetic tones, read the next
letter.

"FATHER:

"I take my pen in desperation, not in hope ; and yet,
perhaps, when you know that the body of my child lies
beside me without my having the means to buy him a
shroud, you may relent. Poor Edward is stretched on his
hard matrass beside the boy, and his hollow cough rings
fearfully through the empty room. Oh! father, if he had

but that old sofa you banished to the garret on the night of my birth-day ball! You will think me crazy to say so, but you are a murderer, father; my boy died for want of nourishment, and you are murdering Edward, too, the best, the noblest —. Oh Heaven, to think of the soft beds in your vacant rooms, and the gilt-edged cups from which you drink your odorous tea, with that white sugar sparkling like diamonds. I have just given poor Edward his nauseous draught in a tin vessel. I have not had time to clease it since my baby was ill.

"My baby, how tranquilly he rests! Would that Edward and I might lie down beside him!

"Father, will God treat his erring children as you do? ' Like as a father pitieth his children'— Oh, Father in heaven, art thou like mine? A change has come upon Edward, father, he is dying—dead."

Dora laid her head upon the table, in tears; but she soon wiped her eyes, and listened, with feminine interest, to another letter:

"*New York.*

"DEAR ISABEL :—

"You must not fail to be here on the 21st of next month as my first bridesmaid. I can take no excuse. My dress is perfect; papa imported it for me. There is and shall be no copy in the city. The pearls, too, are exquisitely *unique.* You can form some judgment of what will be necessary for your own dress by mine. Of course you must be less elegant than the bride.

"Frock with lace trimmings, &c. $150 00
"Veil, ... 50 00
"Pocket handkerchief (the divine thing!) . . . 20 00

" Embroidered gloves, ...   3 00
" Shoes, ...   2 50
" Stockings, ...   5 00
" Embroidered scarf, ... 10 00
" Set of pearls, ... 200 00
" Boquet of natural flowers, ...   5 00

" Come, dearest Isabel, and witness my dress and my felicity!

" Your own, ELEANOR.

" P.S. You know you must appear with me on Sunday. Mamma has bought me a heaven of a bonnet, with feathers."

Dora rolled up her eyes: "And isn't it feathers that's to make that bird?" said she. Upon which she began to speculate on her own wants if she should be married, and decided that ten dollars would be an ample dower for her.

Cousin Lewis, appropriately enough, though accidentally, hit upon a letter of good advice to a bride. I was very much disconcerted, however, at the third paragraph, to see Dora begin to nod; at the fourth, her hands fell in her lap, and her ball of thread rolled on the floor; at the fifth, her head sank on her shoulder, and Cousin Lewis had to support her with his left arm.

" Don't disturb the poor child," said he, kindly, as I began to shake her.

" But, Cousin Lewis," said I, "it is a pity she should lose such excellent advice, particularly if she should marry a parson."

" You know nothing about these matters, Rachel," said Cousin Lewis, sharply. "I will tell her all the advice to-morrow."

So his left arm continued to keep her from falling, and he read on.

"MY DEAR MARY :—

" You ask for advice on the new scene of duties which you have entered. I thank you for the implied compliment contained in such a request. Having watched your growth from the moment that you first blessed the eyes of your fond parents, to this time, when, with conscientious resolutions, and warm affections, you have become the wife of a clergyman, it is with no little interest that I answer it.

" You feel, doubtless, better than I can express, how necessary is true piety to the happiness of one whose husband is devoted to the cause of Christ. Lamentable, indeed, is that connexion, if she go coldly to the house of God,—slight the meeting of household prayer, and give no religious point to the events of life ; but beautiful is the spectacle, where confiding hearts move in pious sympathy, pleased with earth, yet looking toward Heaven ; and when the wave of sorrow comes (as come it must) and rushes over their souls, together bending but a moment with the shock, and then, with a common impulse, resuming their upward view.

" Yet, I would warn you, in the enthusiasm of your aims at religious duty, not to involve yourself in your husband's sphere. Many young ladies, when wedded to clergymen, have made themselves unhappy by extending too widely the circle of their cares. Ardent in the cause of the Master they profess to follow, they imagine that they must devote their time and powers to the flock over which their husband presides. By degrees, family cares press on and crowd their time, and they lose their equanimity of temper amid conflicting duties.

"A minister's wife should show by her deportment, that she is one of his *flock*, and not a leader. A constant and respectful attendance on his ministry, and a deportment which marks that her thoughts are

'For God, through him,'

will secure for her a quiet influence over the minds of his people. She should seem not to be *first*, even in good works; but skilfully and delicately promote the cause of truth through others.

"The best service you can render his people will be to make your husband's home happy; then will he go forth prepared to sympathize with them, and his free spirit will range over the wide sphere of duty in religious joy. Remember that, in common with all men,

'A something of submission, of respect,
Obedience, kindness personal, he loves.
A slighter service so adorn'd will please
Him more than, wanting this, a greater would.'
                                        GOETHE.

"Be not cold to his peculiar taste; if he loves books, cultivate literature, that he may find your intellectual improvement keeping pace in a measure with his own. If music attract him, forward in yourself or in those around you an accomplishment which may soothe his weariness or beguile his care; and while you faithfully study your domestic duties, either in the preservation of neatness and order in your household, or with your needle by his side, let him see that mind is still 'lord of the ascendant.'

" You will probably, as you pass by the period of youth, see those around you who are coming forward to the same animated scene. Be careful not to forget your sympathy with the young ; particularly with those entrusted to you. If you look coldly on scenes which interest them, you allow them to have a set of enjoyments independent of you, which is dangerous to your influence over their characters. Mingle in society in moderation, and watch the little changes in manners that occur there, that they may not be able to teach you. When they begin to direct you on the subject of dress and deportment, they feel that in one point, at least, they have more knowledge than yourself, and you lose just so much authority.

" Society, and usually their own preferences, demand from the families of clergymen the same refinement which belongs to those whose means are much better calculated to allow the acquisition of accomplishments. In cultivating the manners and tastes of young persons under your charge, you must impress on their minds that you are training them to a means of self-support in case of the intervention of pecuniary need, or that you are giving them resources in mental suffering, or providing them with means to appear amiable to others, and form a note in the concert which fine talents are sounding over the whole field of existence, and which, in a manner, speak the praise of Him who gave them. These considerations will repress the mere vanity of display, and daily lessons of piety will chasten and refine the whole.

" I say to you, what I would say to all young wives : cultivate a gentle temper. *You* have a sweet disposition.

Thank God for it, as the best dower for married life. Riches, accomplishments, intellect, fade all away before the genuine smile of good-nature. But do not trust to the gift of sweet temper. None but a woman can know the wear and tear of feeling produced by the minute details of household care. Pray and strive for gentleness, and 'the soft answer which turneth away wrath.' Be willing *not* to have your own way. The contest for power is always a losing one for woman.

> ' Obedience
> Is the best duty !'

In obtaining power, she may chance to lose the sway of stronger affection.

" Farewell, dear Mary. May the God who has blessed you thus far, sanctify and accept the offering of the talents which you and yours have laid before him.

" Your affectionate Aunt,
" CAROLINE."

As Cousin Lewis's voice ceased after reading this certainly excellent letter, Dora started and rubbed her eyes ; it was not many minutes, however, before her sympathies were excited, and her fingers beating time on the table to the musical jingle of the following girlish epistle :

" *Cambridge, Mass.*

" I ought to make excuses due,
    Dear Julia, for not writing you,
    Since, with a kindness prompt and free,
    You gave your charming thoughts to me ;

But I abominate excuses,
And rank them among mere abuses,
As they come marching full and round,
To tinkling instruments of sound,
Without a particle of feeling,
Mere drapery for the heart's concealing.
Your letter was delightful to me,
And made a pleasant thrill run through me,
Like that we feel in smelling flowers,
Or when we listen to soft showers
That fall upon a sultry day,
And chase our languid thoughts away.
So you are reading Anacharsis !
How well kept up that learned farce is,
Showing us sages, states, and kings,
Familiarly as common things.
Stationed once more in this retreat,
Where leisure and excitement meet,
Where studious pleasures, happy, calm,
Show life with every softer charm,
Nothing disturbs seclusion's hour,
Which hovers with its tranquil power,
Save transient visiters, who seem
Like shooting stars, with brilliant gleam,
That dart from out a distant sphere,
Delight my gaze, and disappear.
The Boston question, What's the news ?
Is only answered by reviews,
Or weekly papers, letting out
The business that the world's about,
While the 'last book' unfolds its page
Of interest, in this bookish age.

Charles Lamb, amid some random start,
Throws out sweet whispers to my heart,
While Bulwer's strong, yet poison'd bowl,
I quaff, until my senses roll.
Not to his hand the task is given
To lift the erring soul to Heaven;
Tartarean darkness fills the soul
That yields to his unsound control.
   Some graver things than these I find
Daily to occupy my mind;
Theology, with critic eye,
Causes my lingering doubts to fly;
And history, with reflecting pen,
Teaches of empires and of men.
Then I have evening reveries,
In gazing on the changing skies;
And walks, where, as I look abroad,
My soul springs forward to its God.
Nor even lonely am I then,
Though straying from the haunts of men.
The breeze lifts up a pleasant voice,
The streams, in whispers, say ' Rejoice!'
And nature's tone, wherever given,
Thrills me, like nature's God in heaven.
But how I've written off my time,
Led by the marching steps of rhyme!
Forgive this light and careless letter,
Which leaves me still a heavy debtor
To you, for yours, with its completeness,
Finished, epistolary neatness;
And now, with kind remembrance, due,
Receive, dear girl, a warm adieu.

                              " EMILY."

" And isn't it nice, that?" said Dora, clapping her
hands. " Och! but it dances like Dermot to old O'Con-
ner's harp."

And now the impatient girl's fingers were again thrust
into the saddle-bags, but as she drew out several letters,
I observed that the superscription of one arrested her attention. She became very pale, and broke the seal impe-
tuously, and glanced at the signature. A joyous flush came
over her cheeks, she danced about, waving the letter in the
air, caught me round the neck and kissed me, and threw
herself into Cousin Lewis's arms in a passion of tears.
When she could speak she sobbed out—

" And isn't it father's own handwriting, darling? and
isn't he at Louisville, weeping for his own Dora? And
will not the master" (here she disengaged herself from
Cousin Lewis, and stood before him with her accustomed
courtesy) " take poor Dora to the father that's her own?"
Cousin Lewis was startled. " I had hoped," said he
gravely, " that is, Cousin Rachel and I had hoped, that
Sparrownest would have been your home for life, Dora."

Dora looked down, embarrassed, for my Cousin Lewis's
eyes were fixed upon her, and they were very black and
sparkling, though he was a stricken bachelor.

I withdrew towards the window, but did not altogether
look away. I saw Cousin Lewis take Dora's hand; I saw
Dora blush all up to the eyebrows; I heard Cousin Lewis
speak in a pleading tone. One would not have thought
him to be an old bachelor by his voice. I saw little Dora
tremble, her heart seemed starting from her bosom, and
she began to cry.

" I will not distress you," said Cousin Lewis tenderly.

16*

" Tell me all your feelings, as you are wont to do. Can you love me and be my wedded wife ?"

Dora looked up through her tears, her eyes shone sweetly.

" I will love the masther to the day of my death and after," said she, " but thin I will love Dermot better, and is it a sin is that ?"

Cousin Lewis dropped her hand abruptly, and left the room. He stayed away an hour and then calmly prepared for Dora's journey, and now I never hear him speak her name.

TO TIME—" THE OLD TRAVELLER."

BY WILLIAM H. TIMROD.

THEY slander thee, Old Traveller,
    Who say that thy delight
Is to scatter ruin, far and wide,
    In thy wantonness of might.
For not a leaf that falleth
    Before thy restless wings,
But in thy flight thou changest it
    To a thousand brighter things.

Thou passest o'er the fertile field,
    Where the dead lie stiff and stark,

Where naught is heard save the vulture's scream,
   Or the gorged wolf's famished bark.
But thou hast caused the grain to spring
   From the blood-enriched clay,
And the waving corntops seem to dance
   To the rustics' merry lay.

Thou hast strewn the lordly palace,
   In ruin o'er the ground,
And the dismal screech of the owl is heard,
   Where the harp was wont to sound.
But the self-same spot thou coverest
   With the dwellings of the poor,
And a thousand happy hearts enjoy
   What one usurped before.

'Tis true, thy progress layeth
   Full many a loved one low,
And for the brave and beautiful
   Thou hast caused our tears to flow.
But always near the couch of death,
   Nor thou, nor we can stay,
And the breath of thy departing wings,
   Dries all our tears away.

THE PILGRIMAGE.

BY THOMAS CANTE REYNOLDS.

It chanced that I arrived in Prague just a day or two before the festival of St. Wenceslaus, the patron saint of Bohemia, and of course did not omit the opportunity of witnessing a Roman Catholic pilgrimage. The royal saint is buried in the cathedral of St. Vitus, the metropolitan church of the archbishop of Prague, and the gorgeous chapel which contains his remains is filled with devotees during the continuance of the festival. But the chief centre of attraction is the equestrian statue of St. Wenceslaus, in the Horse Market, a noble oblong square, which lies in the quarter called " the New Town." An altar had been erected in front of the pedestal, the statue ornamented with banners and garlands, and an immense number of tapers placed around and on the statue and the altar, to create a halo of light about the saint, as his devotees crowded around him at night. During the days, several processions of peasants came in, in rustic pomp, from surrounding villages, to unite in the orisons of the " cits " of Prague, and increase the animation and *pittoresque* of the scene. Young girls, clad in white, and bearing garlands of flowers, headed these bands ; and as they defiled slowly into the square, and arranged themselves before the image of the saint, their clear, full voices, guided by the national instinct for music, poured forth a rich melody of praise to the patron of their church and land, chanting, in their soft Bohemian tongue, the ancient hymns in honor of the

royal martyr, which had been handed down through all the
stormy times of this turbulent and unfortunate city. At
night the Horse Market was illuminated, and a great crowd
collected in front of the altar ; some standing, some kneel-
ing, but all respectful, listening. religious in their deportment. On each side of the statue stood an armed sentinel, erect and motionless, apparently unobservant of the
scene before him : discipline had made of him a statue,
and I was reminded by his appearance of the Roman sentinel at the gate of Pompeii, who was found even in such
a scene to sacrifice life to military obedience. This military honor to the saint (for 'twas only such, and not a
mere police regulation), was in strange contrast with those
which the gowned and tonsured ministers of the church
were engaged in paying him. As far as my ignorance of
the Bohemian tongue enabled me to ascertain, the crowd
seemed to be singing rhymed hymns in his praise. A
priest gave out a verse of four lines, one line at a time, and
the spectators joined him in singing it. At the end of
each verse a trumpet sounded a blast, and at the end of
the hymn put forth a lengthy flourish, to my ears by no
means very ecclesiastical in its notes. This scene was
continued until late in the evening, when the greatly
diminished number of the worshippers admonished the
officiating clergy, that it were well to close ; and amidst
the services preparatory to the conclusion of the festival,
I left the scene, and hastened to my hotel.

THE LONE STAR.

BY MARY E. LEE.

FROM restless sleep I woke.   Dark dreams had prest
Heavy upon me, and mysterious thoughts
Of all things terrible, though undefin'd,
Had lain their chilling fingers on my heart,
Freezing the fount of life.
A sense of fearful loneliness hung o'er
My troubled spirit, 'till with stealthy tread
I sought the lifted casement, to look out
Upon the midnight heav'ns ; for I lov'd
Their solemn beauty, and had learn'd to read
Their letter'd volumes, till they grew to be
To my sad bosom, dear, familiar friends :
But all was gloom.   The wearied queen of night
Had sunk on her chill pillow, and the stars,
Those holy comforters, had turn'd away,
Nor left one foot-print of their shining feet,
To guide bewilder'd thought.   No sound was there
Of dissonance or concord ; but silence sat
Upon her ancient throne ; 'mid a deep hush
So boding and profound, that, with each pulse
Throbbing to fever-wildness, I lean'd forth
As if to hear the spirits whispering.
Just then when thought rov'd freest, and I stood
Gazing half-conscious on the sullen clouds
That press'd to the far East, a phantom-train,
Moving in mute procession—when my mind

Was yielding to imagination's sway,
And reason trembled on her steadfast base ;—
A single star look'd out—the blessed thing !
It looked half-trembling, yet so sweetly clear,
'Mid all that gloom and stillness, that I thought
And even now I think (though days have passed),
It was an angel's self that came to soothe
And calm and comfort me ; and then a voice
Soft as a seraph's note breath'd in my ear,
Trust but in heaven ! and then I knelt and pray'd,
'Till the seal'd fountains of my soul gush'd forth,
And I *was* comforted !
Through life that star shall cheer me ; though my path
Should further lead 'mid darkness, and the spots
Where memory loves to linger may be few ;
Though earthly joys may vanish, and the blooms
Of love and hope prove fruitless ; yet with gaze
Steadfast, unchanging, I will look beyond
The clouded present, to my guiding star,
An humble trust in heaven !

A DISSERTATION ON DANDIES.

BY S. A. HURLBUT.

WHAT is a dandy ? Whence comes he, and whither does he tend ? Has he any responsibility for use or abuse of his powers ?

These are questions deserving of serious consideration, and, perhaps, susceptible of a definite solution. Various definitions have been propounded. The author of " Sartor Resartus," the divine Teufelsdröch, whose German industry has searched all records of ancient and modern toilettes, and rummaged out all manner of costumes, from the figleaf of Father Adam down to the coronation robes of European majesty,—defines it thus, as nearly as we recollect: " an embodiment of the divine idea of *cloth*,"—one whose soul is fully and entirely possessed with a due sense of the powers and capabilities of the human frame as a cloth-wearing machine. This is the sublime definition. A more homely one is in the words of an old song:

> " What are dandies made of?
> False wristbands and collars,
> But very few dollars,—
> That's what dandies are made of."

The former appears the more eligible definition; somewhat too abstruse, to be sure, for common apprehension. A dandy is a thing which devotes itself to the glory of its maker-up; an appliance for the exhibition of the skill, talent, and ingenuity of the tailor and men's mercer: it is a walking advertisement of the creative power of the shears and thimble,—of the manner in which the incomplete handiwork of nature is carried out and aided by the intervention of art, padding out the meagre and coercing the superfluous into standard dimensions.

Such is the common, every-day dandy, wholly dependent for the space he fills in the public eye, on the taste of his maker-up. The problem given to be resolved by the "schneider," is this. Given, certain angles and lines as a foundation, and a certain quantity of material upon those angles and lines, to erect a certain figure. A problem requiring, often, as much anxious thought and careful survey, as a rail-road over the Alleghanies. It is wonderful to see how the mind of man triumphs over natural obstacles. In the construction of the great works destined to connect distant portions of the country, does a wide stream cross the line projected, the arched aqueduct rises and spans the rushing current,—the voyager below sees far between him and the blue sky, loaded vessels sweeping their onward way to the distant mart, or a rapid train borne as on the wings of the thunder-cloud. Deep tunnels drive through the solid ribs of mountains, or under mighty rivers, and emerge again into the light of cheerful day. But many, various and startling as are the manifestations of human industry and power, none are more so than the transformation which the wand of the tailor produces in the human figure. It reminds me of a wood-cut illustration of some nostrum for the hair. A poor, miserable, unhappy-looking individual, comes humbly and sneakingly up to the operator, bald as a buzzard, passes under the reviving influence of the composition, and comes out on the other side in a state of boundless ecstacy and rapture. His face is transfigured ; his fingers, trembling with delight, stray joyously through dark masses of curls, the new forests that have sprung up on the once barren heath. Similar to this in kind, though not in degree, is the change effected by the tailor upon the ungainly and ill-compacted figures of his votaries. In the snipping of his shears, in the twinkling of his needle, it is done ; and the forked animal comes out clothed with a far more desirable figure. It may be truly said of him, that his outward man is renewed day by day, or rather re-created, for small vestige is there of the original timbers whereon so fair a superstructure has been raised.

A new birth takes place for him at every dressing hour, —he views himself and ceases to be astonished. It is strange, too, how the thing preserves its identity under such wonderful and startling transformation. Rather, one would suppose, like the little woman whom the pedlar used so shamefully, it would declare, "*I* be not *I*." But as habits grow to us from use, so, ere long, the dandy begins to consider all the externals with which he is endued, as part and parcel of himself; integral and constituent portions of his nature and being. They become a part of his life. In them he lives, and moves, and has his being; and no higher thoughts, no better impulses, reach him through their triple shield. He stands in the focus of a concave mirror, which reflects only himself. Yet this " king of shreds and patches," writes itself *man*.

There is an incipient tendency to dandyism in almost every one. Its first demonstration is made by the new-breeched youngster, in his aspiration after more buttons on his jacket, and becomes quite violent when the era of coats and boots approaches. An awkward delight trembles through every fibre of the boy, when he feels the unaccustomed flapping of the tails; and he ever and anon looks round upon his caudal appendages, as did the jackdaw who borrowed the orient train of the peacock. As the sudden heir to an unexpected legacy, looks on the fair domains now to call him lord; as the happy owner of a prize, that rare individual scarce known to the "oldest inhabitant;" as the lover, just accepted and at the summit of his hopes,—look in joyous amaze around them, and say

in ecstacy, is all this really mine ?—even so does the
neophite in *coathood* doubt the absolute verity of his new
acquisition.   But even as the fortunate heir, or the lucky
purchaser, or the lover himself, soon subsides into the
sober certainty of waking bliss, and from that glides downward into dull possession, or perhaps satiety and wea ri-
ness, so does the *encoated* become familiar with his
garment, and familiarity soon breeds contempt. Coats
will perish in the using, else how could tailors live ?
That tailors should live may be questionable.   I have heard
it argued with great force and solidity, that a tailor, being
but the ninth part of a man, can of course subsist upon one-
ninth of what it costs to support a full man (hence their
partiality for cabbage) ; therefore, if a tailor be paid for
one coat out of nine, he is well paid ; if for two, he is
making money. This conclusion appears irresistible, —
the premises being once admitted.   In fact, it is so clear,
as to have addressed itself to the limited faculties of the
beings now under consideration, and they almost universally act upon it.   Were it not true, how comes it that all
tailors grow rich ?   That the premises are true, one need
only appeal to the established reception of the fact from
time immemorial. As a legal friend at our elbow suggests,
it is a common law principle, anterior to the Norman
conquest, pure Anglo-Saxon.

It might be nice arithmetic, to deduce from the above
maxim, how much manhood there is in a dandy. If a
tailor, the ninth part of a man, can create a thousand dandies, the human portion in each must be in a Homœopa-
thic dose ; each must have an infinitesimal (*not infinite*)
soul. We have hinted at the creation of the dandy ; true
it is, nature hath some portion in him, but of the slender-

est. The art of the patcher nearly rivals the aim of
Frankenstein. "Give me but a *pair* of shoulders," says
one of our eminent *fractions*, " and I will make a *man*."
Shade of Archimedes! thou who wishedst but for a ful-
crum, to move the " great globe itself, and all who it inherit," how puny thy boast! Could'st thou have made a
man out of a *pair* of shoulders? for the genius of a tailor
spurns a *match*. Amid all the melody of thy spheres, art
thou not totally eclipsed? Yet the incomparable cutter-
out was misled by his professional zeal. Alas! he can
only make a dandy! The article is too shallow a counterfeit to pass readily. Thus, we have answered the
question, "Whence comes he?"—namely, from the tailor's? "What is he?"—This has been glanced at, but to
review : he is one who, born a little lower than the angels,
gifted with intelligence, endowed with a soul, has yielded
all these, to be looked at as the last publication of the
" tailor's manual,"—to be gapingly wondered at by the
weak, pitied by the strong; for the unthinking to smile at,
and the grave to pity. On the sunny side in winter, and
the shady in summer, of the fashionable promenade; as
paces the peacock, so paces he, in the attempt to establish
a sensation. Thought has he none, but of what he shall
put on. Imagination, other than of new achievements in
dress, never waves her many twinkling wings over his
brow. Love, the purifier even of the worst, comes to him
only when gazing at the dear form he adores, in a mirror.
Yet the animal is harmless during life; that is to say, it
won't bite. Anger discomposes one's apparel; passion
may put a wrinkle in a coat.

"Whither does he tend? His better part, his clothes,
tend to the rag-shop, through various gradations of subor-

dinate dandyism,—of all colors, ranks and degrees, each lower than the last.

The machine, his body, whereon his clothes have been built,—the skeleton of the peeled dandy—dwindles from day to day, at each remove more difficult of repair, till the angles can no more be rounded, nor the hollow filled; till its glory has departed, and it is fitted and measured at the last, by that tailor whose work is never returned on his hands—the undertaker—to its last surtout, of whose fit he will never complain.

Farther to trace the dandy, beseems us not. At some fitting season we may discourse of the dandy in action, a delicate monster; the dandy in language, an insufferable pestilence to all quiet people; the dandy in literature, the dandy in politics, nay, even the dandy in religion.

So, too, we may show that there are dandies female, as well as masculine, wholly useless, as it is said; for of these matters, thank heaven, we are innocent; but on which we shall seek information from friends too well instructed.

Till then, dear reader, fare thee well.

———

SONG.—TRUE LOVE LIKE MINE.

BY WILLIAM J. RIVERS.

THE vestal flame will cease to burn,
    If fostering hands bring no supply;

And false love's shrine to coldness turn,
  When self-consuming passions die.
      But, lady, love—true love like mine,
      For ever brightens in its shrine.

The mountain rills pass quick away,
  As fleeting as a morning dream ;—
And seas that threat the sky to-day,
  To-morrow sleep beneath its beam.
      But, lady, love—true love like mine,
      Flows ever on without decline.

The playful zephyr steals at noon
  A kiss from every blushing rose ;—
Yet with the whirlwind, mingling soon,
  O'er land and sea tempestuous blows.
      But, lady, love—true love like mine,
      Breathes gently on with breath divine.

The golden sun bids nature smile,
  Yet leaves her with the dark'ning night ;
And bright-faced Luna comes, awhile,
  To soothe us with her waning light.
      But, lady, love—true love like mine,
      Thro' night and day will ever shine.

THE CONVICT.

BY PENINA MOÏSE.

THE turnkey stood irresolute. "Here is gold for you," said the veiled stranger; "it shall be doubled before I quit the prison, if you but admit me to half an hour's conference with Alice Merton." The man still hesitated.

"Are you a *father?*"

"Yes."

"I come to revoke the *curse* of *one*, grey-haired and broken-hearted. I bear a delegated blessing from the death-stricken to the doomed. Will you suffer me to depart without accomplishing this mission of mercy?"

"Pass on," said the gaoler in a husky voice, and placing a taper in her hand, he silently ushered her into the convict's cell.

And who was she, that in her tranquil grace appeared the incarnation of benevolence, and whose voice was like a "vesper melody," when she sought to take the fetter from the filial spirit! It was a being whose lofty destiny had kindled envy in the bosom of a dark dissembler. It was the once confiding friend, whose holiest affections had been made the savage sport of a perfidious rival. It was the proud, the high souled Adelaide Latimer, who lately bent before a vengeful father, and besought him not to withhold the sacrament of nature from his suffering child. She it was that now stood weeping at a little distance from the criminal, who, unconscious of her presence, clasped her sleeping infant to her bosom, while she mournfully exclaimed, "Oh! wake no more, my poor, my helpless babe! Why will not Heaven take my innocent, while yet undreaming of its mother's taint? Alas! upon what callous bosom will my orphan couch to-morrow eve? Would it not be well (added she wildly); would it not be well if I should dash thy tender limbs against those iron bars that shut out hope?" She arose suddenly, as if intending to pursue her horrid purpose, but Adelaide sprang forward, and arresting her uplifted arm, prevented its execution. Alice, transfixed with horror, glared like a maniac upon the form before her. A strange delusion seemed to possess her senses—she called feebly and fearfully on her departed mother, whose shade she fancied had been conjured from the tomb to rescue the desperate offender from this last iniquity. The little Clarence had fallen unharmed upon her bed of straw, and though terrified on being first awakened, had again sunk quietly to rest.

"Is it thus we meet," Alice Merton, faltered out the gentle visitant, raising the taper and throwing back her veil? The prisoner started—for in those sweet tones she heard again the harmonies of childhood—they had then summoned her to fairy sports and flowery scenes. All the pure images time leaves undimmed upon the mirror of remembrance, now floated before her fancy in torturing contrast with her present state. But, alas! that voice had power also over the more turbulent associations of a less buoyant period—and they came thronging like the passions to the magic call of music. She riveted her dark eye sternly upon the speaker—its lightning glance was gone—and it now resembled the blackened corse, on which the subtle fire has spent its fury. Adelaide fixed hers unshrinkingly upon the felon. There was an infant's purity in its clear blue concave—its beam seemed but a reflection caught from the Heaven to which it had so often been upturned.

"What brings thee here, Adelaide Latimer? By what caprice of taste hast thou resigned the luxury of adulation for a descant on depravity? But, I bethink me now, thou hast a saintly reputation, and perhaps in some ecstatic vision may'st have dreamed thy pious rhetoric would move the malefactor, although the man of God has failed to do it. Superfluous condescension! The seed of righteousness can never vegetate within a bosom seared as mine has been. My father's curse, like the red desert blast, prostrated me in my pilgrimage, and shed a desolating influence over every human feeling. Away! No whining valedictory, no mockery of lip-contrition awaits the hawking hireling of scandal-mongers. The bride of Clement de la Mere scorns to abase herself before her haughty rival."

A blush, that brilliant traitor that o'ermasters pride, rushed to the cheek of Adelaide, but recoiled as suddenly to the heart, whose guarded secret it had thus betrayed.

With a powerful effort, however, she regained her composure, and thus addressed the delinquent:

"Alice, thou art no longer the *accursed*. The dreadful interdict that barred thee from communion with the holy, exists no more. My purpose here was not to taunt thee for thy past transgressions, but to bestow a blessing in thy father's name."

The criminal uttered a convulsive cry, and sank senseless at the feet of her injured and magnanimous friend. Adelaide knelt beside her, and applied the restoratives

17

with which she had come provided. She soon revived,
and, burying her face in her hands, wept long and bitterly.
Those tears seemed to dispel the mists that veiled the
light of another world from her view. She threw her
fettered arms around Adelaide's neck, and, in an agony of
remorse, repeatedly exclaimed—

"My God! my gracious God! bless her, and pardon
me! But oh! why came he not to his condemned and
erring child? Would not his grey hairs have been far
more touching orators than all the ghostly counsellors that
ever preached a crusade against evil morals? Why, on
the eve of execution, comes he not to mitigate its horrors,
and foretoken, by his presence, that my Heavenly Father
will not exclude the felon from his kingdom?"

"Perhaps," answered Adelaide, "perhaps his spirit
even now is pleading for thee before the last tribunal—it
was but fluttering on the verge of eternity when I left
him."

"My father dead?" shrieked the unfortunate convict.
"Oh God! endue me now with strength to burst my
chains, that I may cling one moment to his corse, and
gasp out my repentance. My child," continued she,
straining him to her breast—"the brand no longer darkens
thy young brow—the curse revoked, effaces the hereditary
blight that would have marred thy future bold aspirings.
But thou hast lost the only one on earth whose kind
adoption might have redeemed thy tarnished name from
my transmitted ignominy."

Adelaide bent down to soothe the affrighted infant,
whose fingers, becoming entangled in her ringlets, were
so tenacious of their grasp, that she could not release herself without leaving some of the hair in his hand. The

benign enthusiast regarded this little incident as a token that destiny designed to intermingle, through her means, some golden threads in his dark web of fate. She caught him in her arms, and exclaimed with energy—

" There is no orphanage for thee, sweet boy, while Adelaide has power to shield and cherish thee. Yes! thou shalt be a substitute for every severed bond ; and never shalt thou know thy parent was aught else than guiltless."

" Stay !" said Alice, withdrawing her son, while her whole frame quivered with emotion. " You are yet ignorant of the flagrant wrong inflicted by his mother. Your noble conduct has subdued the fiend within me—it cannot longer wrestle with an angel. Necessity demands that, in reverting to the past, I should be brief. Know, then, that when your love for Clement de la Mere was confided to me, I was aware that you were idolized by him ; for, observing our friendship, he had been unreserved in his communications on that subject. You little dreamt, however, how far beyond the bound of female delicacy my unsolicited affection went for that fatal being : neither was he suspicious of my feelings. Under these circumstances, I determined to supplant you, if possible. For this purpose, I assumed the mask of frankness—feigned even to violate your confidence, that he might be spared the mortification of a rejection—assured him your heart was preoccupied ; and finally succeeded in convincing him, that his pursuit of you was hopeless. The sympathy I manifested for his sufferings (for he was almost frantic) insensibly increased his esteem for me, and, as if to impose upon himself the necessity of forgetting you, in a moment of grateful excitement, he offered me his hand. We were married. But alas! my imperious temper, so artfully suppressed before my triumph was achieved, now boldly shook off all restraint. Our hapless union was constantly clouded by domestic tempests. It was during one of these, more violent than usual, that I sarcastically imputed his infelicity to his unmastered affection for you; and tauntingly upbraided him with his want of penetration, in not discovering that his tenderness had been amply requited. Never shall I forget the look with which he sought to read my soul at that moment.

" ' Swear by your hope of salvation that this is true,' shouted he, stung to madness by my implied treachery.

" Unprepared for such a result, I trembled and hesitated.

" ' Woman, trifle not with me!' added he fiercely— ' swear that you are not *now* playing me false, or by *my* hope of salvation, I'll cast you from my door as portionless as you entered it!'

" I verified my assertion by the desired oath. He walked rapidly and frequently across the hall: at length, turning suddenly upon me, he said, in a voice half stifled with anguish—

" ' Farewell! between us now there is an eternal barrier; my banker must henceforth become the guardian of your comfort.' "

" He then rushed from the house, to which he never more returned."

Adelaide's sobs now became audible.

" Has no trace of him been since discovered?" inquired she.

" After the birth of my child, a fellow-officer from the field of Waterloo, sought me out to deliver a watch, which he said was De la Mere's dying bequest to his innocent offspring."

A faintness now seized Adelaide, but she roused herself, and continued to listen with an intense interest.

" Retribution overtook me from that hour," resumed the delinquent ; " the banker, with whom he had deposited a liberal sum for my support, failed soon after. His desertion had roused all the furies in my bosom ; I resolved upon what I conceived the most refined species of vengeance—I dishonored his name, and leagued myself with the most degraded of my sex. Then it was that my father's curse rendered me reckless, and I passed insanely through every gradation of guilt, until I became an incendiary. For this enormity it is that justice has decreed the scaffold. My heart would have remained stony and impenitent, had not your merciful interposition won the paternal benediction. Can you forgive me *now*, Adelaide Latimer ?"

The noble sufferer replied to this appeal by pressing the little Clarence to her heart, and firmly pronounced a solemn vow that, in weal and in wo, then and for ever, the child of Alice Merton should be unto her as dear as if nature herself had established the strongest links of affinity between them.

The entrance of the turnkey reminded them that they must now separate. For some minutes they remained locked in each other's embrace ; then kissing the eyes, forehead, and lips of her unconscious babe, Alice surrendered it to her noble friend.

A short paragraph in a paper of the ensuing evening, announced that the mortal course of the convict had been terminated in the most impressive manner ; and that the sympathies of the multitude, assembled on that occasion, had been powerfully elicited by the fortitude and meekness with which she expiated her crime.

IMITATION OF A SONNET OF MANZONI.

BY JOHN PARKER.

ERE on the cross the bleeding Saviour died,
He, for the sins of man, in anguish sigh'd ;
At that sad sigh, the grave gave up its prey,
And darken'd was the glowing orb of day.
In depths profound that sigh was heard by one,
Who first had seen the glories of the sun ;
Adam received the sigh that nature shook,
And on the scene of wo was forc'd to look ;—
Returned to see once more the world he lost,
And which to save, such precious blood-drops cost ;—
" Who, then," he trembling ask'd, " thus tortur'd dies,
And why are veil'd in gloom, and wo, the skies ?"
" The Son of God," a solemn voice replied,
" Who for thy sins, sad mortal, thus hath died,
This is the fruit of that accursed tree,
But by this death you will from sin be free."
With horror struck, his face then Adam veil'd,
Yet not before as " God" he Christ had hail'd—
" See, then," he said, as turn'd on Eve his eyes,
" See for thy crime, e'en God himself now dies."

The abyss profound re-echoed with the word,
And still in storms the accusation's heard.

THE FOUNTAIN OF YOUTH

BY W. HAYNE SIMMONS.

THE voyage of Ponce De Leon, a Spanish adventurer, in search of a *Fountain of Youth,* fabled to be situated somewhere in Florida, is well attested by the historians of his time. There exists a Spanish poem on this subject, of a burlesque character, in which the fount is supposed to have been at last found, and is described as crowded by visiters, anxious to partake of its sanative and rejuvenating effects. Many of the *young* and of the *prematurely old* are among the *company at the Springs;* and are represented as equally *needing,* and equally desirous of experiencing the *benefits of the waters.* Numerous ludicrous scenes are described as occurring among these youthful debauchees, imbeciles, and invalids—many o them being unexpectedly reduced to infancy, and others *under age,* by the arch-efficacy, and rather too *literal* realization of the powers of the fountain. They are thus placed in situations of distress truly *bizarre* and amusing. This *reductio ad absurdum* of the fiction, or current story of the day, appears to have been one of the chief objects of the author of the poem. If the virtues of the celebrated *Mineral Springs* on the Suwaney were known to the Indians, and if the accounts we have of the cures, *revivals,* and restorations of crippled limbs, wrought by their waters, be all correct, the above fable, which was so strangely and seriously credited by the early Spanish adventurers, may be traced to a likely source, and may thus have had some foundation in fact.

" Both Siloe this, and Jordan doth excel—
    The English Bath, and eke the German Spa,
    Nor could Cephisse nor Hebrus match this well."—Spencer.

As these life-giving springs may now be easily *found*, and as at least one of the attributes of youth—health, may be acquired by drinking their waters; a *voyage* or journey in *search of them*, by our summer excursionists, would be both a more advisable and less arduous undertaking than it was in the days of the unfortunate Ponce De Leon.

THE FOUNTAIN OF YOUTH.

Beguiled by visions vain,
  Full long the adventurer stretched his sail,
    O'er seas unknown ;
    Bound on a voyage wild and lone,
The wonderous fount to gain,
By Indian fable placed
  In secret vale,
And land sequester'd far in ocean's trackless waste ;
  The draught miraculous to fill,
  That chased of age the wintry chill,
And spite of time,
  Made bright the brow once more,
    New vigor to life's weary springs could give,
And youth's new blooming prime,
  With all its joys restore.

There sun-bows fresh the flowery purlieus crowned,
And bowers of laughing bliss rose radiant round ;
Here youth immortal, from the enchanted wave,
Bright as the morn, victorious o'er the grave,

His graceful limbs in careless beauty thrown,
  On surge-like shell,
    Whose foamy prow,
  The winged loves and blisses gay impel,
    With smiling brow,
  Holds high the Amreeta cup,
Filled with the elixir bright, the ambrosial dew,
    Of life to the pilgrim pale,
  By age down grown,
    And bids him drink it up,
  And with the draught forget his sorrows flown ;
    Bids him retrace the vale
  Of years, and to the bowers of youth return ;
  Bloom with its bloom, and with its fires re-burn,
And crop its joys anew.

Such was the vision fair of western skies
That play'd before the fond sea-wanderer's eyes,
Like mirage o'er the watery syrt receding,
And onward still its follower, treacherous leading.

Oh, vain the thought ! Oh, wild the dream !
  Again, on earth, to find
    The flowers, death-trodden on life's weary way,
That glittered in its morning beam
    A space, fair smiling with the hues of hope,
Those blooms that will not last,
  E'en then when soft the dallying wind,
    And laughing, vernal season woo their stay ;
    But flee, a fragile race, the pageants of a day,
    That do but ope,
  To fade and leave behind

The tears that swelled within their infant eyes,
As if prophetic of the coming blast
  And changing skies
    That shed no twilight gleam,
  And see no star arise
      After their sun has set.
    Oh! rather sure, in Lethe's stream,
      'Twere happier to forget
The past, and all the pangs remembrance brings,
  The promises bright
Of hope's false rainbow, that delusive springs ;
    Whether midst sorrow's tears,
    Or in life's morning sky its smile appears ;
The sad mockery to prove
  Of youth, without its joys renewed ;
O'er buried love
And friendship lost, to weep ; affection's blight
    To feel ; the weary cares
  Of age, and all its solitude,
Without its promis'd rest ;
  Like cold Aurora* over regions dead,
Wandering unblest,
  Where the pale hours nor dews nor blossoms shed,
Hoping, in vain, the day that rises never ;
Beauteous and sad, forlorn and restless, ever ;
Environ'd still by wastes of death and ever-during night.

* The polar aurora.

MOWBRAY AND SHELTON-PLACE—THE SEATS OF THE CLIFTONS AND SOMERVILLES.

BY WM. WRAGG SMITH.

MOWBRAY, or St. Giles—the former the more modern, the latter, the ancient name by which the family seat of the Cliftons was known—contrasted greatly in appearance with Shelton-place. There was an air of gloomy grandeur about Mowbray—the provincial architecture of the large, square brick mansion, with its thick, solid walls coated over with ivy and the green damp of age—and its steep, well-tiled roof, tall chimneys, and quaint dormar windows, whence the frightful owl on a winter's night would startle the silence with shrill and thrilling pæans to the Fates, or in the quiet of a waning spring twilight, the solitary whippoorwill utter his melancholy wail of love to his shy partner in the neighboring coppice. The majestic oaks—those " paternal trees"—those hoary patriarchs of the quiet homestead—almost locked their giant arms, and mingled their venerable beards of moss across the heavy, gothic-looking pediment of the pillared front, and cast their shadows, " broad and brown," around. On passing the double substantial pillars of the pasture gate, the mansion was approached through one of the most magnificent avenues of these sombre trees to be found in Carolina. The pasture itself formed a circular area of some hundred acres, the open waste of which, for the most part grown up with brown grass and increased rather than relieved in its aspect of desolation by the little forests of pine

saplings which had sprung up on the extreme edges, contributed much to this character of gloom.

The only softer features in the picture were, a short
avenue of elm trees whose livelier, feathery foliage flaunt-
ed over the margin of an oblong artificial basin on the right
of the house, and a glimpse of the river winding its tor-
tuous course through green fields of marsh, whose desert
expanse, terminating in the insipid horizon of dark and mo-
notonous pines, formed the principal prospect from the ter-
race or belvedere at the back. But what chiefly gave that
character of interesting solemnity—that depth of gloomy
coloring which threw a shade of mellow sadness over Mowbray, and inspired the solitary rambler through its seques-
tered grounds with feelings amounting to romance, were—
the "orchard" on one side, and the "wood-walk" on the
other ;—simple names for objects in the landscape which
it would require the dark pencil of a Poussin adequately
to portray ;—homely names for holy haunts which religion
might people with the ghosts of the dead, and poetry embellish with the shadowy forms of Dryads and Hamadryads. The one was a dark, dense grove, within whose
deep and solemn recess reposed the family burial ground.
The cedar and wild orange had here found a rich and congenial soil, and mingled their dark masses with those of
the live oak and magnolia. A gurgling brook, driven along
its deep and narrow bed by the united waters of two distant streams, passed through the middle of the orchard, and
filled with its hollow murmurs the imposing silence of this
sylvan retreat. Here, in the deep bottom, might be seen
a few tall and gloomy cypresses intermingled with the
huge swamp pines. The long moss here revelled in the
damp air, and now in pendant festoons, now touching the

ground in stately perpendicular columns, gave to the solemn
place the likeness of a vast cathedral of which it formed
the gothic arches and gloomy pillars. The giant grape
vine grappled with the sturdy lords of the forest, scaling
their very summits, and hanging out ladders, as it were, to
heaven; and as such they were actually consecrated by
the superstitious negro domestics of Mowbray, who firmly
believed that where these vines grew to such a size and
height near the grave-yard they were made use of by
spirits to let themselves down by to the earth when re-visit-
ing their mortal habitations.

The other dark and heavy mass of foliage in the back-
ground to the left, known as the wood-walk, was composed
of a noble forest, chiefly of oaks, some of enormous size,
which curtained the serpentine margin of the river. An
irregular path wound through the wood ; and at intervals
or openings, where the scenery was most romantic and remarkable, rustic seats were placed. Here it was some
isolated monster of a thousand years growth, whose cir-
cumference it might have taken the outstretched arms of
four men to compass, and whose broad boughs were so
many horizontal trees with their pendant moss curtaining
a rural bower that would have suited the primitive loves of
Dido and Æneas, and may have once been the trysting
place of the aboriginal Cacique and haughty Queen of a
hundred palmetto isles. Here some freak of nature invited the attention :—a huge limb that, sinking beneath its
weight, had buried itself in the ground, and like a river
that has disappeared, sprung up again to the surface ; or a
colossal trunk had been uprooted from its position on the
margin of the gully or creek, and formed a natural bridge
across it :—and here a limpid spring gushed from the side

of the mossy bank where the wild violet and glossy-leav-
ed partridge-berry mantled the ground with their refreshing verdure ; and the brook trickling along a margin where
the sun never penetrated, and concealed among the rank
fern and the spreading leaves of the big water-dock and
curious Arum, lost itself finally in a little swamp of cedars
and myrtle below. Near its source the tall and stately
magnolia reared its compact and symmetrical head of dark
and shiny foliage against the bright blue sky, or mingled
in the soft moonlight its zephyr murmurings with the continuous serenade of the mocking bird.

Such were the principal features of the scenery immediately around this ancient residence, and they were
heightened by their solitude. Mowbray stood almost
alone in a district of country where the earliest settlements clustered, and Carolina hospitality first acquired
celebrity. Now the revolutions in agriculture and in
fortunes, had long since returned to the deer his native
ranges, and dismantled of its honors the roof of the provincial patrician. The country was deserted. Its neigh-
borhood was broken up : its mansions had been levelled
with the dust. The shantee of the vagabond stranger
curled its primitive smoke over the walls where once
reigned splendor and refinement. The woodman's axe
resounded where the roll of carriages was wont to be
heard. The hundred armed oak that had outlived centuries was hurled from its time-honored site, a hecatomb to
the infernal demon—*money*. The thistle had usurped the
place of the rose, and the broom grass waved its sere
head in cheerless mockery over the parterre. The hog
rooted in the garden, the cow lowed beneath the ruined
basement arch. Such was the picture of desolation

which many a spot presented. The few old residences which still remained, were either isolated or almost abandoned, and gradually decaying, or had fallen into the hands of strangers. Mowbray stood alone, like one of a past generation who has outlived kindred and fellows, or like a proud man in solitary exclusion from the world.

As the heavy gate groaned on its hinges, and Moultrie cantered on his way to Shelton-place, the lover's mind was just in the mood to dwell and expatiate upon the features in the solitary scenery which we have attempted to describe. But now they became yet more striking. Mowbray was an oasis to the desert that surrounded it. There was nothing to relieve the eye from the painful monotony of the interminable pine-barren with its arid sands and dismal tupelo ponds. At length, when there did come a break in the scene, it was some torn-down fence along the road-side with its remains of substantial bank upon which a forest now grew, and wide ditch choked up with weeds and under-brush, or filled with green stagnant water, and then a rotten post or crumbling brick pillar—the ruins of a gate—with a vista of some lane that was once an avenue, now leading up to an old field in the centre of which might be discovered a chimney and two or three oaks.

But the reader is now at Shelton-place, and introduced to a very different scene. Shelton-place was distant ten miles or more from Mowbray, and situated on one of those rivers whose fertile alluvial constitutes, under the later and improved system of Carolina rice culture, what is called *tide swamp*, in contra-distinction to *inland swamp* which our ancestors used to cultivate. Here everything bore the marks of a modern era. The few trees which

were scattered around the dwelling were not of natural
growth. The environs were bare and open. Rice fields
and corn fields bounded the site of the plantation as far
as the eye could reach ; and all was cheerful with cultivation. The grounds contiguous to the house were laid
out with some taste, but all was modern and artificial.
There were no solemn sweeping shades of moss-crowned
avenues—no memorials of antiquity—no dim alcoves of
Nature—no vast and venerable solitudes. But there
were pleasing bouquets, shrubberies and flowers breathing
perfume, and musical with the notes of hundreds of songsters, hedges of Cherokee rose, and interjacent lawns,
and green oatfields separated by neat white fences. The
mansion was of very late date, large and commodious,
built of wood and painted white, with a white and green
verandah. Its furniture corresponded, being all of modern
style. Here was not seen, as at Mowbray, the tall,
old-fashioned clock of dark mahogany, with its ample
enamelled dial, standing in the corner of the dim ante-
room, like a spectre cased in starch apparel, and counting
the solemn seconds with its quaint, loud, and almost
human-like tick ; but, in lieu, the elegant bronze time-
piece, surmounted by a flying Cupid, clicked delicately
and musically on the marble mantel-piece. The parlor
at Mowbray boasted not, as that at Shelton, of its chaste
tall French mirrors, satin ottomans, elegant new mahogany or maple chairs, centre-table, and bookcase, stylish
in appearance, but veneered and flimsy. Modern refinement, and the taste for present display, had made not the
slightest innovation upon its old-time simplicity and substantial magnificence. The single mirror, of modest size,
in its elaborately-carved ebon frame, set off well with a

few gilt mouldings, still retained its place between the windows over the spindle-legged card table. The heavy family sofa, with its chintz cover, filled the space opposite; and the solid carved mahogany arm chairs, dark with age, showed their prim, tall backs around the room, and looked, in their white dimity petticoats, the personification of so many respectable old quaker ladies. In place of the centre table, stood a small work-table with grotesque claw feet, the workmanship of the time of Elizabeth; and the bookcase was a massive piece of furniture, invaluable from the circumstance of its having accompanied the ancestors of the Cliftons in their emigration to Carolina. It consisted of a library above, and underneath a complete escrutoire and drawers with all the useful appurtenances, the whole curiously wrought of ebony inlaid with ivory. To behold Shelton-place—the neatness and stylishness about it—the costliness of the furniture, and the luxury in which Mr. Somerville lived both in the town and country, one would have thought him rich. But Mr. Somerville had been initiated at an early age into the mysteries of fashion and high life in the circles of the New York merchants and Wall street brokers, among whom he had been in the habit of spending his summers, and had in youth contracted a taste for splendor and lavish expenditure, for speculation and borrowing on credit. This extravagant mode of life, based upon no regular business (for his planting at the South could not be called such, being conducted in the same spirit of speculation, and with an expense instead of a profit), had soon dissipated his resources. He then thought it was time to look about for a matrimonial speculation, and while he disguised the state of his affairs, and continued to keep up the same appearances on the strength of bank loans and sums borrowed on mortgage, he succeeded in winning his way into the good opinion of the Shelton family, and was considered a good match for their daughter, whom he married ; and on the day that he drove up four-in-hand to his newp ossessions,—his wife's plantation, Shelton-place,—his own was brought to the hammer.

———

ON THE REVERSES OF THE SPANISH ARMS.

BY WILLIAM CRAFTS.

THE sun has set on Spain !
    Its proudest height,
    Supremely bright,
Saw Saragossa fall,
And, with its latest rays,
    It plays
On brave Gerona's wall.

High o'er the Pyrenees
    The Gallic flood,
    A stream of blood,
Pours its destructive sway.
It whelms Castilian pride,
    And wide
Sweeps havoc and dismay.

Spain, all thy glory's gone !
    Charles's spirit
    None inherit—
Sons unworthy of your sire !
Lost, for ever lost to fame,
    The name
That set the world on fire !

Freedom waves her flag in vain !
    The priest-rid race,
    Ignobly base,
Invite the tyrant's chain.
Vainly does Albion dare
    The war,
For pseudo-patriot Spain.

The blaze of Austria's fame
    Could not illume
    The living tomb,
Where superstition reigns ;
To Austria's war-struck shell,
    The cell
Returned no kindred strains.

With proud indignant wave,
    The Danube rose
    Against its foes,
But sullen Ebro still,
Sees foreign minions ride
    Its tide,
Nor murmurs at their will.

Spain! were all thy patriots true,
    How bright for thee
    The page would be,
That now laments thy doom.
Hid is thy laurel wreath,
    Beneath
The cypress' funeral gloom.

Snatch from the closing earth
    A verdant leaf,
      For every chief
Who fought for thee so well—
Let freedom's sorrows lave
    Their grave ;—
Sweets to the brave, farewell!

———

MIDNIGHT—LAST DAY OF THE YEAR.

BY MARY E. LEE.

IT is a solemn hour!—Creation sleeps
In death-like slumber 'neath the mantle fold
That night hath thrown around her, and no note
Disturbs the dream of Nature, save at times
The rude wind-spirit's chariot as it sweeps
Through the star-banner'd fields of ether blue.
Silence is all around!   Silence so deep,
That one might think this Earth a picture-world,

A shadowing out of some celestial sphere,
By an unrivalled hand, where all is full
And perfect loveliness, and naught remains,
Save but the master-touch to waken *life*.

Yet hark ! that distant sound.   Methought it seem'd
The knell of parting Time, as on his swift
Yet noiseless wing he moved unwearied by
To bear of human deeds the open scroll,
Up to that presence-chamber, where no act,
Or careless word, or fragment of a thought,
Is pass'd unchronicled, but all is mark'd
By the recording Angel's lightning-pen,
As with a sunbeam in the Book of Life.

The midnight clock strikes twelve ;—It breaks the spell
That weigh'd upon my senses ; yet e'en now,
Phantoms of thought crowd fast within my brain,
And deep reflection waves her thrilling wand,
And in sad cadence bids me search the web,
Of the past year, and see if conscience true,
Can find some golden thread or tissue fair
Throughout its varied texture. —— ——
Alas ! I may not scan the sullied page
That memory spreads before me : 'tis too like
A waste and desert land, where each green spot
Makes desolation clearer, or yet else
Like to some fragile bark, that wildly toss'd
Amid a stormy sea, at distance seems
Naught, save a noteless atom.   'Twas a vain
And idle dream to build the boasted pile
Of past determination, on a base

So frail as Earth's poor strength ; 'twere better far
To lay it with an offering fit, of tears
And prayer and supplication, on that Rock
That heeds nor passion's waves nor mortal blasts,
The Rock of Ages !   Yet I bless thee too,
Departed year ! for thou hast planted deep
Within my chasten'd soul, a precious germ
Of holy purpose ; a small mustard-seed
Of humble resolution, that may grow,
If nurs'd by constant care and pure desire,
To an unfading plant.

                Thou ! that dost sit
Wrapt in thy floating garments of dense cloud
And solemn grandeur, on the boundless height
Of Heaven's majestic summit, at whose base
Rolls ever onward with increasing force,
Eternity's strong current : Thou ! whose name
Is Love, and dwell'st in love, O Father ! grant
That through the coming year I may not move
As thro' a mazy labyrinth, form'd of paths
For ever vacillating ; but may urge
With steady footsteps all my future course,
Towards that narrow way, whose vista shows
The *crystal gate of Heav'n !*

THE LEPER OF CAPERNAUM.

BY MARY E. LEE.

" No hand but mine shall tie his evening bouquet," exclaimed Zara, springing from the couch where, in an inner
apartment, she had reposed during the sultry mid-day
hours, her cheek crimsoning with a flush of love and
modesty. She tossed aside the beautiful flowers, just
proffered her by her favorite slave, the young and pretty
Ulla, whose pleasant duty it was to cull every evening a
choice nosegay from the extensive garden, and to present
it, with smiles of welcome, to the noble Julius, when, at
eventide, he entered the quadrangular court, into which
he was regularly ushered, while an attendant hastened to
inform the lovely Zara of his arrival. " I alone will bless
his coming in," she murmured, as, leaning towards a mirror of polished brass, encased in jewels, she twined her
long dark hair into a graceful knot, fastening it with a simple silver bodkin, and scarcely noticing the new and spotless robe, which her admiring maidens confined with a
girdle of pearls round the slender waist. She sprang
lightly through the open lattice, and in a few moments her
merry laugh was heard from the furthest recesses of the
garden, as selecting the choicest blossoms from the lavish
waste which the eager Ulla threw into her extended lap,
she soon twined a luxuriant cluster, in which her lover's
favorite flowers were most conspicuously displayed.
There was the blushing almond, whose tint only rivalled
her own fair cheek; the jasmine, with its carved and fault-

less waxen cups, from which the butterfly loves best to sip the morning dew ; the honeysuckle, that Eden-home for the never-wearied bee ; the rose and pomegranate, vieing in scarlet brilliancy and pink-shelled delicacy of color ; the balsamic shrub, and the variegated myrtle ; all met together, and formed a bouquet, as fragrant and thornless as the path of existence over which the maiden's light footsteps had glided from birth.

The tribe and family of Zara, of the house of David, was one of the most wealthy and influential in the city of Capernaum ; and when, at the last feast of Tabernacles, she became espoused to the young and accomplished heir of the rich Rabbi, Simon, their parents rejoiced over the unmingled cup of worldly bliss, which seemed presented by so fit an union ; and although their prophet had foretold that "from Bethlehem shall come the governor, that shall rule my people Israel," yet, in those days of Roman bondage, every Jewish family indulged the delightful hope, that from them might spring the promised Messiah.

Her light task ended, the happy maiden hastened to lay it in one of the many carved vases, filled with exotics, which were tastefully arranged around the marble basin of a sparkling fountain, whose cool sprinklings refreshed and invigorated those delicate foreigners, even when the meridian heats were at their height ; then reclining against a column, round which a luxuriant parasite had been taught to twine its soft foliage, she took her lute from Ulla's hand, and while her face beamed with the lustre of youth and beauty, and her bosom heaved with sighs of tranquil bliss, she commenced an Eastern love-song, the words of which, though hardly distinguishable at first, soon gushed in a torrent of melody from her tutor'd lips :

Awake! my silver lute!
String all thy plaintive wires,
And as the fountain gushes free,
So let thy memory chant for me
　The theme that never tires.

Awake! my liquid voice!
Like yonder timorous bird,
Why doth thou sing in trembling fear,
As if by some obtrusive ear,
　Thy secret should be heard?

Awake! my heart—yet no!
As Cedron's golden rill,
Whose changeless echo singeth o'er
Notes it had heard long years before,
　So thou art never still.

My voice! my lute! my heart!
Spring joyously above
The feeble notes of lower earth,
And let thy richest tones have birth
　Beneath the touch of love.

The sun was fast sinking behind the lofty mountains which border the lake of Genesareth, and its parting rays were reflected back in prismatic hues by the ever-restless fountain, when Zara carelessly threw aside her lute, and with a beating heart, listened for those footsteps, which never failed to rejoice her every sense.

"Tell me, Ulla," she inquired, "is yonder hibiscus yet gilded with the day-beams? for it is just at the mo-

ment of their farewell, that Julius ever greets me beneath
its clustering foliage."

" Ah! lady," exclaimed the pretty slave, on returning
from her brief survey, " the shadows are already twinnig
their dark net-work over its branches, and the singing-birds
chant but feebly in their golden cages."

" Strange," murmured Zara, as for the first time boding
doubt and disquiet threw their light clouds over her childish
features, " strange, that I should *wait* his coming. Surely
nothing yet ever detained him from my presence ; he, who,
for love of me, neglects his hunting-spear, his fishing-nets,
his fairy-like shallop, and his beautiful horse, all that forms
the pastime of his city companions. O, no ; none of
these have made him linger ;" and, with nervous restless-
ness, she hastily paced the extended walks, and seemed
plunged in a deep and painful revery.

Presently, with quivering lips, she turned to the sympa-
thizing slave, exclaiming, " Haste ! Ulla, haste ; for just
now I call to mind that his cheek was paler than its wont,
yesterday, and although he named them idle fears, yet did
my watchful eye detect a strange languor in his animated
features. Here, maiden, take this pretty bodkin, which I
know thou yearnest after ; it shall be my reward for thy
light-footed speed."

The agile Ulla caught the gay bauble from the extended
hand of her mistress, and bounding over the Mosaic pave-
ments of the noble dwelling, she passed through the wide
court, reached the low and dark outer gate, common even
to the finest Jewish mansions, and drawing her wimple
closely around her, she hurried down the narrow street, and
was soon lost in the distance.

*   *   *   *   *   *   *   *   *

Day after day of melancholy abstraction, or delirious grief, followed the first agony of those tidings which informed the terror-stricken Zara that her beautiful betrothed! the fountain of her gladness! the day-star of her existence! was stretched powerless on the couch of sickness; and the languor attending every movement, the dulness of senses, the change of voice, and, most fearful sign of all, the small, but ever increasing spots, which had shown themselves on his polished limbs, each revealed but too surely, that that disease of all others the most revolting, that scourge of the East, loathsome, scaly, flesh-decaying leprosy was his dreadful doom.

Cowering in a dark corner of her high and luxurious chamber, where all the refinements of taste and fancy were lavished to excess, her veil drawn in thick folds over her wasted countenance, every gladdening beam of day shut out by the purple tissues of Tyre, which were extened over each lattice-work of brass, so lately thrown open to admit the balmy breezes of the lake, Zara sat, with her weeping parents and relatives on either side, and like the heart-stricken friends of Job, " None spake a word to *her*, for they knew that her grief was very great."

But leaving any further description of the maiden's present sorrow, at being thus deprived of the overflowing draught of love and bliss, when the ambrosial nectar was even at her lips, let us visit another dwelling—that of the parents of the unfortunate youth—and see how the deadly poison of disappointment worked into their very life-blood; when, after weeks of shivering unbelief, mingled with maddening fears, they were compelled to admit the fearful truth, they turned almost with loathing, from the marred and distorted features of their idol-son. Oh! what a lesson for pride! What a sight for ungoverned love to behold! In vain did they lay rich offerings of gold and silver and precious stones, with the best of their flocks and herds, on the altar of the living God; in vain did they conceal that disfigured form from the gaze of anxious and inquiring friends; in vain did they sit in ashes, and lay aside their costly garments for the rough and fretting sack-cloth; they felt that the disclosure must, at last, be made, and when, at the command of the unfortunate youth himself, the holy priest was summoned to their stately dwelling, the servant of the Lord beat his breast in sorrow, and the tears of sympathy bedewed his snowy beard, as in loud, but broken accents, he cried, " Unclean! unclean !"[1]

Let us draw a curtain over that separation, when, according to the strict Jewish laws, the bewildered and agonized parents were compelled to thrust from their portal the sole object of their earthly hopes, and to see him depart, broken-hearted and alone, unto a desert place beyond the city's walls, where in companionship with others afflicted like himself, the wretched Julius almost rejoiced as he felt his strength daily diminishing, and marked how the flesh, once so smooth and perfumed, fell from his bones, even as if he were already dead. Educated in the holy tenets of the faith of his fathers, he dared not murmur against the will of heaven, but even as the tried patriarch, " he laid his finger on his lips, and bowed himself."

Yet were there hours, when the voice of prayer and supplication arose from the desert hut which he inhabited, and often at midnight, his wakeful companions were startled from uneasy slumber, as seeking for aid, where alone it may be found, the pious Julius sobbed aloud such texts as these : " My flesh and my heart faileth, but God is the strength of my heart, and my portion for ever." " Save me, O God, for the waters have come into my soul. Deliver me out of the mire, and let me not sink." " Oh, that I were as in months past, as in the days when God preserved me ; when his candle shined upon my head, and when by his light I walked." " I will remember the years of the right hand of the Most High." " I will say of the Lord, he is my refuge and my fortress ; my God, in him will I trust."

One comfort was left to this helpless son of sorrow, and although he even feared that in blessing he might curse them, yet, when each morning he visited the spot where it was customary for the friends of the lepers to place needful nourishment, so that they should not endure the horrors of starvation, in addition to their irremediable sufferings (no leper being allowed to dig the earth or scatter seed), his soul rejoiced, even while it sickened, as he saw the lavish store of viands, the most delicate and costly, which never failed to be supplied ; and it would have added to his grief, had he known that those parents themselves fed on naught but bread and herbs, that they drank but sparingly of the fountain, and hardly allowed themselves needful repose ; trusting yet, that by such severe penance, the right arm of the Lord might be stayed, and their son restored unto health.

The spring and the summer had departed, yet the heavy chains of grief and despair became only more firmly riveted around the soul of Zara. Her form once so rounded, and buoyant as the fawn of the mountain, was now emaciated and rigid ; the hues of the grave rested on her pale cheek ; and like a frail blossom, struck by an untimely

wind, so her life withered beneath the tempest of affliction, and although her father repeated many good texts
from the phylacteries of the Pharisees, and better yet, un-
rolling a portion of the book of Psalms (the priceless
inheritance of his forefathers), would read from its consoling pages; the intolerable load of sorrow was only for a
brief time lifted from her mind, to fall again with added
strength, and destroy every bud of coming peace within.
Yet, sometimes, memory would have its rightful sway, and
seated at the lofty lattice which overlooked the spreading
sea of Galilee, her spirit would take flight to happier days;
and like some bird, which, escaping from its prison-cage,
beats its bright wings in glorious ascent to the blue upper
sky, or revels in the green shadows of the breezy forest,
so would she spend visionary hours in gazing on some
distant boat, fancying it the one in which her lover once
darted across the golden lake; or strike a few sweet notes
from her unstrung harp; or bending over the withered
bouquet which she had carefully cherished since that fatal
evening, as if every leaf and flower were endowed with
a peculiar charm, she would yield herself to delicious
spells, until some   dden and wounding thought broke the
pinion of imagination, and forced the unwelcome truth into
her inner soul.

In the wilfulness of a diseased mind, she suffered no
attendant to approach her, save the young slave mentioned in the opening page; and when the child in
thoughtless prattle recalled the happy days of her court-
ship, she would listen in silent attention, until her eye-
lashes glistened with cooling tears, and a passionate burst
of weeping worked out its own consolation.

It was on one glorious autumn evening, that she sat

gazing with thoughtful brow on the tranquil expanse of waters, over which the setting sun was tossing a brilliant shower of diamonds, while a few purple clouds hung their misty shadows across the mountain-tops, as if to conceal from mortal vision the glories that lay within. Light skiffs, of every form and size, glided like golden arrows over the polished mirror of the lake, and as the chant of the oarsmen was borne along by the swelling breeze, it fell like spiritual music on the senses. One boat of small and mean dimensions shot apart from the rest, and entered into a little cove among the mountains. One form descended from its side to the beach, when the strokes of its oars were once more heard, as it cleaved the waters in the direction of Capernaum.

"Look! lady," exclaimed the gazing Ulla, who had stood in pleased silence, viewing the busy scene of life beneath; "look! yonder is the strange prophet, of whom all men speak. Even now hath he vanished among the hills, and my brother Philip, who followed him yesterday, to listen to his sermon on the mount, declares that he speaketh as never man spake. Would that I too could listen to his instructions, for they say that his words are as the fruitful seed, falling among the furrows, and although my brother says that 'there is no beauty that we should desire him,' yet is his face beaming with mercy, 'for he is a man of sorrows, and acquainted with grief.'"

"Speak, maiden; I would hear more of him," exclaimed the startled Zara, as she felt, although unconsciously, the soothing influence of her words; but she hardly sprang from her seat, before sinking back again, as if ruled by habitual despondency, she languidly, though reprovingly added, "Hold thy peace, Ulla, for knowest thou not that the holy Pharisees have witnessed against him, and it was but an hour ago, that my father's wrath was kindled, even in this very chamber, when thy weak-minded, irresolute brother told us of his purpose to leave our indulged and well-furnished household, and follow this impostor, as my father named him."

"Oh, lady, repeat not my master's hasty words," exclaimed the ardent Ulla, "for even if he be not the Messiah, as some say, yet has Philip's heart warmed towards him, because of the words of pleasantness and truth that proceed from his lips; and when the prophet opened his mouth and taught the multitude, saying, 'Blessed are they that mourn, for they shall be comforted,' my brother had hope, even for you, dear mistress." Thus speaking, the affectionate girl clasped Zara's wasted hand in both of hers, and bowed her young head in silence and sorrow.

Zara wept, as the accents of the child breathed faith and hope into her soul, and when, with secresy and caution, the maiden whisperingly added, "I have something yet more wonderful to tell you," she suddenly lifted her head from her bosom, and clasping her hands nervously together, till the thin blood colored their fingers with unwonted crimson; "Keep nothing from me, Ulla, for 'as the hart panteth after the water-brooks,' so doth my sick and drooping spirits yearn to learn every saying of this wonderful teacher."

It was an affecting and tender sight to see that Jewish maiden, as eagerly straining Ulla to her side, with her long hair thrown back in profusion from her blue-veined temples, and her white, statue-like features only revealing

life in the strange and unnatural flash of the dilated eyes,
she drew from her a hurried and confused confession of all
the rumors which had been circulated respecting the
despised Nazarene ; and when the child told, although
hesitatingly, how Philip had heard that the sick were
healed, and the lepers cleansed, and the sorrowful made to
sing for joy, a new life entered into Zara's emaciated and
worn-down frame, the tingling blood rushed from every
avenue of the heart, and she even dared to hope that " the
Son of Righteousness had indeed risen with healing in
his wings."

* * * * * * * * *

The sun had just risen over the desert sands, which lie
northward of Capernaum, and the carrion bird already
hovered there, in search of fresh prey, when the outcast
lepers, quitting their uneasy beds, moved slowly to the
place where their vessels were placed every noon to be
filled at evening, by their sorrowing friends, to whom the
tidings of their death would have imparted comfort instead
of grief.

Julius felt his heart beat ready to bursting, when on
taking his rightful portion, he found a bouquet of flowers,
bound together by a slight well-known golden bracelet,
which in the first days of his betrothal, he had one evening
fastened round the wrist of his beloved Zara. The clasp
which confined it, contained a small ivory tablet, on which
they had been accustomed to return words of love, when,
in playful jest, the laughing Zara would exile her pleading
lover to the farthest recesses of her garden, and employ
the willing Ulla to bear him this bauble, filled with the
secret and delicate fancies of her untaught spirit. Eagerly
seizing on the precious gift, he touched the yielding spring,

and judge of his delight, wonder, and contending doubt
and hope, when the following words met his eye :

"Oh! my beloved, a well-spring of life hath burst forth
in the desert of my soul. The Teacher, of whom we
once heard, hath visited Capernaum. He healeth all manner of sickness and all manner of disease. Hasten to
meet him, and thou mayest yet be made whole."

A faintness, even unto death, came for a moment over
the feeble frame of the youthful leper; his reason grew
dizzy and weak, and he would have fallen, if one of his
astonished companions had not caught him in his arms,
and laid him at the door of his hut.

"Long hath he called for death," muttered one, who
had been, through weary, weary years, an occupant of
that gloomy retreat, "now his desire hath come upon him;
would it were even so with me!"

Julius revived as these words reached his ear, and wrap-
ping his garments around him, he arose, as if endued with
sudden strength; and while his frame shook as with
an ague-fit, he declared unto his companions the blessed
hopes which were awaked in his bosom, and besought them
to accompany him across the desert plain, unto the open
road leading to Capernaum, by which the Saviour might
probably pass.

But life seemed no longer desirable to the distrustful
lepers; their spirits and bodies were equally broken and
exhausted, and when, after earnest but fruitless entreaties,
the disappointed Julius bade them farewell, they would not
even bless the poor wayfarer, but scoffed at and reviled
him, until he was ready to sink with shame and doubt.

Minutes seemed to increase to years, as with failing and
tortured limbs, the sufferer slowly crossed the burning

sands, which separated him from the home of his childhood. Yet even in the midst of bodily anguish, the music
of new-born hope refreshed his inner spirit; and as his
mind wandered to the cool border of his native lake, or
drank in the fresh perfume and delicious shade of the
well-remembered gardens, or lingered entranced over the
joyous meeting with friends, and parents, and loved one ;
or thrilled with indescribable emotion as he sought to
picture the ecstacy of that moment, when He, the Wonderful, the Unknown! yet the already reverenced and
blessed Physician, should break down the hateful barrier
between life and death, which had made him an exile from
the haunts of men, and should restore him, in renovated
and buoyant health, to be once more the ornament and
treasure of his bereaved home, he regarded not the wasting
discomfort of that arid desert, where the hot sand and
parching sky shared equal and undisputed empire, but was
able to exclaim in devout fervor, "The Lord is *my*
keeper.—The Lord is *my* shade upon my right hand.
The sun shall not smite *me* by day; but the Lord shall
preserve *my* going out and *my* coming in, from this time
forth, and even for ever more."

Yet when with feet blistered and bleeding, and brow
throbbing even to delirium, he reached the verdant pathway, and saw no object save the thicket's variegated
shrubbery, and heard no sound, save the distant murmur
of the city's crowds, his heart died within him, and
sinking down by the road-side, he tried to close his straining eye-balls on the intense glare of the cloudless sun.
" Death hath come upon me at last," he muttered. " My
tongue splitteth for lack of moisture, and the God of my

fathers hath forsaken me ;" thus saying, in utter despondency, he lay down to die.

A few moments had elapsed, when the footsteps of a wayfarer were heard in the thicket; the leper's glazed eye opened nervously, and a convulsive movement was apparent in his limbs, as his vacant vision rested on the features of a stranger, tall in stature, his hair waving in graceful masses from his innocent yet thoughtful brow; while inborn and awful dignity mingled with calm humility, clothed every attitude, as it were, with their faultless drapery.

With a look of ineffable benignity he drew near, and bent over the dying sufferer, his beaming eye speaking volumes of compassion; but before a word could proceed from his parted lips, and suddenly, as if some magic were brought by his presence, the leper's rigid features relaxed with life. "God of my fathers, it must be himself!" broke from his electrified tongue; and springing up, but only to throw himself again at the Saviour's feet, he exclaimed, while a sun-burst of rapturous hope and thrilling faith kindled his pallid face, "Lord! if thou wilt, thou canst make me clean."

With a heavenly smile, in which power, and compassion, and joy, and gratitude, and love, and truth, and divine purity, met like the seven hues of the rainbow, in mysterious but beautiful union, "Jesus put forth his hand, and touched him, saying, I will, be thou clean, and immediately his leprosy was cleansed."

* * * * * * * * *

Years rolled by, and found the two Jewish families, into whose private history we have thus briefly intruded, among the most devoted followers of "Him who should redeem Israel." Their homes and hearts were ever open to welcome the true disciples of the risen; Saviour and when at their decease, houses and lands, with coffers of rich garments and precious stones, came into the possession of Julius and Zara (whom the sacred Priest had long since united in the marriage tie), the grateful and pious pair, regardless of this world's fleeting and empty honors and applause, " sold them, and brought the prices of the things that were sold, and laid them at the Apostles' feet, and had all things in common, with the least of the brethren."

THE WILDERNESS.

BY WM. HAYNE SIMMONS.

'Twas a still noon of sunshine and of shade,
And o'er the forests and the prairies stole
Shadows and gleams, as o'er the tranquil soul
Its wayward fancies float. The hills afar
Shone sudden out, and now the streamlet near
Was veiled in night, and fierce the sultry star
Basked in the woods—while fleeting glooms arrayed
The treeless wilds ; and thus their April play
The beams and clouds continued all the day.
No sound, save the cicada's voice, I heard,
Who chirped rejoicing in the burning air ;
Or locust dinning from the bristly pine,
Perched on its topmost bough of glossy green—

For, driven by th' oppressive hour, each bird
To mossy depths, where ne'er the golden line
Of sunbeam reached, had slunk—and panted there.
The bright-winged summer-duck alone was seen
Coasting the forest-lake, amidst its reeds
Seeking its food with long-immersed head,
The darting minnow tribes, or sappy seeds,—
Stirring the bottom oft with busy beak;
His gorgeous hues upon the waters shed
A glory—and in the mirror dark appears
His image, gliding as with life endowed;
Each tint that on the wild flower lovely burns,
Or on the clouds of morning glows by turns,
Seems struck at heat upon his plumage fair,
Unfading thence; and midst the brilliant crowd,
But more distinct by neighb'ring contrast made,
Amber and emerald hues; and, like Cacique
Of the wild flock, a gaudy crest he wears,
Oft bristled up in fear, or reared in pride;
Or close smoothed down to pass beneath the spray,
Stretched o'er his moving path, that glides away,
And bears him on to deeper solitudes,
Through dreary ways, but to the trout beside
Known, amidst roots and wat'ry thickets rude.
Oft by the sable trunk, stretched in the shade,
Like fallen Titan, by its mighty bulk
Above the flood upreared—with plumes composed
He sits for hours by the grass enclosed,
Happy in his beauty and secure retreats.
O'er head he sees the fierce-eyed wild-cat skulk
On lofty boughs safe o'er the water's brine;
There to the cane close clings the green-skinned frog;

Or, rolled up on the lichen-covered log,
Near basks the snake, where falls the casual beam
From the high leafy ceiling ;—the noon heats
Thus safe he shuns within these twilight chambers,
Or over trunks and tangled vines he clambers,
And forth his female leads, and downy team,
On the black flood, like some fair cloud of morn
Growing more radiant in the rear of night.
In that deep solitude with wild delight
Their young ones sport and dive ; or with quick eye
The light moscheto mark, or gilded fly
Pursue, on ice-like wing that wanders by.
Thy temple, Nature ! here, by hands unseen,
Reared, and thy altar drest with living green,—
Oh, echo not the bleeding victim's cries !
But joyous notes like happy hymns that rise ;
While grateful incense from each shrub and flower
Ascends to Him, the blest, all-bounteous Power !
Who, ere his favor yet was sought by blood,
Thus bade thee smile ! and gave thy innocent brood
To sport and play, and saw that it was good !
And bade man learn, within thy sacred fane
Thy ways are peace, thy service joy, not pain.

AUTUMNAL DAY IN CAROLINA.

BY WILLIAM H. TIMROD.

Sleeps the soft south,—nursing its delicate breath,
  To fan the first buds of the early spring ;
And summer, sighing, mourns his faded wreath,
  Its many colored glories withering
Beneath the kisses of the new-waked North,—
  Who yet in storms approaches not, but smiles
On the departing season, and breathes forth
  A fragrance as of summer,—'till, at whiles,
All that is sweetest in the varying year,
  Seems softly blent in one delicious hour,
Waking dim visions of some former sphere
  Where sorrows, such as earth owns, had no power
To veil the changeless lustre of the skies,
  And mind and matter formed one paradise.

BIOGRAPHICAL AND BIBLIOGRAPHICAL

NOTES

Biographical and Bibliographical

NOTES

These notes have three purposes: (1) to provide capsule biographies of The Charleston Book
authors; (2) to provide a list of the contributions of each author to the volume; (3) to iden-
tify possible sources, when known, for those
contributions. The capsule biographies are not
documented, because they are derived primarily
from such standard works as the Dictionary of
American Biography, Appleton's Cyclopaedia of
American Biography, Caroline May's American
Female Poets, The Letters of William Gilmore
Simms, John Belton O'Neall's Biographical
Sketches of the Bench and Bar of South Carolina,
U. R. Brooks's South Carolina Bench and Bar, the
Biographical Directory of the Senate of South
Carolina, the Biographical Directory of the
South Carolina House of Representatives, Joseph
I. Waring's A History of Medicine in South
Carolina, denominational histories of Charleston
and South Carolina churches by Dalcho, Thomas,
Howe, Elzas, and others, the Library of Southern
Literature, William Gilmore Simms's Essays on
the Literary and Intellectual History of South
Carolina, and George Armstrong Wauchope's The
Writers of South Carolina. Some additional
information has been gleaned from the WPA's sur-
vey of Charleston tombstone inscriptions at the
South Carolina Historical Society, from pub-
lished and manuscript genealogical materials in
the Society, from the City of Charleston Year-
book, from the South Carolina Historical
Magazine (particularly "The Memoirs of
Frederick Adolphus Porcher," edited by Samuel

Gaillard Stoney), and from the Transactions of the Huguenot Society of South Carolina. Simms's sources for his selections cannot all be positively identified: many items had been reprinted in numerous places before Simms put together The Charleston Book; other items have yet to be traced to any source.

ALLEN, WILLIAM.

Simms remembered him as "another of these promising lads of literature" in Charleston in the 1820s. "His newspaper articles," Simms wrote, "were very numerous. Specimens of his verse will be found in the files of the 'Courier'" for 1824 and 1825; he wrote them under pseudonyms such as "J.A.O., Rinaldo, St. Eustace, etc. His labors were unrelaxing, and he wrote in good measured cadences. He was the writer of more than one novel, or romance, of the old English narrative school, which were never published. He was a slightly made, thin, nervous person, of spasmodic eagerness and impulse, and dabbled in chemistry as well as literature. His death ... took place at Haddrill's Point [near Charleston], while [he was] still very young ...." It was the result of a chemistry experiment.

Selection

p. 228: "Stanzas"

ALLSTON, WASHINGTON (1779-1843).

Artist and author from an Episcopal planter family of Georgetown County. Selling much of his patrimonial estate in 1801, upon graduation (with indifferent grades) from Harvard, Allston moved to Europe to study art. In 1818, he returned permanently to the States, but not to Charleston, where his friends Charles Fraser (q.v.) and John Cogdell lived. Rather, he went to New England, home of both his first and second wives. He lived there until his death.

His "tale," Monaldi, was written in 1822 for a
serial, The Idle Man, published by his close
friend and later brother-in-law, Richard Henry
Dana; it was separately published in 1841.   A
friend of Coleridge and Wordsworth, Allston also
published widely as a poet.   Reviewing "The
Writings of Washington Allston," in the Southern
Quarterly Review, 4 (Oct. 1843), Simms concluded
that the poems were the product of an educated
and   accomplished,   but   not   a   professionally
polished, pen.   Richard Henry Dana, Jr. collected   the   poetry   and   unpublished   lectures   by
Allston on art for an 1850 volume, Lectures on
Art, and Poems, by Washington Allston, Esq.

Selections

p. 13:   "Rosalie," quoted by Simms from
         Rufus Wilmot Griswold, ed., The
         Poets   and   Poetry   of   America
         (Philadelphia, 1842) in an arti-
         cle on "The Writings of Washing-
         ton Allston," Southern Quarterly
         Review, 4 (Oct. 1843), 385-386.

p. 285: "The   Kindness   of   Contemporary
         Criticism," from Monaldi: A Tale
         (Boston,   1841),   32-37.   (Nine
         paragraphs are omitted altogether
         from the beginning and end of the
         chapter   in   which   this   episode
         occurs.)

p. 304: "The   Tuscan   Maid,"   quoted   by
         Simms from Griswold's The Poets
         and Poetry of America in an arti-
         cle on "The Writings of Washing-
         ton Allston," Southern Quarterly
         Review, 4 (Oct. 1843), 388-389.

BACHMAN, JOHN (1790-1874).

New York-bred naturalist and Lutheran minister, Bachman was called to Charleston's St.
John's Lutheran Church in 1815.   First president
of the South Carolina Lutheran synod and founder

of South Carolina's Lutheran theological seminary, he also taught at, and was a trustee of,
the College of Charleston and was active in the
Literary and Philosophical Society of Charleston. He wrote books and articles on a variety
of theological and scientific matters (including
the unity of the human race), but he is best
remembered for his collaboration with John James
Audubon on The Vivaporous Quadrupeds of North
America. He maintained personal and professional ties with scientists around the world, among
them Alexander Wilson of Philadelphia and the
Baron von Humboldt. He also was a leader in the
early days of the American Association for the
Advancement of Science, a founder of the Elliott
Natural History Society, and a member of the
South Carolina Institute.

Selection

p. 30:   "Morals of Entomology," from the
         Southern Literary Journal, 2 (Aug.
         1836), 409-427. (The first forty-
         six paragraphs are omitted.)

BLACKWOOD, V. GARDNER.

An 1845 graduate of the College of Charles-
ton, Blackwood was possibly a grandson of either
Thomas Blackwood, President of the Planters' &
Mechanics' Bank, or John Blackwood, merchant,
both of whom were Irish immigrants active in the
First Baptist Church of Charleston.

Selection

p. 283: "To Henrietta"

BRYAN, GEORGE S. (1809-1895).

Charleston Unionist and lawyer, he was enrolled at the bar in 1831, after having read law
with Thomas S. Grimke (q.v.). A member of the

Conversation Club and a trustee of the College
of Charleston, he helped found the Carolina Art
Association on the eve of the Civil War. As a
Whig leader allied with H. S. Legare (q.v.) and
J. L. Petigru (q.v.), he earned notoriety for
his political writings under the pseudonym,
Crawford. With Petigru and B. F. Perry of
Greenville, he was a leading anti-secessionist.
Between 1866 and 1886, he served as U. S.
Circuit Court judge for the District of South
Carolina. Frederick Porcher remembered him as
having "greater inclination for elegant litera-
ture than for the mysteries of law" and being
"devotedly fond of party politics." He was,
Porcher continued, a vain but amiable man "of
cleverness and taste." Author of a tribute to
Charles Fraser (q.v.), in 1857 he gave an
address on The Character of The Poet as Man and
Genius (Philadelphia, 1858) before the literary
societies of the Military College of South
Carolina.

Selections

p. 208: "Song"

P. 296: "The National Sabbath," apparently from "An Oration, Delivered
before the Washington Society on
the 4th July, 1838." (See, "Passages from an Oration," Southern
Literary Journal, 4, n.s. [July
1838], 68-72.)

CARROLL, BARTHOLOMEW RIVERS, JR.

Son of a Scotch-Irish school master and
brother of both Charles and Edward Carroll
(q.v.), good friends of Simms, he married Eliza
Adeline, daughter of wealthy sea island cotton
planter Ephraim Mikell, in 1833. It was seven
years earlier that he and his brother Edward had
stopped attending the College of Charleston
Grammar and English School. Between January
1836 and December 1839, Carroll edited The
Southern Agriculturist, and in 1837-1838, he

also edited the four volumes of the new series of The Southern Literary Journal, taking over from Daniel Whitaker (q.v.). Like Simms and his brothers, he attended St. Paul's Episcopal Church. Frederick Porcher remembered him from Literary and Philosophical Society meetings as "very intelligent and never at a loss for facts to support his views." Porcher noted, too, that Carroll "had tried several fields of labor, but at last setled down into that of a teacher, in which he was eminently successful."

Selection

p. 266: "Mental Structure of Hugh S. Legaré," from "Sketch of the Character of the Hon. Hugh S. Legaré," Southern Quarterly Review, 4 (Oct. 1843), 355-357, 358-359. (In all, two-thirds of the piece were omitted.)

CARROLL, CHARLES R.

Barnwell District planter and Charleston lawyer, Carroll was enrolled at the bar in 1826. It was in his newly opened office that Simms read law, and it was with him that Simms lived much of the time between the death of his first wife and his second marriage. While living together in 1833, the two co-edited with another bachelor The Cosmopolitan, an occasional. Like Simms, Carroll attended St. Paul's ("the planters'") Church in Charleston.

Selection

p. 134: "Women," from the Southern Literary Journal, 3 (Nov. 1836), 180-183.

CARROLL, EDWARD.

Brother of B. R. and Charles R. Carroll

(q.v.) Edward died while still a young man as
the result of a fall from a horse. He attended
the College of Charleston until 1826 and St.
Paul's Episcopal Church.

Selection

p. 227: "Here are Roses"

CLAPP, JOHN MILTON (1810-1857).

Associate editor of the Charleston Mercury
under John Stuart (q.v.), Clapp became editor of
the Southern Quarterly Review in 1847, when John
E. Carew bought the Mercury. Albert Rhett was a
graduate of Yale, brother of Robert Barnwell
Rhett, fire-eater politician from Beaufort, and
brother-in-law of John Stuart. His death
brought forth obituaries in New York as well as
Charleston.

Selection

p. 149: "The Death of Albert Rhett"

CRAFTS, WILLIAM (1787-1826).

Son of a Boston-bred Charleston merchant,
Crafts graduated from Harvard in 1805 and was
admitted to the South Carolina bar in 1809. He
was first elected to the state House of Representatives in 1810 and served the last six years
of his life as a state senator. In 1817, he
gave the Phi Beta Kappa address at Harvard. Two
years later, he helped found the New England
Society of Charleston. He was a frequent contributor of theater criticism to the Charleston
Courier and other local journals, and several
volumes of his verse were published along with a
number of his orations. The Rev. Dr. Samuel
Gilman (q.v.), a fellow Harvard graduate,
collected A Selection in Prose and Poetry from
the Miscellaneous Writings of the Late William
Crafts, which appeared in 1828.

Selection

p. 22:   "The Pilgrims of New England,"
         from A Selection in Prose and
         Poetry ..., 195-207. (In all,
         eighteen paragraphs are omit-
         ted.)

p. 41:   "Love Asleep," from A Selection
         in Prose and Poetry ..., 359.

p. 295: "Love's Benediction," from A
         Selection in Prose and Poetry
         ..., 360.

p. 382: "On the Reverses of the Spanish
         Arms," from A Selection in Prose
         and Poetry ..., 377-378.

DANA, MARY STANLEY BUNCE PALMER (1810-1883).

Born in Beaufort, South Carolina, Dana was
sister of Presbyterian cleric Dr. Benjamin
Morgan Palmer. In 1835, at age fifteen, she
married Charles E. Dana of New York; following
his death, she married Episcopal cleric Robert
D. Shindler in 1848. The volume which first
brought her notice was The Southern Harp (1840),
a collection of her poems set to familiar tunes.
Others of her volumes published before The
Charleston Book include The Northern Harp
(1841), The Temperance Lyre (1842), The Parted
Family and Other Poems (1842), and a novel,
Charles Morton (1843). Her Letters Addressed to
Relatives and Friends, Chiefly in Reply to
Arguments in Support of the Doctrine of the
Trinity appeared in 1845; The Young Sailor and
Forecastle Tom in 1846. When recommending her
inclusion in Evert Augustus Duyckinck's
Cyclopaedia in 1854, Simms described her as "of
Charleston."

Selection

p. 164: "Song"

DEBOW, JAMES DUNWOODY BROWNSON (1820-1867).

Son of a native of New Jersey, DeBow was orphaned in Charleston as a boy. He worked his way through the College of Charleston, graduating at the top of his class in 1843. The next year he was admitted to the bar. Shortly thereafter he succeeded D. K. Whitaker (q.v.) as editor of the Southern Quarterly Review. Then, in late 1845, after attending the Memphis Commercial Convention and receiving encouragement from Joel Roberts Poinsett (q.v.), John C. Calhoun, and others, he moved to New Orleans to start the Commercial Review of the South and Southwest, better known as DeBow's Review. DeBow accepted appointment to the chair of economics at the newly formed University of New Orleans in 1848 and soon thereafter became director of the short-lived Louisiana Bureau of Statistics as well as a founder of the Louisiana Historical Society. Made superintendent of the U. S. Census by President Pierce, he directed the seventh census (1850) and compiled a Statistical View of the United States (1854). Quitting the Census Bureau in 1855, DeBow lectured widely, presided over the 1857 commercial convention at Knoxville, Tennessee, and wrote on American subjects for the Encyclopaedia Britannica, all the while continuing to edit his Review. During the Civil War, he acted as chief agent for the purchase and sale of cotton by the Confederate government. At the war's end, he started the Review again and served as president of the Tennessee Pacific Railroad Company.

Selection

p. 242: "Beautiful"

DICKSON, SAMUEL HENRY (1798-1872).

Son of a Presbyterian schoolmaster, Dickson was educated first at the College of Charleston, then at Yale. He received his M. D. from the University of Pennsylvania, submitting a History of Yellow Fever in Charleston in 1817 as his

thesis. Returning to Charleston, he became active in the Conversation Club and the Medical
Society of South Carolina and, with several
fellow Society members, began to offer courses
in medicine. This led to the establishment in
1824 of the Medical College of South Carolina
under legislative authority. In the wake of a
split between the faculty of the Medical College
and the members of the Medical Society, Dickson
resigned his professorship. However, the next
year he agreed to serve as the dean of the newly
formed Medical College of the State of South
Carolina. He also served as a College of
Charleston trustee and, in the 1850s, became
very active in American Medical Association
affairs. He left South Carolina for good in
1857, when he assumed a professorship at Jefferson Medical College in Philadelphia. He nevertheless continued his involvement in Charleston
affairs, being active for instance in the
Elliott Natural History Society. A temperance
advocate, he addressed the South Carolina
Society for the Promotion of Temperance in 1830.
In 1842, he delivered the Phi Beta Kappa address
at Yale. His _Poems_ appeared in 1844. He also
was a frequent contributor to the _Southern
Literary Messenger_ and the _Southern Quarterly
Review_. His _Essays on Slavery_ appeared in 1845.

Selections

p. 70:   "The Characteristics of Civili-
         zation," from _An Oration Deliv-
         ered at New Haven, Before the Phi
         Beta Kappa Society_, August 17,
         1842 (New Haven, Conn., 1842),
         41-47.

p. 88:   "I Sigh for the Land of the
         Cypress and the Pine" (presum-
         ably from Dickson's _Poems_, though
         the annotator has been unable to
         locate a copy of the volume in
         South Carolina).

p. 300: "The Influence of Letters upon
         Happiness," from _An Oration
         Delivered at New Haven_ ...,

29-32.   (In all, Simms excerp-
ted approximately twenty-five
percent of this oration for
this selection and the other
one noted above.)

DINNIES, ANNA PEYRE (1816-1886).

Though born in Georgetown, South Carolina,
Dinnies was raised in Charleston, where her
father, Judge W. F. Schackleford, moved when she
was young. In Charleston, she studied at the
female seminary kept by David Ramsay's daughters. Married at age fourteen to journalist
John C. Dinnies after a four-year literary
correspondence, she moved to her husband's home
in St. Louis, Missouri, moving again sixteen
years later to New Orleans. She had written a
good deal already before her marriage, but only
began publishing voluminously after having moved
west. Principally a writer of stories and
poems, she contributed to various magazines
under the pseudonym, Moina. In 1845, an illustrated volume of her verse, The Floral Year,
appeared.

Selection

p. 40: "The Wife," reprinted from an
unknown source in the Southern
Rose, 5 (Sep. 3, 1836), 8, and
again in the Southern Cabinet, 1
(Feb. 1840), 109.

DUKES, JOSEPH H.

Leaving the College of Charleston in 1834
without graduating, Dukes was admitted to the
bar in Columbia in 1839. He moved from Charleston to New York in 1859-1860. Simms considered
him an "old friend" and recommended him as "a
fine gentleman, of fine ability, a young man of
excellent Charleston family, and a batchelor
[sic!]." This was in 1860, when Simms also

noted that Dukes had abandoned poetry for "more
lucrative employments."   While in Charleston,
Dukes gave addresses before the Washington
Society in 1842 and "The Firemen of Charleston"
in 1844. At the close of the Civil War, he composed a memorial inscription for the tomb of
James Louis Petigru (q.v.).

Selection

p. 298: "The Charter Oak"

ELLIOTT, STEPHEN (1771-1830).

Born in Beaufort of a planter family,
Elliott graduated in 1791 from Yale before
coming home to plant and continue the family
tradition of service in St. Helena's Episcopal
Church. In 1794, he was elected for the first
of several terms in the South Carolina House of
Representatives from St. Helena's Parish.   In
1808, he began four years of service as state
senator from the Parish. While in the Senate,
he was an author of the 1811 Free School Act and
the Act of 1812 creating the Bank of South Carolina.   Following passage of the latter bill,
Elliott was elected as the Bank's president and
moved to Charleston, where he served in that
capacity from 1812 until his death. There, too,
he became a founder and president of the Literary and Philosophical Society, president of the
Charleston Library Society, a founder with
Samuel Henry Dickson, and professor of natural
history, at the South Carolina Medical College,
a trustee of the College of Charleston, and in
1828, cofounder and coeditor with Hugh Swinton
Legare of The Southern Review, modeled on the
Edinburgh Review and arguably the leading
southern journal during its four-year existence.
Elliott remains best known perhaps for his two-
volume Sketch of the Botany of South Carolina
and Georgia (1821-1824), based on a collection
he made between 1800 and 1808.

Selection

p. 5:   "The Completeness and Variety
         of Nature," from the Southern
         Review, 1 (Nov. 1828), 408-431.
         (Only a quarter of the essay is
         included. All references to the
         two works which occasioned
         the review are omitted, only
         Elliott's leading generalizations
         being kept.)

FARMER, HENRY TUDOR (1787-1828).

An 1819 graduate in medicine at the University of New York, Farmer wrote his thesis on
arthritis. He was elected a member of the Medical Society of South Carolina in 1819 and in
1820 delivered "An Address ... before the Franklin Library Society." The year before, his
Imagination: The Maniac's Dream and Other Poems
had been published in both London and New York.
Farmer was a member of St. Michael's (Episcopal)
Church in Charleston, and with William Crafts
(q.v.) and Edwin C. Holland (q.v.), contributed
to the Omnium Botherum as well as the Charleston
Courier. In recommending him for inclusion in
Duyckinck's Cyclopaedia, Simms wrote: "Farmer
was an Englishman, a man of decided and various
talent, an amateur actor of great merit, but
desultory, dissipated, indolent, without aim.
This was when I knew him. He was then 45 or
50." In Simms's estimate, Farmer ranked highest
"of the poets of the day in Charleston, when
Crafts, Harby [q.v.] and Holland were in
vogue...." Simms got Farmer's papers with the
intention of editing a complete edition of the
poems but died before completing the project.

Selection

p. 20:   "The Woes of Modern Greece: A
         Prize Poem"

FRASER, CHARLES (1782-1860).

Educated at the College of Charleston, Fraser was admitted to the bar in 1807, practicing until 1818. Then, having accrued a competency, he began to devote himself largely to the art which had always occupied his leisure and attention. Like his friend Malbone, he concentrated on miniatures. By the time of his death, he had painted many of Charleston's most prominent citizens, including numerous personal friends. He was a frequent traveller, often visiting his Winthrop kin and Washington Allston (q.v.) in Massachusetts and his friend Thomas Sully in Philadelphia. Though eschewing "[l]iterary reputation," Fraser was nevertheless a frequent contributor to periodicals such as the American Monthly Magazine and the Magnolia, and he was as frequently a speaker before local societies such as the Conversation Club. In addition, he served on a variety of boards, including the College of Charleston board, and was a member of numerous organizations, such as the South Carolina Institute. Fellow college trustee George S. Bryan (q.v.) wrote a biographical sketch of him on the occasion of the 1857 retrospective exhibit put on in Charleston in Fraser's honor.

Selections

p. 46:   "Claude Lorraine," quoted in [William Gilmore Simms], "The Writings of Washington Allston," Southern Quarterly Review, 4 (Oct. 1843), 371, from the Magnolia, 2, n.s. (May 1843), 315.

p. 165: "Gardening"

p. 332: "Nature Made for Man," from the Magnolia, 2, n.s. (June 1843), 383.

GILMAN, CAROLINE (1794-1888).

New England-born and an ardent Episcopalian, Gilman began contributing poetry to the
North American Review about 1817. Three years
later, she married the Rev. Samuel Gilman (q.v.)
and moved with him to Charleston, where he became rector of the Second Independent (Unitarian) Church. In 1832, Mrs. Gilman started
the Rosebud, one of the earliest children's
magazines in the United States. Changing the
name and format of this journal twice and making
the magazine suitable for older readers in the
process, Gilman continued publication through
seven volumes, finally stopping because of ill
health in 1839, after having ridden out the
panic of 1837 which had cut deeply into her sub-
scriptions (and income). Not only did she provide a forum for South Carolina writers such as
Anna P. Dinnies (q.v.), Mary E. Lee (q.v.),
Frederick A. Porcher, William James Rivers
(q.v.), William Gilmore Simms, and William Henry
Timrod (q.v.) through the Rosebud, Southern
Rosebud, and Southern Rose, she also brought
numerous northern and European writers to the
attention of her subscribers in a dozen states;
among them were Harriet Beecher Stowe, Nathaniel
Hawthorne, Byron, Goethe, Lamartine, Manzoni,
Schiller, and Tromlitz. Furthermore, she
contributed serial novels, poetry, and historical materials herself. These would be collected
and published in a half-dozen volumes. Gilman
continued to write until nearly her death.

Selections

p. 145: "My Garden," from the Southern
Rose, 6 (Apr. 28, 1838), 280-
281.

p. 333: "The Lost Mail" from the Southern
Rose, 6 (Mar. 3, 1838), 216.

GILMAN, SAMUEL (1791-1858).

New England-reared and Harvard-educated,
Gilman was a school teacher and then a tutor at

his alma mater between 1812 and 1819, when he married and, with his wife Caroline (q.v.), moved to Charleston to accept the charge of the Second Independent (Unitarian) Church. At that point, he had already achieved recognition as a poet, having both given the class poem at his graduation and contributed translations in verse from Boileau to the North American Review. In Charleston, he continued to devote five or six hours a day to reading and writing and frequently supplied verse translations (particularly from French and German) and religious and literary essays to his wife's magazine, the Rosebud, (later, the Southern Rosebud and, still later, the Southern Rose) as well as the Boston Christian Examiner and the London Monthly Repository. Serving for sixteen years as chaplain of the Washington Light Infantry, Gilman was active in the Conversation Club. He gathered many of his non-theological writings in Contributions to Literature, published just two years before his death.

Selections

p. 61: "French Literature," from "Remarks on French Literature," Magnolia, 2, n.s. (Apr. 1843), 224-225.

p. 206: "The Silent Girl," from the Southern Rose, 4 (Sept. 19, 1835), 16, reprinted from the Southern Rose Bud.

GRIMKE, THOMAS SMITH (1786-1834).

Charleston-born and Yale-educated son of a wealthy lawyer and jurist, Grimké gave up thought of entering the Episcopal ministry at his father's insistence and read law instead in the office of Langdon Cheves. A partner in the firm of Robert Y. Hayne, sometime U. S. Senator for South Carolina, he served as a state senator from 1826 to 1830 and as a vestryman at Simms's and the Carroll brothers' church, St. Paul's

(Episcopal). An ardent Unionist and advocate of temperance, world peace, and educational reform, he also served as a trustee of the College of Charleston, was a frequent contributor to the Calumet, journal of the American Peace Society, and wrote on literature and education for the Southern Review and other journals. In addition, he gave numerous addresses before the Literary and Philosophical Society, the American Sunday School Union, and other organizations. A selection of his writings, Reflections on the Character and Objects of all Science and Literature, appeared in 1831. Included in it is Grimké's Phi Beta Kappa address at Yale in 1830.

Selection

p.42: "The Secret of Oratorical Success"

HARBY, ISAAC (1788-1828).

Grandson of a lapidary to the Emperor of Morocco, he was born in Charleston, where he attended Dr. Best's Academy. He read law briefly with Langdon Cheves but gave it up, returning to teach first in an academy which he opened on Edisto Island, then in one which he started in Charleston. In 1807, while still teaching, he briefly edited a weekly journal of "original essays, criticisms, communications" entitled The Quiver. Then, in 1814, he bought the Investigator with a friend and renamed it the Southern Patriot and Commercial Advertiser. In its pages, he and his partner supported President Madison. Selling out in 1817, Harby continued his journalistic career in the City Gazette and Commercial Daily Advertiser. There, over the pseudonym Junius, he urged Andrew Jackson's nomination for the presidency. A theater critic first in Charleston and, then during his last year, in New York, Harby also wrote several verse plays with political subjects. Two were performed and published in Charleston: The Gordian Knot (1810) and Alberti (1819). Harby was a founder in 1824 and leader of Reform Judaism. A selection from the Miscellaneous

Writings of the Late Isaac Harby, Esq., edited by former political ally Henry L. Pinckney (*q.v.*) and fellow Reform Jew Abraham Moise, appeared for the benefit of Harby's family in 1829.

Selection

p. 46: "The Fall of Jerusalem," from "Discourse before the Reformed Society of Israelites," in *A Selection from the Miscellaneous Writings* ..., 55-87. (Just four pages of the "Discourse" are included.)

HASELL, WILLIAM SORANZO (1780-1844).

Son of Susannah Hasell and Parker Quince, William Soranzo changed his name to Hasell. He delivered the class poem at his graduation at Yale in 1799. Simms had to get his name for *The Charleston Book* from Charles Fraser (*q.v.*), who described the recently deceased Hasell as "a very worthy and excellent fellow." Hasell counted among his kin Thomas S. Grimké (*q.v.*), the Rutledges, the Middletons, the Rhetts, and other prominent low-country families.

Selection

p. 50: "Alfred: An Historical Poem," from the pamphlet of the same title which was published anonymously in Charleston in 1800. Simms included the entire poem.

HOLLAND, EDWIN C. (1794-1824).

Editor in 1818 of the Charleston *Times*, he was a vigorous early defender of slavery. With Henry T. Farmer (*q.v.*), William Crafts (*q.v.*), and others, he contributed to *Omnium Botherum*, a satirical occasional directed against Thomas Bee's *Omnium Gatherum*, and to the Charleston

Courier. "The Pillar of Glory" won first prize
in a national competition conducted by the
Philadelphia Portfolio in 1813; the poem was set
to music by Jacob Ekhard, Sr., organist at St.
Michael's (Episcopal) Church, Charleston, as was
Holland's second patriotic entry in the contest,
"Rise, Columbia, Brave and Free."   Both scores
and poems were distributed with the issue of the
Portfolio in which the results of the contest
were announced.

Selection

p. 122: "The Pillar of Glory," from the
        Portfolio, 2, 3d ser. (Nov.
        1813), 542 et passim.   (Note:
        the poems and scores are unpagi-
        nated inserts which could be
        removed for use at the piano.)

HURLBUT, STEPHEN AUGUSTUS (1815-1882).

   Born in Charleston, Hurlbut was admitted to
the bar there in 1837, having read law in the
office of James Louis Petigru (q.v.).   In 1845,
as a result of "some unedifying frolic," according to Petigru's biographer and grandson, James
Petigru Carson, he moved to Belvidere, Illinois,
where he became active in state and national
politics.   In March 1861, President Lincoln sent
him to make contact with Petigru and other anti-
secessionists in Charleston.   The mission proved
abortive, and Hurlbut was temporarily imprisoned
as a spy.   On his return north, he was com-
missioned a Brigadier General in the U. S. Army;
he commanded the Fourth Division at Shiloh.
Promoted to Major General in 1862, he was
assigned command of the Department of the Gulf,
where he remained until relieved of command in
June 1865 after charges of corruption.   Returning to Illinois and Republican Party politics,
he was followed by charges of drunkenness and
dishonesty.   Appointed U. S. Minister to Columbia in 1869, he returned in 1872 to serve two
terms in Congress.   He died shortly after
appointment as U. S. Minister to Peru in 1881.

Selection

p. 229: "The Wreckers: A Tale of the Sea"

p. 289: "Music," from the Southern Rose, 7 (Mar. 16, 1839), 237.

p. 355: "A Dissertation on Dandies," from the Magnolia, 1, n.s.   (Oct. 1842), 254-56.

IRVING, JOHN BEAUFAIN (1800-1881).

Born in Jamaica, Irving was educated for the ministry at Rugby and Cambridge but went on to study medicine in Philadelphia.   In 1823, he applied for his license to practice medicine in South Carolina.   For a time Sheriff of Charleston, he later became a rice planter on the Cooper River.   A popular lecturer, Irving edited the tri-weekly Rambler, a journal of the arts, between 1843 and 1844, when a medical appointment took away the leisure he had used for the purpose.   Secretary of the South Carolina Jockey Club for thirty years, he wrote a History of the Turf in South Carolina.   He was a founding member in 1849 of the South Carolina Institute. After the destruction of his plantation in 1865, he moved to New Jersey to live with his German-educated son, artist John Beaufain Irving, Jr. He remained there until his death, becoming manager of the Jockey Club of New York.

Selection

p. 272: "A Glimpse of a Ghost," from A Day on Cooper River (Charleston, 1842), 38-41.

KING, MITCHELL (1783-1862).

Born in Scotland, where he studied science and metaphysics, King was apprenticed to a

Scottish merchant in Prussia, became dissatis-
fied and returned home. Setting out for London
in 1804 with hope of getting a position in East
India, he missed the East India fleet but got
passage to Malta. Giving up finding a post to
his liking there, he took a return passage, only
to be captured by Spanish privateers. He
escaped on a vessel bound for Charleston, where
he started a school. Gaining the attention of
Dr. Buist, principal of the College of Charleston through some newspaper verse, King then
hired on at the College of Charleston, where
Hugh Swinton Legaré (q.v.), was his pupil.
Beginning to read law in 1807, he was entered
before the bar in 1810, the same year in which
he had become headmaster of the College's grammar school. A founder of the Charleston Philosophical Society in 1809 and, then, the Literary
and Philosophical Society (1813), he lectured
before the former organization on astronomy. He
was twice recorder and judge of the city court
and twice president of the St. Andrew's Society.
During Nullification, he was an ardent Unionist,
as were Legaré, Petigru (q.v.), and Simms. King
served as a trustee of the College of Charleston
from 1817-1862, was president of the board from
1847 until his death, and served as acting president of the College in 1844. He was a trustee
of the Medical College of the State of South
Carolina from its founding and president of its
board from 1837. At his death, he left a
library of 2,500 volumes to the College of
Charleston.

Selection

p. 77: "The Resolve"

LEE, MARY ELIZABETH (1813-1849).

Daughter of a Charleston lawyer, educated
by tutors until the age of ten, Lee then attended female seminaries. She divided her time
between Charleston and Camden, contributing her
own poems and stories as well as translations
from German to the Southern Rose, the Orion, the

Southern Literary Messenger, the Magnolia, Graham's Magazine, the Knickerbocker, and numerous other journals. Her Historical Tales for Youth "was the outcome of a successful competition for a prize offered by the Massachusetts Educational Board for books to be introduced into school libraries." Samuel Gilman edited the Poetical Remains of Mary Elizabeth Lee, which appeared in 1851.

Selection

p. 141: "The Last Place of Sleep," from the Magnolia, 1, n.s. (Aug. 1842), 92.

p. 354: "The Lone Star"

p. 384: "Midnight--Last Day of the Year," from the Southern Rose, 4 (Jan. 9, 1836), 80.

P. 387: "The Leper of Capernum"

LEGARE, HUGH SWINTON (1797-1843).

Born in Charleston, Legare lost his father at an early age, then at five, got fever from a smallpox innoculation and, as a result, would have stunted limbs for the rest of his life. Legare studied under Mitchell King (q.v.) at the College of Charleston before going to Moses Waddell's Willington Academy and, then, at fourteen to the South Carolina College, where he graduated in 1814 at the head of his class. After reading law with King, he went to Europe in 1818. There he and William C. Preston, a Virginian who would serve South Carolina in the U. S. Senate, traveled with Washington Irving, studied French in Paris, went to Edinburgh, met George Ticknor, and studied Roman law, natural philosophy, mathematics, and chemistry at the University. Legare returned to South Carolina in 1820 to manage his family's faltering John's Island cotton plantation. The next year, he began to practice law. From 1824 to 1830, he represented Charleston in legislature. Then, in 1830, he succeeded fellow Unionist James Louis Petigru (q.v.) as state attorney general. In consequence of an argument which he made before the U. S. Supreme Court while in this capacity, he was offered the post of charge d'affairs in Brussels. He accepted, thus escaping the nullification-embittered atmosphere of South Carolina. Remaining for four years, he studied Roman and civil law, meeting Savigny, and learned both German and Dutch. Upon his return to South Carolina in 1836, he was elected to Congress but then, like political ally Richard Yeadon (q.v.), lost his bid for reelection two years later because of his opposition to the independent treasury bill supported by John C. Calhoun. He returned to the practice of the law and entered Whig Party politics. In 1841, newly elected President John Tyler of Virginia appointed him U. S. Attorney General. Then, when Daniel Webster resigned the secretaryship of state, Tyler appointed Legare secretary ad interim. Shortly thereafter, Legare died. His sister, with more devotion than accuracy, edited his selected writings for publication in two volumes over the next two years. They were drawn from the Southern Review, which Legare had edited with Stephen Elliott (q.v.) between 1828 and 1832, from the New-York Review, from published orations and congressional debates, and from his official and private correspondence with Secretary of State Edward Livingston, Alfred Huger, Thomas C. Reynolds (q.v.), and others. The writings range over political and diplomatic matters, Greek and Roman literature and history, classical education, English literature, and the writings of fellow Charlestonians such as William Crafts (q.v.), whose work and dilettantism the rigorously academic Legare sharply criticized.

Selections

p. 14:   "The Study of the Classics," from "Classical Learning," Southern Review, 1 (Feb. 1828), 1-49. (Only pages 45-48 are given.)

p. 290: "The Greek Language," from "Classical Learning," <u>Southern Review</u>, 1 (Feb. 1828), 1-49. (Only pages 40-42 are given.)

LEGARE, JAMES M. (1823-1859).

Son of John D. Legare, founding editor of the <u>Southern Agriculturalist</u> and recording secretary of the Horticultural Society of Charleston, James studied at the College of Charleston at the same time as James D. B. DeBow (<u>q.v.</u>), William Henry Trescot, and Henry Samuel Dickson, son of Dr. Samuel Henry Dickson (<u>q.v.</u>). From the College of Charleston, Legare went to the Roman Catholic St. Mary's College in Maryland, his father believing the rigors of Catholic discipline being beneficial. Upon graduation, Legare read law in the offices of James Louis Petigru (<u>q.v.</u>) and began both to contribute verses to the <u>Rambler</u>, edited by John Beaufain Irving (<u>q.v.</u>), and <u>Simms's Magazine</u> and to exhibit his paintings. Then, because of ill health, Legare moved to Aiken, where he taught while continuing to paint and write. From there, he contributed to the <u>Southern Literary Messenger</u>, the <u>Southern Literary Gazette</u>, the <u>Knickerbocker Magazine</u>, and <u>Putnam's</u>. At this time, too, he became a confirmed Episcopalian. In 1848, his only collection of verse, <u>Orta-Undis</u>, was published by the cousin of Hugh Swinton Legare's Boston friend, George Ticknor. Longfellow praised the volume, and he and Legare began a correspondence. In 1852, Legare set up a laboratory where he continued work on the inventions which he hoped would make him wealthy. He received several patents but few profits.

Selection

p. 189: "Du Saye: A Legend of the Congarees"

p. 216: "Childhood Among the Tombs"

LEVIN, LEWIS CHARLES (1808-1860).

Born to a Jewish family in Charleston, Levin attended the South Carolina College before moving about 1828 to Mississippi, where he read law while teaching school. After living in Maryland, Kentucky, and Louisiana, he settled in Philadelphia, where he was admitted to the bar in 1838. He became a prominent temperance leader and served as editor of the Temperance Advocate. Later, he helped form the Native-American Party and edited the Philadelphia Sun. Riding the strong anti-Catholic feeling in Philadelphia, Levin was elected to Congress in 1844, 1846, and 1848 and became an outspoken partisan of nativism. He died a victim of insanity.

Selection

p. 163: "The Frozen Dew-Drop"

MACKEY, ALBERT GALLATIN (1807-1881).

Son of a Charleston physician, politician, and journalist, Mackey graduated from the Medical College of South Carolina in 1832. At the outbreak of the Seminole War, he, like William Henry Timrod (q.v.), volunteered for service. Returning to Charleston, according to Joseph I. Waring, "he joined the Medical Society in 1839 and was physician to the Alms House in 1840." In 1844, he gave up medicine to devote himself full-time to journalism and writing. At different times, he edited the Southern Patriot, the Southern and Western Masonic Miscellany, and the Charleston Sun. Many of his own writings were on freemasonry. An ardent anti-secessionist, like George S. Bryan (q.v.) and James Louis Petigru (q.v.), he presided over the state constitutional convention of 1868. Some time after that, he moved to Washington, D. C.

Selections

p. 209: "The Parchment Eater"

p. 216: "Childhood Among the Tombs"

MOISE, PENINA (1797-1880).

Daughter of a Jewish refugee family from St. Domingue (Haiti), she lost her father at the age of twelve and had to quit school in order to help support her family. She continued to read and write in her spare moments, however. By 1830, her verse and prose were being published in the Charleston Courier and elsewhere. Her Fancy's Sketch Book appeared in 1833 and includes a poem "On the Death of My Preceptor, Isaac Harby, Esq." (q.v.). Her volume of hymns for a congregation Beth Elohim, the reform synagogue which Isaac Harby had helped found, went through four editions.

Selections

p. 94: "Miriam"

p. 363: "The Convict"

MULLER, ALBERT ARNEY (b. ca. 1793).

A major in Francis Marion's brigade during the Revolution, legislator, and powder receiver for Charleston, Muller's father died in 1793. As a deacon in 1817-1818, Muller was at Grace Church, Sullivan's Island, near Charleston. Then, in 1819, as an ordained minister, he officiated at St. James, Goose Creek, before taking charge of Christ Church across the Cooper River from Charleston. He left there in 1823, moving to Pennsylvania. In 1829, he spoke at the annual convention of the Episcopal Church in Mississippi. In recommending him to Evert Duyckinck in 1854 for inclusion in Duyckinck's Cyclopaedia, Simms wrote: "Rev. Albert A.

Muller--author of a volume of Poems some of which are of remarkable beauty .... Muller was a man of irregular habits & doubtful moral--what has become of him I don't know." Reminiscing still later, in 1868, Simms wrote of Muller's "slender volume of poems, chiefly of religious character," that it "argued a great improvement in the purity of local verse."

Selections

p. 27: "Sunset at Rome: A Prize Poem"

p. 293: "The Marriage Feast," from Gospel Melodies, and other Occasional Poems (Charleston, 1823), 57-59.

p. 325: "The School Girl Watching the Stars"

MURDEN, ELIZA (fl. ca. 1808).

A Mrs. Murden and her daughters operated a female seminary in Charleston in 1831. Eliza's Poems by a Young Lady of Charleston appeared in 1808 and was subscribed to by, among others, John S. Cogdell, Henry Farmer (q.v.), William Flagg, Charles Fraser (q.v.), Peter Freneau, Thomas S. Grimke (q.v.), Elias Marks, John Parker, Jr. (q.v.), William Hayne Simmons (q.v.), and John Blake White (q.v.). In the Advertisement, Murden explained that she turned to poetry "as a relief from more serious occupations" and found it "the solace of her leisure hours." Her second volume, Miscellaneous Poems, was published in New York in 1827. Subscribers who had not subscribed to the earlier volume included the Rev. Dr. John Bachman (q.v.) and the Rev. Edward Phillips (q.v.). Several of the poems are to Henry T. Farmer.

Selection

p. 241: "The Volunteer"

PARKER, JOHN (1787-1849).

A Charleston attorney and Cooper River rice planter, Parker was admitted to the bar in 1810 and was a vestryman at St. James, Goose Creek Episcopal Church. He was almost an exact contemporary of Manzoni (1785-1873), the Italian poet and novelist.

Selection

p. 370: "Imitation   of   a   Sonnet   of Manzoni"

PETIGRU, JAMES LOUIS (1789-1863).

Born in Abbeville District, South Carolina, Petigru entered Moses Waddell's Academy in Willington, South Carolina in 1804 and, two years later, the South Carolina College. Graduating in 1809, he taught for three years in Colleton and Beaufort Counties while reading law. In 1819, he accepted James Hamilton, Jr.'s offer of a partnership in a Charleston law firm and moved to the city. Three years later he was elected state attorney general. An ardent Unionist during the Nullification controversy, he continued to play an important, if backstage, role in local politics through the 1850s. He was appointed U. S. District Attorney in 1850 and elected code commissioner for South Carolina in 1859, completing a Portion of the Code of Statute Law of South Carolina, 1860-1862 just before his death. He was a founder and the first president of the South Carolina Historical Society and a long-time member of the Literary and Philosopohical Society, which he had helped revive in the 1830s, after the death of Stephen Elliott (q.v.). In 1848, he delivered the centennial address before the Charleston Library Society, and in 1855, he delivered the semi-centennial address at South Carolina College. He also addressed colleges throughout the South, contributed to the Southern Review and other publications, and maintained an extensive law

practice. S. A. Hurlbut (q.v.) and James M.
Legare (q.v.), among many others, read law in
his offices.

Selection

p. 89: "The True Glory of America," from
        the Charleston Courier, July 4,
        1844. (Note: the text of this
        Moultrie Day [June 28] oration is
        included in James Petigru Carson,
        Life, Letters and Speeches of
        James Louis Petigru [Washington,
        D. C., 1920], 228-236.)

PHILLIPS, EDWARD (ca. 1804-1855).

     Phillips was an Episcopal clergyman. Mission
priest at St. Stephen's Chapel under the auspic-
es of the Protestant Episcopal Domestic Missionary Society, he at other times held the charges
of St. Thomas and St. Dennis, just north of
Charleston, and the Church of the Holy Apostles
in Barnwell. JOHN STEVENS COGDELL (1778-1847)
was a Charleston lawyer and painter who took up
sculpting in 1825 at the suggestion of Washington Allston (q.v.); he exhibited at the Boston
Atheneum, and his busts were placed in the
Capitol, the National Academy of Design, and the
Philadelphia Academy as well as in the Charleston Library Society. He was elected a state
representative in 1810, 1814, 1816, and 1818,
when he was made state comptroller general. In
1821 he was appointed naval officer of the
Charleston customs house; in 1832 he became
president of the Bank of South Carolina, serving
until his death. Bishop THEODORE DEHON
(1776-1817) was born and educated in Boston,
graduating from Harvard in 1795. His first
charge--in 1798--was Trinity Church, Newport,
Rhode Island. His first visit to Charleston was
in 1803. In 1809, after having declined the
rectorship of St. Phillip's, Charleston, he
accepted the call of St. Michael's there. The
next year he helped found, and became the first
president of, the Protestant Episcopal Society

for the Advancement of Christianity in South
Carolina. Elected bishop of the diocese in 1812,
he died of yellow fever five years later.

Selection

p. 271: "Cogdell's Bust of Bishop DeHon,"
from Chicora, 1 (Oct. 1842), 101.

PINCKNEY, HENRY LAURENS (1794-1863).

Son of Charles Pinckney and Mary Eleanor
Laurens, Henry Laurens Pinckney was schooled by
his father and the Presbyterian Rev. George
Buist. After graduating in 1812 from the South
Carolina College, he read law with his brother-
in-law Robert Y. Hayne. In 1816, he was elected
to the state legislature, where he served
through 1832, rising to the House speakership in
1830. Between 1823 and 1832, he owned and
edited the Charleston Mercury, a states-rights
journal which had possibly the largest circulation of any paper in the state. In 1829, 1831,
and 1832, Pinckney served as intendant, or
mayor, of Charleston. From 1833-1837, he served
in Congress, losing his bid for reelection in
1836 because of disagreements with John C.
Calhoun. Returning to Charleston, he again
served as mayor, in the process overseeing the
conversion of the College of Charleston to a
municipally supported institution, a project to
which Richard Yeadon (q.v.) also gave active
support. Subsequently, Pinckney served as
collector of the port (1840-1841), as a state
legislator (1844-1845), and as a city tax
collector (1845-1863). He was a frequent
speaker before literary, patriotic, and civic
groups as well as on politics.

Selections

p. 95: "The Spirit of the Age," from
"The Spirit of the Age": An
Address Delivered before the Two
Literary Societies of the Univer-
sity of North Carolina (Raleigh,

N. C., 1836), 9-14.   (In all,
twenty-two pages were cut.)

p. 320: "Delights of Knowledge," from An
Oration on the Pleasures and Advantages of Knowledge, and the
Necessity of Moral as well as
Mental Cultivation, to Individual
Excellence and National Prosperity; Delivered before the Literary Societies of the University
of Georgia. August 3d, 1837 ....
(Athens, Ga., 1837), 9-11. (In
all, seventeen pages were cut.)

POINSETT, JOEL ROBERTS (1779-1851).

    Son of a Charleston physician and an English
woman, Poinsett studied at Timothy Dwight's
academy in Connecticut, then at St. Paul's
School in England, at the medical school of the
University of Edinburgh, and at the military
academy at Woolwich. Returning to South
Carolina, he read law with Henry W. DeSaussure.
Soon after, he set out on a long tour of Europe
and the Near East, meeting Necker, Napoleon,
Metternich, Goethe, and Alexander I of Russia.
Hoping to secure a military appointment in 1808,
when war with Britain threatened, he returned to
the U. S.   The appointment eluded him, but he
finally received a posting as special agent to
Buenos Aires and Chile.   Arriving in 1811, he
developed ties with leaders of the Spanish
American independence movement.   At the over-
throw of his Chilean friends, the Carrera
brothers, Poinsett returned to South Carolina in
1815.   Elected to the state legislature in 1816,
he became chairman of the legislative Board of
Public Works in 1818, devoting himself to internal improvements.   In 1821, he succeeded Charles
Pinckney in Congress, remaining until 1825.
Appointed the U. S.'s first minister to Mexico
in 1825 by his friend, Andrew Jackson, he held
the post for four years.   He then returned to
South Carolina, becoming a leader of the
Unionist Party in the Nullification controversy.

Because of the obloquy his actions then brought
on him and following his marriage in 1833, he
went into retirement until 1837, when President
Van Buren appointed him Secretary of War. Four
years later, Poinsett retired again to his plantation near Georgetown. From there he continued
to resist secessionist sentiments and to support
the arts and sciences. Having helped establish
the South Carolina Academy of Fine Arts with
Washington Allston (q.v.), Samuel F. B. Morse,
John S. Cogdell, Thomas Middleton, Stephen
Elliott (q.v.), and others in 1821, he went on
to help found the National Institute for the
Promotion of Science and the Useful Arts and to
collect for the American Philosophical Society
and the Historical Society of Pennsylvania. He
also participated in Charleston's Literary and
Philosophical Society and Horticultural Society
and served for eight years on the College of
Charleston Board of Trustees.

Selections

p. 105: "Etruscan   Remains,"   from   the
        Southern Literary Journal, 2
        (Apr. 1836), 81-89.

p. 306: "Literature and the Fine Arts,"
        from Discourse on the Objects and
        Importance of the National Insti-
        tution for the Promotion of
        Science, Established at Washing-
        ton, 1840, Delivered at the First
        Anniversary (Washington, D. C.,
        1841), 44-47.   (In all, forty-
        five pages were cut.)

PORTER, BENJAMIN FANEUIL (1808-1868).

    Son of a cabinet maker, Porter was largely
self-educated. Having read law with William
Crafts (q.v.), he was admitted to the bar in
1825. Three years later he moved to Chester,
and from there, to Alabama. Not finding employment as a lawyer and having studied some medicine with Dr. Thomas Legare of Charleston, he

set up medical practice, not to return to the
law until 1834.   He was elected to the state
legislature   in   1832,   serving   until   elected
reporter for the state supreme court in 1835.
In 1840, he was elected judge, but resigned a
year later over politics.   Then, in 1848, he
returned to Charleston, where he established a
practice, staying several years.   While in
Charleston, he helped found the South Carolina
Institute.   Writing in about 1859, Porter noted
for John Belton O'Neall: "in the intervals of
professional employment, I have studied every
branch of the sciences and philosophy.   I have
become a fair Latin, and a good French scholar.
Taking a fancy to the Civil Law, I have explored
it from the earliest fragments, through Paul,
Ulpian, the Institutes, Pandects, Novels, and
Code, to the Spanish and French law, and in it
found   the   true   source   of   the   principles   of
jurisprudence."   Moreover,   he   continued,   "By
temperance and industry, I have found time to
spend many hours to the advocacy of education,
and every means of improving this country: to
write occasionally for the papers and magazines,
and to prepare works on the law, &c., which may
one day find their way to the press.   I have
prepared a translation of 'Heinnecius Elements
of the Institutes.'"

Selection

p. 199: "Trial   of   Milo--Oration   of
        Cicero," from "The Visit of Atti-
        cus to Rome"

PORTER, WILLIAM DENNISON (1810-1883).

Graduating with second honors from the
College of Charleston in 1829, Porter taught
school while reading law.   He was admitted to
the bar in 1833, became clerk of court of
Charleston in 1836, served as a magistrate from
1840-1864, as city attorney from 1848-1860, as
state representative from 1840-1848, as state
senator from 1848-1865, as president of the
senate from 1858-1865, as lieutenant governor

from 1865-1868, as president of the tax payers'
conventions of 1871 and 1874, and as master in
equity in 1878. Treasurer of the Charleston
Library Society, trustee of (1) the South
Carolina College (1858-1868), (2) the College of
Charleston (1860-1864), and (3) the Medical
College of South Carolina (1875), director of
Magnolia Cemetery, solicitor of the Charleston
Savings Institute, commissioner of the Charles-
ton public schools, captain of the Washington
Light Infantry, and member of the Charleston
Chamber of Commerce, the South Carolina Insti-
tute, and Grace (Episcopal) Church, Charleston,
he was a frequent public speaker before literary
and civic organizations and wrote often on
public questions under the pseudonym "Rutledge."

Selection

p. 154: "The Value of the Arts and
Sciences to the Practical
Mechanic," from the Charleston
Courier, April 12, 1843.

REYNOLDS, THOMAS CAUTE (1821-1887).

Born in Charleston, Reynolds was educated in
Virginia, where his family had moved while he
was a boy. He graduated from the University of
Virginia in 1842, after having studied at Berlin
and Heidelberg and traveled through Europe,
carrying letters of introduction from Hugh
Swinton Legare (q.v.). Speaking French,
Spanish, and German fluently, he was appointed
secretary to the U. S. legation at Madrid in
1846, having been admitted to the bar two years
earlier. In 1850, Reynolds moved to St. Louis,
where he quickly established himself as a secessionist and Know-Nothing leader. He served as
U. S. district attorney for Missouri from 1853-
1857 and was elected lieutenant governor in
1860. Following the death of Governor Jackson,
Reynolds became governor, holding the office
through the Civil War. At the war's end, he
fled to Mexico, not returning until 1868. In
1874, he was elected to the state legislature.

In 1876 he served as a member of the U. S. com-
mission to visit Latin America. His death was
by suicide.   Reynolds contributed to the
Southern Literary Messenger and the Southern
Quarterly Review. His De Vera Judicii Juratorum
Origine, Natura et Indole was published in
Heidelberg in 1842; it shows Legare's influence.

Selections

p. 250: "German Graveyards"

p. 352: "The Pilgrimage"

RHETT, JAMES SMITH (1797-1855).

Born in Beaufort and admitted to the bar in
1819, Rhett was a planter in Christ Church
Parish, just north of Charleston. He served as
a trustee of the College of Charleston from 1831
until his death and was a state senator for all
but one year between 1837 and 1848. An Episcopalian, he was buried in St. Philip's church-
yard, Charleston, where John C. Calhoun had been
buried five years before.   Ironically, unlike
his ardently pro-Calhoun and pro-Nullification
brothers Albert and Robert, he was a Unionist.
He was an occasional contributor to the Southern
Review and Southern Quarterly Review and also
delivered an Eulogium on the Life and Character
of Thomas S. Grimke (Charleston, 1835). Grimke
was a kinsman.

Selection

p. 181: "The Ocean Spirit"

RICHARDSON, MAYNARD DAVIS (1812-1832).

Simms summarized Richardson's life in an
1854 letter to Evert Duyckinck: "Maynard Davis
Richardson, son of Hon. John S. Richardson, one
of the Judges of the Courts of Common Pleas at
the State of South Carolina, was born in

Charleston on the 1st. day of January 1812--died 12th. Oct. 1832--established at Sumter, [S. C.] the Southern Whig newspaper--wrote Political & Literary Essays--Poetry--his Remains, edited with a Memoir by Mr. Simms, consists of prose & verse, essays more or less elaborate--a vol. of some 300 pages--a promising youth cut off in the very beginning of his career[.]" Richardson graduated from South Carolina College in 1830. Though he was not reared in Charleston, Simms claimed him for the city, because "it was ... at the College of Charleston, and while in the seminaries of that city that the capacities of his mind ... first began to develop themselves." Richardson also was a Unionist editor at the same time as Simms, starting at the age of twenty.

Selections

p. 132: "The Power of Beauty," from William Gilmore Simms, ed., The Remains of Maynard Davis Richardson, with a Memoir of His Life (Charleston, 1833), 224.

p. 184: "Pursuit of Happiness," ibid., 14-144.

p. 318: "The Winter Scene," ibid., 223.

RIVERS, WILLIAM JAMES (1822-ca. 1910).

First honors graduate at South Carolina College in 1841, Rivers returned to Charleston and started a private school near the College of Charleston. His Catechism of the History of South Carolina appeared in 1850. In 1855, he helped form the South Carolina Historical Society. A year later, he was elected professor of Greek at his alma mater, where, in 1857, he delivered the annual address before the Cliosophic and Euphradian literary debating societies. His topic, "The Connection of Epic Poems with the History of the Times in Which They Were Written, Illustrated from Homer,

Virgil, Tasso, and Milton," combined his historical and poetic interests.   In 1857, too,
Rivers   followed   custom   by   delivering   his
inaugural   address   as   professor   in   the   state
house of representatives; its title was "On the
Study of Greek Literature."   In addition, he
edited the first volume of the Collections of
the South Carolina Historical Society. Volumes
two and three came out under his editorship in
1858 and 1859, at the same time as he was contributing numerous articles to Russell's Magazine.   He gave the South Carolina Historical
Society's annual address in 1861, speaking "On
the Development of the Power of the Colonial
Assembly as Indicative of Our Early Progress
Toward Constitutional Self-Government."   Starting in the following year, he began compiling a
roll of South Carolinians killed in Confederate
service,   gathering   12,000   names   by   December
1865.   In 1867, he gave a lecture on "The
Characteristics of Henry Timrod's Poetry, and
His Rank as a Poet," which was published and
sold with two of Rivers' own poems the next year
to raise money for a tombstone over Timrod's
grave in Trinity Churchyard, Columbia. Over the
next several years, Rivers contributed to the
Southern Presbyterian Review and lectured at
South Carolina College "On the English and
Classical in Our Literature," "On the Interpretations of Classical Mythology," and on related
subjects. Then, in 1873, he accepted the presidency of Washington College in Maryland. Three
years later, he gave the twenty-first address
before the South Carolina Historical Society and
spoke before the National Educational Association   on   higher   education   in   the   South.
Addresses and Other Occasional Pieces by William
J. Rivers, formerly Professor of Greek Literature in the South Carolina College was privately
published in Baltimore in 1893.

Selection

    p. 253: "The Sisters," from the Magnolia,
           1, n.s. (Oct. 1842), 254.

SHEPPARD, THOMAS RADCLIFFE (1778-1809).

In 1868, Simms described Sheppard as "a well
known citizen of Charleston some sixty years
ago, ... one of our early native poets, whose
verses we have seen. They were creditable,
mostly elegiac of character, and written upon
well known English models such as Grey's Elegy.
Shepherd's [sic!] widow survived him many years,
and Shepherd's farm is still to be identified on
Charleston Neck, along with the field-works
thrown across the Neck, when we expected inva-
sion in the War of 1812 with Great Britain."
Henry T. Farmer (q.v.) included an elegy to
Sheppard in his Imagination, the Maniac's Dream,
and Other Poems. Sheppard founded the Charleston Times, and Political and Commercial Evening
Gazette in 1800 with Thomas C. Cox, who continued as publisher after Sheppard's death.
Edwin C. Holland (q.v.) later edited the paper.

Selection

p. 249: "The Night Storm"

SIMMONS, JAMES WRIGHT (ca. 1790-1858).

Younger brother of William H. (q.v.) Simmons
attended Harvard, traveled widely in Europe, and
worked for both the New York Mirror and the New
York Courier before emigrating to Texas, where
he became comptroller general of the Republic
and worked on the Galveston Banner. In 1828, he
and Simms started the Southern Literary Gazette.
Simms later described his friend's writing as
"highly charged with original thought and fancy,
and highly beautiful in expression." Reviewing
his literary career in 1868, Simms noted that
Simmons had "published in Europe and America, a
score or more of volumes. He was a poet, drama-
tist, essayist and reviewer. His prose is singularly vigorous and compact, copious and
affluent without being diffusive. His first
essay was in verse. When scarcely of age, he
published, somewhere about 1817, we believe,
'The exile's Return'--a poem of considerable

length, in several cantos, in the octo-syllabic
verse, after the school of Byron. Numerous
volumes of poems and dramas followed this, the
titles of which are not now remembered.
'Manfredi" was a tragic drama, and there were
dramas on the subject of Caius Marius and some
other historical topics. He dramatized Scott's
romance of The Bride of Lammermoor, under the
title of 'The Master of Ravenswood,' which was
played the usual three nights on the Charleston
boards. He was the writer, also, of a satire
upon the 'American Boards;' of a poem after the
school of Don Juan, called 'Blue Beard,' and a
volume of essays in prose, in London, called
'American Sketches' [to which William Hayne
Simmons contributed as well]. He is also the
author of an elaborate treatise on the 'Moral
Character of Lord Byron,' which was especially
approved by Sir John Cam Hobhouse. His latest
production is a poem entitled 'The Greek Girl'
issued from the Boston press in 1852. He no
longer lives, dying ... at the mature age of
sixty-nine. Small of person, Mr. Simmons was
lithe and spare, with a handsome Byronic face
and head. His endowments, naturally large and
various, must have realized him larger and more
various successes, had his will not too stuborn-
ly resisted the training of circumstances and
the exactions of society. He seemed to prefer
the audience, 'fit though few,' which consoled
Milton. Mr. Simmons was also a frequent writer
not only for the 'Southern Review,' but other
Southern periodicals, such as 'The Magnolia,'
'Southern and Western Magazine,' etc."

Selections

p. 67:   "Sumter," from "General Sumter,"
         Southern Literary Journal, 5
         (Jan. 1837), 326-327.

p. 254: "Thoughts on Spring," from the
         Magnolia, 4 (May 1842), 307-308.

p. 310: "The Temple of Jupiter at Olym-
         pia," from The Maniac's Con-
         fession, a Fragment of a Tale
         (Philadelphia, 1821), 99-103.

SIMMONS, WILLIAM HAYNE (1784-1870).

Educated in medicine at the University of Pennsylvania, Simmons "at an early period," according to Simms, "removed to Florida, where he cultivated, on a moderate estate, an orange plantation, dividing himself between the interests of his plantation and the attractions of his muse." Simms added: "The coercions of the former necessarily made his intercourse with the muse so many liasons. But his mind still continued active; he kept up his intercourse with Carolina and wrote occasionally for the pages of the Southern Quarterly, and some of his essays were comprised in a volume entitled 'American Sketches,' published by his brother in London. He was, if we rightly recollect, one of the commissioners with General Gadsden in forming that treaty with the Seminole Indians, which stipulated for their removal to the West--a condition which led to the war with that people, and their final expulsion after five years of miserable struggle in the swamps of Florida." In the course of the war, "the orange groves and all the property of Dr. Simmons were rested from him, while his negroes were carried off by the red men." Author of a History of the Seminoles, he wrote what Simms thought were "the most beautiful specimens of American descriptive poetry which has [sic!] ever been published, possessing the rare excellence of being at once poetical in expression and true to nature." Simms concluded, however, that "His muse ... has been indolent, and the reproach lies at his door, of leaving unused, large resources of mind and knowledge, which might have brought him equal fame and profit." Simmons' 1857 verse collection Alasco was a revision of his Onea and Other Poems.

Selections

p. 102: "The Bell-Bird of Brazil," from "Brazilian Scenery," the Magnolia, 4 (Feb. 1842), 67-68.

p. 275: "National Views," from Southern Literary Journal, 1 (Dec. 1835), 266-270.

p. 371: "The Fountain of Youth," original
publication not located; however,
a revised version appears in
Alasco (Charleston, 1857), 89.

p. 401: "The Wilderness," similarly,
appears in revised form in
Alasco, 113-118. (Simms thought
this poem one "of special
beauty," an example of Simmons'
"fine resources of fancy," as
well as of "the exquisite delicacy of his taste and the high
polish of his style and manner.")

SMITH, WILLIAM WRAGG (1808-1875).

In 1854, Simms wrote to Evert Duyckinck of
Smith's Poems (Charleston, 1842), a translation
from Lamartine as well as "other minor poems."
In his view, "the translation [is] in tolerably
smooth Spenserian stanzas. The miscellanies
are light, musical & tolerably graceful. Mr.
Smith is a man of queer moods, very solitary in
habit--musing and contemplative, about 45. He
comes of one of our old families. Has written
for the South. Review. Is a planter on Ashley
River." His father, William Loughton Smith, a
congressman and one-time minister to Portugal,
left him Ashley Barony. Though never married,
William Wragg Smith had natural children by
Theresa Hedley, to whom he in turn willed the
estate. A collateral descendent, Judge H. A. M.
Smith, described him as a "gentleman of education and culture, who contributed his investigations and publications to the knowledge of the
botany of the low county of South Carolina." He
was a founding member of the Elliott Natural
History Society, to whose transactions he made
numerous contributions. He also contributed
humorous sketches to the Southern Literary
Journal when it was edited by B. R. Carroll
(q.v.).

Selections

p. 240: "Melody"

p. 375: "Mowbry and Shelton-Place--The
        Seats of the Cliftons and Somer-
        villes"

SPIERIN, GEORGE HEARTWELL (1787-1803).

Son of Irish immigrants to New York, Spierin
was educated by his father, a graduate in divinity of Trinity College, Dublin. In 1791, the
family moved to Virginia, where Spierin's father
opened an academy. Then, in 1798, the family
moved again, this time to Georgetown, South
Carolina. Once more Spierin's father opened an
academy. Spierin was reading Ceasar at seven
and Horace at nine. By the time of his death at
age sixteen, he had already written a large body
of poetry. A selection was gathered and published in Charleston in 1805.

Selection

p. 259: "Ode to Fancy," from Poems of the
        Late George Heartwell Spierin, of
        Charleston, South-Carolina, Stu-
        dent of Law (Charleston, 1805),
        94-95.

STEWART, MARY E.

A contributor to the Southern Rose edited by
Caroline Gilman (q.v.).

Selection

p. 153: "The Flight of Time"

STUART, JOHN A. (1800-1852).

Beaufort-born and reared, Stuart was a
brother-in-law of Robert Barnwell (Smith)
Rhett. When Simms visited Beaufort in March
1831, Stuart was editing the Gazette there.

"Its political tenets," Simms wrote, "are for a
strict construction of the Constitution, and
during the late session of our Legislature, it
advocated and we believe still advocates the
call of a Convention of the people of the State,
in order, properly to determine in what sense
our relations with the General Government should
be understood. Its course, however, was dignified and gentlemanly." Stuart brought the same
states rights principles and correct conduct to
the Charleston Mercury a year later. He had
bought the paper from fellow Nullifier Henry
Laurens Pinckney (q.v.) and would remain as publisher until the mid-1840s. John Milton Clapp
(q.v.) was assistant editor in Stuart's last
years with the paper. The following selection
is similar to the humorous and realistic
sketches which Stuart contributed to the
Southern Literary Journal when B. R. Carroll
(q.v.) was editor.

Selection

p. 217: "The Boat Chase"

TIMROD, WILLIAM HENRY (1792-1838).

Son of a German Lutheran immigrant, Heinrich
Deimroth, Timrod was a bookbinder. His A Vision
and Other Poems was published in Charleston in
1814. Simms "knew Mr. Timrod well" and remembered that "at his humble shopboard" he "met
several of the young men of letters, or in some
way distinguished--Judge Bryan [q.v.], Charles
Carroll [q.v.], Mayrant, and others." Timrod
himself, Simms recalled, "was a good talker,
full of life and geniality, with no small share
of humor. He was of gently frank, and amiable
nature, burly of figure, but of round, lively
expressive face. At whiles, between talking and
working, he would read us, every now and then,
his literary labor of the night before. He was
for a long time particularly engaged upon a
drama of art, i.e., an art subject, such as the
German class as 'art novels,' which he elabo-
rated with great care and finish." In Simms's

estimate, Timrod's "blank verse was good; well rounded, musical in its periods, and possessed of very considerable force. Portions of this drama ... were published in the 'Southern Literary Journal'...." Simms remembered, too, that Timrod "also wrote some sweet and delicate sonnets. His volume of poems was remarkable for its music, and the flexibility of his verse. His was no halting muse, no spavined jade, though she may have lacked in power." If Simms's memory served him correctly, Timrod also was an editor, having started a weekly during the War of 1812 under the title The Evening Spy; no issues are known to have survived. Whatever the faults of memory, Simms continued, there was "no doubt" that Timrod "published scores of poems and essays which were never collected...." Simms added: "Freed from the necessity of manual labor, and with proper culture, Mr. Timrod might have taken high rank, even at a period when there was a host of clever litterateurs in the field." It was not only manual labor which deflected Timrod, however. Timrod served in the Seminole War as "the captain of the German Fusileers, a corps of naturalized citizens, who could date their origin back to the beginning of the Revolution of 1776, and were distinguished by their gallant conduct, especially at the unfortunate siege of Savannah, where the ancestor of Mr. Timrod, who was a native German, placed himself honorably on the record, as a member of the corps." Returning to Charleston from Florida, Timrod "resumed his labors at the accustomed work-bench, cheerfully and merrily as ever...." Although his health was impaired, he also resumed writing, "mostly in almanacs, which he had interleaved for this purpose, the printed calendar serving the purpose of showing when the poem was written." He continued thus "to the hour of his death."

Selections

p. 124: "Hymn of the Exile"

p. 304: "The May Queen--A Sonnet"

p. 350: "To Time--'The Old Traveller,'"

from the Southern Rose, 5 (Oct.
29, 1836), 40.

p. 404: "Autumnal Day in Carolina"

WHITAKER, DANIEL KIMBALL (1801-1881).

Son of a scholarly Massachusetts minister,
Whitaker took a B. A. at Harvard in 1820 and won
both the Boylston Medal for his 1823 M. A. thesis on "The Literary Character of Dr. Samuel
Johnson" and the Bowdoin Medal for oratory.
After private study, he was licensed to preach,
but bad health caused him to seek a warmer climate. Between 1823 and 1833, he planted rice
and cotton in South Carolina, then moved to
Charleston, where he read law, entered into a
successful practice and established the Southern
Literary Journal, which he edited from its
inception in 1835 until B. R. Carroll (q.v.)
took it over in 1837, after the conclusion of
the third volume. Five years later, Whitaker
started the Southern Quarterly Review, bringing
out the first volume in New Orleans (in the hope
of wider circulation) before returning to
Charleston, where J. D. B. DeBow (q.v.) assisted
him in the editing in 1844. Three years later,
John Milton Clapp (q.v.) became editor, when
Whitaker returned to law practice again and
then, with his first wife, Mary, started Whitaker's Magazine in 1850, taking it from Charleston to Columbia the next year. That venture
lasted two years more, then Whitaker returned
once more to law until the advent of the
Buchanan administration, when he received a
civil service posting, which he kept in the
Confederate government. At the war's end, he
returned to New Orleans, where he established
the New Orleans Monthly Review in 1874, editing
it until 1876. A frequent contributor to the
Washington National Intelligencer, the Charleston Courier, and the New Orleans Times as well
as his own publications, he was called "one of
the best essayists in North America" by Edgar
Allan Poe. Though his second wife was a
daughter of eminent South Carolina Baptist

leader Samuel Furman and he himself was a Con-
gregationalist by upbringing, Whitaker converted
to Catholicism in 1878.

Selection

> p. 313: "The Necessity of a Southern
> Literature," from "The Periodical
> Press," Southern Quarterly Re-
> view, 1 (Jan. 1842), 51-55. (In
> all, the essay is sixty-two pages
> long.)

WHITE, JOHN BLAKE (1781-1859).

Born near Eutaw Springs, South Carolina,
White started to read law in Columbia, then in
1800 decided to go to England to study art with
Benjamin West. Failing after his return in 1803
to establish himself as an artist in either
Charleston or Boston, he took up the law again,
but this time in Charleston. Admitted to the
bar in 1808, he was, "with Harby [q.v.], James
W. Simmons [q.v.], ... Samuel Gilman [q.v.],
Edward Jones, and a few others," Simms recalled,
one of "those chiefly who contributed to the
society, and its light literature through the
columns of the newspaper, or the pages of the
periodical in Charleston, during a ... period
..., say from 1816 to 1824." Between 1806 and
1839, White saw several of his plays performed
and published: Foscari, or the Venetian Exile
(1806), The Mysteries of the Castle (1807),
Modern Honor (1812), The Triumph of Liberty, or
Louisiana Preserved (1819), "The Forgers; a
Dramatic Poem," which appeared in the March 1837
Southern Literary Journal, and Intemperance
(1839). In 1833, his "Grave Robbers" was exhibited at the Boston Atheneum, and in 1840, the
South Carolina Institute awarded him a gold
medal for historical painting. He was an ardent
temperance and prison reform advocate.

Selection

> p. 125: "The Dungeon and the Gallows,"

from "Capital Punishment," <u>South</u>
<u>ern Literary Journal</u>, 1 (Jan.
1836), 302-310. (The first and
the last paragraphs are omitted.)

WURDEMANN, J. G. F. (1810-1849).

Having been educated "in European medical
centers," according to Joseph I. Waring, Wurdemann "came to Charleston and joined the Medical
Society in 1834.   In 1836 he was appointed
demonstrator of anatomy at the Medical College
of the State of South Carolina," where he worked
alongside of Samuel Henry Dickson (q.v.).   A
Lutheran, Wurdemann attended St. John's, the
church of Dr. Bachman (q.v.), with whom he also
corresponded on natural history.   "The city of
Charleston," Waring notes, presented Wurdemann
"with a handsome silver goblet for his chari-
table services to the needy." Waring continues:
"For the last eight years of his life Dr. Wurdemann suffered from tuberculosis and sought a
congenial climate in Cuba, Florida, and Aiken,
South Carolina. During these years he published
articles on Florida and the West Indies in the
<u>Southern Journal of Medicine and Pharmacy</u> and
the <u>Boston Medical and Surgical Journal</u>."   He
also contributed to Charleston's literary
periodicals. While in Florida, furthermore, he
established Enterprise, a health resort.

Selection

p. 328: "Campos Santos," from either
<u>Notes on Cuba</u> (Boston, 1844),
28-37, or, more probably, the
serial form of this passage which
bears the same title, "Campos
Santos," and is in the <u>Magnolia</u>,
2, n.s. (Mar. 1843), 156-158.

YEADON, RICHARD (1802-1870).

Son of a Charleston banker, Yeadon was educated in private academies in Charleston, then
at South Carolina College, where he graduated
second in his class in 1820. Returning to
Charleston, he attended services at the Circular
(First Independent) Congregational Church, read
law in the offices of Thomas Bennett and
Benjamin Hunt, and was admitted to the bar in
1824. Soon after, he joined the Forensic Club,
the nucleus for a short lived law school presided over by Hugh Swinton Legare (q.v.), among
others. Having entered into partnership with
Charles Macbeth, Yeadon became a special magistrate for Charleston District. He joined the
Union Party in 1830, contributing articles to
the Charleston City Gazette, edited by fellow
Unionist Simms. With the ascendency of the
Nullifiers in elections the next year, Yeadon
lost his magistracy; then in 1832 he became editor and co-owner of the Charleston Courier. He
lost in a race for the state legislature that
year but ran successfully in 1836 on a compro-
mise ticket put together by John C. Calhoun and
James Louis Petigru (q.v.). Like Legare, however, Yeadon then went against Calhoun by supporting the rechartering of the National Bank
and, like Legare too, was defeated for reelection in 1838 by a Calhounite. In the same year,
as a city councilman, Yeadon led the successful
campaign to have the College of Charleston
become the first municipally supported college
in the U. S.; he became a trustee in 1840,
serving until his death. In 1842, he helped
Daniel Huger defeat Calhounites Robert Barnwell
Rhett and Francis W. Pickens in the race for the
vacant U. S. Senate seat. Yeadon, like Legare,
was firmly identified with the Whig Party by
this time. When the Whigs suffered a crushing
defeat in South Carolina in 1844, Yeadon retired
from editorship of the Courier and set out on a
grand tour of Europe. He returned to practice
law and serve in city government. He also wrote
descriptive essays, gave speeches up and down
the East Coast, helped found the South Carolina
Institute and the South Carolina Historical
Society, and chaired the committee which planned

the establishment of the Charleston High School.
Then in 1856, he returned to editorship of the
Courier to combat the Republican presidential
ticket of Charlestonian John C. Fremont. At the
same time, he went on a speaking tour of the
North, urging the preservation both of slavery
and the Union. With this Unionist stand, he
outpolled all other candidates from Charleston
in the state legislative elections of 1856; four
years later he was barely reelected. Following
Lincoln's election, Yeadon gave up his Unionism
and the next year turned the Courier into a pro-
Jefferson Davis paper, the only one in South
Carolina to support the president throughout the
war. Yeadon also outfitted the Yeadon Light
Infantry and the Willington Rangers, raised
money for the construction of the gunboat
Palmetto State, invested heavily in Confederate,
state, and local bonds, continued to serve in
the legislature, and was a trustee of South
Carolina College from 1863-1865. At the war's
end, Union forces temporarily confiscated the
Courier and looted Yeadon's Charleston house.
Returning to Charleston from Aiken, Yeadon
resumed his law practice but only occasionally
wrote for the paper which he had edited for the
preceeding nine years.

Selection

p. 142: "Death of Hugh S. Legare"

www.ingramcontent.com/pod-product-compliance
Lightning Source LLC
Chambersburg PA
CBHW020229110726
47898CB00004B/1198